ArtScroll Mesorah Series®

Rabbi Nosson Scherman / Rabbi Meir Zlotowitz

General Editors

מגילת אסתר
עם פירוש גנזי המלך

TREASURES

Published by
Mesorah Publications, ltd

THE KING'S

A wealth of commentary and insights on

MEGILLAS ESTHER

BY RABBI ELIEZER GINZBURG

FIRST EDITION
First Impression . . . February 1996

Published and Distributed by
MESORAH PUBLICATIONS, Ltd.
4401 Second Avenue
Brooklyn, New York 11232

Distributed in Europe by
J. LEHMANN HEBREW BOOKSELLERS
20 Cambridge Terrace
Gateshead, Tyne and Wear
England NE8 1RP

Distributed in Israel by
SIFRIATI / A. GITLER—BOOKS
4 Bilu Street
P.O.B. 14075
Tel Aviv 61140

Distributed in Australia & New Zealand by
GOLDS BOOK & GIFT CO.
36 William Street
Balaclava 3183, Vic., Australia

Distributed in South Africa by
KOLLEL BOOKSHOP
22 Muller Street
Yeoville 2198, Johannesburg, South Africa

ARTSCROLL MESORAH SERIES®
THE KING'S TREASURES

ISBN
0-89906-368-3 (hard cover)
0-89906-369-1 (paperback)

Typography by Compuscribe at ArtScroll Studios, Ltd.

Printed in the United States of America by Noble Book Press
Bound by Sefercraft, Quality Bookbinders, Ltd. Brooklyn, N.Y.

This sefer is dedicated by

Mr. and Mrs. Dovid Lipins

in honor of their children

Chaim and Sorah Leah Fisher **נ״י**

Yuri Moshe and Rochel Rivka Shoshana **נ״י**

Shalom Eliezer Halevi and Esther Pearl Ginsberg **נ״י**

Habachur Noach Chaim Lipins **נ״י**

Mr. And Mrs. Dovid Lipins
are backbones of
the vibrant Torah community
of Cleveland Heights, Ohio.
They are respected around the world
as models of chessed,
whose lives are dedicated
to help and generously support
Torah causes.

In memory of
Grandparents and Relatives

יוסף בן נפתלי הי״ד
אשתו דאברא בת יצחק הי״ד

בניהם	בנותיהם
אברהם ואפרים הי״ד	**טויבע** הי״ד
נשיהם ומשפחתם	**ופייגא** הי״ד

Frommer

יעקב בן שמואל הי״ד
אשתו מלכה בת שלמה זלמן ע״ה

בנם
חיים בן ציון ארי׳ הי״ד
Benedikt

יצחק בן אלימלך הי״ד
אשתו רייזיל בת דוד הי״ד
Tag

אהרן בן יוסף פנחס הי״ד
אשתו אסתר בת יוסף ע״ה
Greenberg

Dedicated by
Mr. and Mrs. Yosef Frommer

◆§ Author's Preface

In the introduction to his commentary on *Megillas Esther*, *Rambam* explains that the *Megillah* contains a unique aspect which sets it apart from all other works of Scripture:

"Moses recorded his prophecies, as the verse says, 'Moses wrote this Torah and gave it to the Kohanim, the sons of Levi, the bearers of the Ark of the covenant of Hashem, and to all the elders of Israel' (*Deuteronomy* 31:9). Likewise, the Prophets recorded the prophetic visions that were revealed to them, and David and the Ten Sages composed the Book of Psalms [in a spirit of prophecy]. King Solomon, too, wrote down his prophetic visions.

"In contrast, the decision to write *Megillas Esther* was undertaken despite the fact that the author had not merited Divine inspiration. Only when the *Megillah* was actually being written did Divine inspiration pervade his being. This [spirit of prophecy] enabled him to record historical events from a Godly perspective. For example, the verse says, 'The Jews that were in Shushan assembled again on the fourteenth day . . . but they did not lay their hand on the spoils' (9:15) — if it were not for Divine inspiration, how could the author, a mortal being, know that 'they did not lay their hand on the spoils'? Only Hashem could possibly know who took and who did not take from the spoils!

"This realization obligates one to study the *Megillah* closely and uncover its profound allusions."

Now that we have defined the distinguishing factor that makes the *Megillah* unique among Scriptural works, we must procede to understand the reason for this intrinsic difference. The answer is provided by the *Maharal*:

"There are those who wonder, 'If the miracle of Purim was so great, why did Hashem not perform an open miracle as in the days of the Hasmoneans, when the single flask of oil lasted eight days?' The answer is that the very fact that the miracle of Purim had to be kept concealed indicates that it emanated from a lofty heavenly realm that is far too sublime to be overtly manifested in our corporeal reality. This also explains why Hashem's Name does not explicitly appear even once in the entire *Megillah*, but is only hinted at in selected passages. Indeed, all the events recorded in the *Megillah* are shrouded in secrecy. . ."

Clearly, then, we see that the miracles of Purim emanated from גנזי המלך, "the King's concealed treasures." It is for this reason that the contents of the *Megillah* could not be fathomed by the author prior to writing them down, and why they only emerged when the quill touched the parchment paper.

Taken at face value the *Megillah* seems a simple and straightforward work, but when one plumbs its depths, one discovers an infinite treasure house of eternal meaning.

Throughout the many years of exile, as we have wandered from nation to nation, from one civilization to another, we have carried the message of the *Megillah* along with us. It has imbued us with strength and perseverance, and enabled us to draw vast spiritual riches directly from the "King's concealed treasures."

I pray to the Almighty that all those who study what I have written will become inspired and grow stronger in their belief of Hashem; that they will believe with greater conviction in His ability to redeem the Jewish People in their darkest hour, when seemingly insurmountable difficulties threaten our very existence. May the radiance of "the King's concealed treasures" illuminate the murky darkness that is enveloping our present generation!

I write these words with deep gratitude to the *Ribbono Shel Olam*, Who has granted me the privilege of presenting this work to the English-speaking public.

I am indeed fortunate to have such a close friend as Rabbi Meir Zlotowitz, who undertook to publish this *sefer*. Under his guidance and supervision, ArtScroll's talented staff diligently applied themselves to present my *chidushei Torah* to the English public in a concise and appealing manner, while carefully preserving the original message I wished to convey. My sincere thanks to Rabbi Moshe Schapiro, the gifted *talmid chacham* who translated, adapted, and edited the *sefer*.

In just a few words, I would like to express my gratitude to Mr. Yossi Frommer and his wife for their continuous support of my literary efforts in Torah. I also welcome this opportunity to thank Mr. Dovid Lipins and family of Cleveland, Ohio for his warmth, friendship, and support on behalf of my literary efforts. May the *Ribbono Shel Olam* grant them all ברכה, הצלחה, and שמחות.

Finally, I would like to express my deep appreciation of the constant support and assistance I have always received from my wife תחי', who has played a major role in all aspects of my publications.

May we merit to see the fulfillment of all the words of the Prophets, and be granted the spiritual riches of "the King's concealed treasures."

Eliezer Ginsburg
Tu Bishvat 5756

THE KING'S TREASURES

בִּרְכוֹת הַמְּגִלָּה

BLESSINGS OVER THE MEGILLAH

Before reading *Megillas Esther* on Purim [both at night and again in the morning], the reader recites the following three blessings. The congregation should answer *Amen* only [not בָּרוּךְ הוּא וּבָרוּךְ שְׁמוֹ] after each blessing, and have in mind that they thereby fulfill the obligation of reciting the blessings themselves. During the morning reading, they should also have in mind that the third blessing applies to the other mitzvos of Purim — *shalach manos*, gifts to the poor, and the festive Purim meal — as well as to the *Megillah* reading.

[These blessings are recited whether or not a *minyan* is present for the reading.]

בָּרוּךְ אַתָּה יהוה אֱלֹהֵינוּ מֶלֶךְ הָעוֹלָם, אֲשֶׁר קִדְּשָׁנוּ בְּמִצְוֹתָיו, וְצִוָּנוּ עַל מִקְרָא מְגִלָּה. (קהל – אָמֵן.)

בָּרוּךְ אַתָּה יהוה אֱלֹהֵינוּ מֶלֶךְ הָעוֹלָם, שֶׁעָשָׂה נִסִּים לַאֲבוֹתֵינוּ, בַּיָּמִים הָהֵם, בַּזְּמַן הַזֶּה. (קהל – אָמֵן.)

בָּרוּךְ אַתָּה יהוה אֱלֹהֵינוּ מֶלֶךְ הָעוֹלָם, שֶׁהֶחֱיָנוּ, וְקִיְּמָנוּ, וְהִגִּיעָנוּ לַזְּמַן הַזֶּה. (קהל – אָמֵן.)

B*lessed are You, HASHEM, our God, King of the universe, Who has sanctified us with His commandments and has commanded us regarding the reading of the Megillah.* (Cong. – *Amen.*)

B*lessed are You, HASHEM, our God, King of the universe, Who has wrought miracles for our forefathers, in those days at this season.* (Cong. – *Amen.*)

B*lessed are You, HASHEM, our God, King of the universe, Who has kept us alive, sustained us and brought us to this season.* (Cong. – *Amen.*)

I

1. וַיְהִי בִּימֵי אֲחַשְׁוֵרוֹשׁ — And it came to pass in the days of Ahasuerus.

The Sages said, "A tradition has been handed down to us by the people of the Great Assembly: Wherever it says, 'and it came to pass in the days of. . .,' the words convey anguish. [As for the verse,] 'And it came to pass in the days of Ahasuerus,' it refers to Haman. . ." (*Megillah* 10b).

It is difficult to understand why the Sages attributed the anguish implicit in this verse specifically to Haman, since ostensibly, they could just as well have attributed it to Ahasuerus.[1] This is evident from the Sages' numerous etymological interpretations of Ahasuerus' name, all of which emphasize his wickedness.

For example, they say he was called Ahasuerus (אֲחַשְׁוֵרוֹשׁ) because "in his day he caused the faces of the Jewish People to become as black as the bottom of a pot" (הוּשְׁחֲרוּ פְּנֵיהֶם שֶׁל יִשְׂרָאֵל בְּיָמָיו כְּשׁוּלֵי קְדֵרָה) referring to the dark facial appearance characteristic of individuals who have fasted for long periods of time. This is a fitting description of the Jews in those days, for they declared numerous fasts to beseech Hashem to intervene on their behalf and revoke the evil decrees instituted against them by the King.[2] Similarly, the Sages suggest he was called Ahasuerus because "whoever remembered him would exclaim, 'Woe upon his head!' " (אָח לְרֹאשׁוֹ), or because "in his day, everyone became poor" (הַכֹּל נַעֲשׂוּ רָשִׁין בְּיָמָיו) (*Megillah* 11a).

The following analogy further illustrates Ahasuerus' wickedness: "They [Ahasuerus and Haman] could be compared to two people, one of whom had a mound in his field, and the other a pit. The owner of the pit thought, 'If only he would sell me that mound!' while the owner of the mound thought, 'If only he would sell me that pit!' Some time later, they met each other. The owner of the pit said to the owner of the mound, 'Sell me your mound.' His response was, '[Please,] take it for free!' " (ibid. 14a). The owner of the pit corresponds to Haman, who "bought" the Jewish People from Ahasuerus, and the owner

1. In every instance when these words occur in Scripture, the person or event responsible for the anguish felt by that particular generation is immediately identified. For example, one verse says, "And it came to pass in the days of Amraphel. . ." (*Genesis* 14:1), and in the very next verse, we learn that a major war was fought in the region. Similarly, after the introduction, "And it came to pass in the days when the Judges judged. . .," the same verse goes on to tell us that "there was a famine in the land" (*Ruth* 1:1). Our verse, however, does not specify the cause of that generation's suffering, unless we interpret the word אֲחַשְׁוֵרוֹשׁ to be that cause. Why, then, did the Sages avoid this more fitting interpretation?

2. We can well understand, then, why the Sages decreed that the miracles of Purim be celebrated with feasting and rejoicing, since the faces which were dark from fasting and anxiety suddenly had reason to radiate in exuberant joy. Thus, it is only fitting that feasting replace fasting and rejoicing replace weeping, in fulfillment of the verse, "Instead of the thorn shall rise a cypress, instead of the nettle shall rise a myrtle" (*Isaiah* 55:13).

1/1 [1] And *it came to pass in the days of Ahasuerus — the Ahasuerus who reigned from Hodu to*

of the mound is a reference to Ahasuerus. With this analogy the Sages teach us that, like Haman, Ahasuerus also wished to destroy the Jewish People.

We see, then, that the anguish implicit in the verse, "And it came to pass in the days of Ahasuerus," could very well have been attributed to Ahasuerus. If so, why did the Sages attribute it to Haman?

The answer lies in the *Rambam*'s commentary to the *Megillah,* where he writes that in all five occurrences in Scripture of the words, "And it came to pass in the days of. . .,"[1] the suffering alluded to by the verse eventually came to an end, and in its stead came happiness and joy. In light of this pattern, Ahasuerus could not have been the subject of our verse, for the suffering which he inflicted upon his generation did not cease. The Sages infer this from the words, הוּא אֲחַשְׁוֵרוֹשׁ ("the [*same*] Ahasuerus"; 1:1), which imply that Ahasuerus remained as wicked when the story of Esther ended as he had been when it first began. This is corroborated by the verse, "King Ahasuerus levied taxes on both the mainland and the islands" (10:1) — the Sages teach that as a consequence of these taxes, the entire generation became poor (*Megillah* 11a).

Haman's reign of terror, on the other hand, *did* come to an end. This is why the Sages attributed the suffering implicit in our verse to Haman and not to Ahasuerus.

הוּא אֲחַשְׁוֵרוֹשׁ — The [same] Ahasuerus.

The Sages dedicated nearly seven pages of the Talmud (*Megillah* 10-17) to expound upon numerous verses in the *Megillah.* Nowhere else in the Talmud do we see such a prolific discussion of any Biblical text. Therefore, the

1. Listed below are the five occurrences of these words in Scripture, followed by a later verse which announces the joyous event that brought that period of anguish to an end:

a. Regarding Abraham it says, "And it came to pass in the days of Amraphel" (that Lot was captured in a war (*Genesis* 14:1). A later verse states, "[Abraham] divided [his forces] against them [and attacked] that night, he and his servants" (ibid., 14:15).

b. At the beginning of the Book of *Ruth* it says, "And it came to pass in the days when the Judges judged" (that there was a famine) (*Ruth* 1:1). A later verse states, "She then arose. . .to return. . .for she had heard in the fields of Moab that Hashem had remembered His people by giving them food" (ibid., 1:6). The last verses in Ruth go on to tell us that Naomi's return led to the birth of King David.

c. There is a verse in *Isaiah* (7:1) that says, "And it came to pass in the days of Ahaz" (a wicked king). A later verse announces the birth of the righteous Hezekiah (*Isaiah* 9:5).

d. In *Jeremiah* (1:3) it says, "And [the word of Hashem] came to [Jeremiah] in the days of Jehoiakim" (foretelling the destruction of Jerusalem). In another verse God promises, "I shall return to Jerusalem with mercy" (*Zechariah* 1:16).

e. In the *Megillah* we read, "And it came to pass in the days of Ahasuerus." Later, we learn, "On the very day that the enemies of the Jews expected to gain the upper hand over them, it was turned about: The Jews gained the upper hand over their adversaries" (*Esther* 9:1).

question must be asked: What did the Sages see in the *Megillah* to justify such lengthy elucidation?

One answer is that the *Megillah* brings the Jewish People more joy than any other holy work, and hence the Sages were naturally drawn to discuss it at greater length.

Another answer is that the Sages recognized the unique qualities of Purim. This is apparent from the words of the *Tur* (*Orach Chaim* 693), who writes, "Since [Purim] is a day of miracles, on which [the Jewish People] were redeemed, we should beseech [Hashem] to have mercy upon us, and redeem us in the future just as [He redeemed] us in the past." Evidently, the Sages saw a correlation between Purim and the final redemption,[1] and hence declared the day of Purim an opportune time to implore Hashem to redeem the Jewish People.

With this principle in mind, we can well understand why the Sages expounded upon the *Megillah* so extensively. In part, their words are an expression of their love of Purim and what it represents. However, they were also driven by a desire to impart their teachings to future generations in order to strengthen the broken spirit of the Jewish People. The Sages perceived that the words of the *Megillah* have the power to console the Jewish People, as well as to infuse them with faith in the final redemption.

Following are some of the parallels that can be drawn between Purim and the future redemption:

1. The *Megillah* ends with the words, "he was concerned for the welfare of all his posterity" (10:3). Concerning the final redemption, the Sages say, "[Elijah will not come] to distance or bring close, but only to make peace between them, as it says, 'Behold, I will send you Elijah the Prophet, and he will reconcile the hearts of parents with their children, and the hearts of children with their parents" (*Malachi* 3:24). This, too, is the meaning of the verse, "he was concerned for the welfare of all his posterity."
2. The verse says, "Many are the designs in a man's heart, but it is God's plan that will be fulfilled" (*Proverbs* 19:21). In reference to this verse the commentators say in the name of R' Bunim of P'shis'che that "God's plan shall be fulfilled" through the very deeds of that man, even though his plans may actually conflict with God's ultimate design. This principle will become clearly evident to all in the days of Messiah.

   On Purim, too, this principle became clearly evident to all — Haman and his sons were hung upon the very post which they had readied for Mordechai.
3. Mordechai became Ahasuerus' viceroy, a position which even Moses did not attain in Egypt. For it says, "Moses was very great in the land of Egypt, in the eyes of the servants of Pharaoh and in the eyes of the people"

---

1. *Sefer HaChaim* (p. 154), written by the *Maharal*'s brother, refers to the *Megillah* as ספר גאולה (lit., "Book of Redemption").

(*Exodus* 11:3) — he was respected by Pharoah's *servants and subjects,* but not by Pharaoh himself.

Mordechai's high position coincides with the verse, "Aliens will rebuild your walls; their kings will wait upon you" (*Isaiah* 60:10), which refers to the days of the Messiah.[1]

4. The verse, "Many of the people professed themselves Jews, for the fear of the Jews had fallen upon them" (9:17), echoes a messianic theme: According to the *Ibn Ezra,* the verse, "For then I will make the people pure of speech so that they shall call out in Hashem's Name" (*Zephaniah* 3:9), teaches that in messianic times the nations of the world will emulate the Jewish People and pray to Hashem in Hebrew.

הוּא אֲחַשְׁוֵרוֹשׁ — The [same] Ahasuerus.

The Sages infer from these words that Ahasuerus remained as wicked when the story of Esther ended as he had been when it first began (*Megillah* 11a). Even though Ahasuerus witnessed Haman's good fortune suddenly and inexplicably decline, and the Jewish People miraculously redeemed from the hands of their enemies, he remained completely unchanged.

In truth, the end of the *Megillah* itself hints to the fact that Ahasuerus was still as wicked as ever, for the verse says, "King Ahasuerus levied taxes on both the mainland and the islands" (10:1). The explanation is as follows:

R' Yosef Nechemiah, the Rav of Krakow, often wondered why this verse was included in the *Megillah.* After all, every verse that appears in Scripture was deemed by the Sages to contain an eternal message that would remain relevant to all future generations. Ostensibly, however, this verse has no bearing whatsoever on the miracles that took place, nor does it shed light on the condition of the Jewish People in those times.

R' Yosef Nechemiah answered as follows: As any student of Jewish history knows, in every country where Jews have wandered, their industrious endeavors and consequent prosperity have always aroused the jealousy of the local population. In response, heavy taxes were levied against them, and the brunt of filling the state's coffers was placed squarely on their shoulders. The Jews living in Shushan were no exception. After the miracles of Purim, however, Ahasuerus found himself in a quandary, since his Jewish subjects were held in high regard by the populace, as the verse says, "Moreover, many from among the people of the land professed themselves Jews, for the fear of the Jews had fallen upon them" (8:17). Thus, he no longer had public support to extort the Jews, which meant that he would have to find other means by which to raise taxes. His only alternative was to levy taxes

---

1. *Sefer HaChaim* (p. 153) points out that prior to Mordechai no Jew had ever held such a high position in the Persian Empire. Mordechai's rise to power was viewed as such a rare phenomenon that it even earned a place in ancient Persia's historical annals. In fact, I was told by someone who recently left Iran that Mordechai and Esther are still mentioned in public-school history books *to this very day.*

א/ב ב וְעַד־כּוּשׁ שֶׁבַע וְעֶשְׂרִים וּמֵאָה מְדִינָה: בַּיָּמִים הָהֵם
כְּשֶׁבֶת ׀ הַמֶּלֶךְ אֲחַשְׁוֵרוֹשׁ עַל כִּסֵּא מַלְכוּתוֹ אֲשֶׁר

---

against his own people, and this he did, as the verse says, "King Ahasuerus levied taxes on both the mainland and the islands" (10:1).

However, Ahasuerus' gracious gestures towards the Jewish People were purely symbolic, for in his heart he hated the Jews as intensely as ever. This is alluded to by the irregular spelling of Ahasuerus' name in the latter verse: אֲחַשְׁרֹשׁ. By omitting both *vavs* (ו), the verse reveals that Ahasuerus did not make these conciliatory gestures towards the Jews wholeheartedly, but only because he had no choice.[1]

הוּא אֲחַשְׁוֵרוֹשׁ הַמֹּלֵךְ מֵהֹדּוּ וְעַד־כּוּשׁ — The [same] Ahasuerus who reigned from Hodu to Cush.

The Sages infer from this verse that Ahasuerus was not of royal descent, but assumed the throne through his own efforts. At first glance, this fact hardly seems significant, and appears to have little bearing on the miracles of Purim.

In truth, however, no verse in the *Megillah* is irrelevant. This is evident from the Vilna Gaon's explanation of why the Sages decreed that one must hear every single word of the *Megillah* reading on Purim:[2] "From the beginning of the *Megillah* to the end, every single verse, every sentence, has the effect of magnifying the extent of the miracle." Having established this principle, we will now proceed to explain why this verse is pertinent to the story of Purim:

The *Megillah* tells us that "Vashti the Queen also made a feast for the women in the royal house of King Ahasuerus" (1:9). This in itself was quite audacious of her — she made a feast in her honor *on the very same day* that the elaborate celebration in honor of the King was taking place! Furthermore, the *Lekach Tov* points out that Vashti purposely held her feast *in the royal house of King Ahasuerus,* referring to the King's private chamber, which only he was allowed to enter. If these salient facts are indicators of the relationship between the royal couple, it seems that domestic harmony was a rare commodity in Ahasuerus' palace.

As we progress further in the *Megillah,* the tension between the royal

---

1. Similarly, the Sages (*Bava Metzia* 87a) infer from *Genesis* 23:16, where the name "Ephron" is spelled without a *vav,* that Ephron spoke insincerely when he made his grandiose offer to give his field to Abraham as a gift. In the end, he revealed his true nature by taking far more money from Abraham than the property was really worth.

2. In *Orach Chaim* ch. 604, note 48, the *Mishnah Berurah,* citing the *Magen Avraham,* says: "The listener must focus his hearing on listening to every single word from the mouth of the person reading [the *Megillah*]. If the reader or the listener misses even one word, he has not fulfilled the *mitzvah,* and he must read [the *Megillah*] once again."

Cush over a hundred and twenty-seven provinces — 2 that in those days, when King Ahasuerus sat on his royal throne which was in Shushan the

---

couple escalates into open conflict: "On the seventh day, when the heart of the King was merry with wine, he ordered. . .to bring Vashti the Queen before the King wearing the royal crown, to show off her beauty to the people and the officials. . . But Queen Vashti refused to come at the King's command. . . The King therefore became very incensed and his anger burned in him" (1:10-12).

The *Vilna Gaon* points out that Vashti is first referred to as "Vashti the Queen," and later as "Queen Vashti." From this, the Gaon detects an undercurrent in their confrontation, indicating that there were deeper roots to their animosity which are not explicitly mentioned in the *Megillah.* Their real point of contention was as follows:

When Ahasuerus summoned Vashti, he relayed a message to her which in effect said, "You are a common woman, and the only reason you are Queen is because I appointed you. Therefore, you must obey me!" This is why the first verse places Vashti's name before her title of Queen — in Ahasuerus' opinion, she was nothing more than Vashti, the common woman, whom he had decided to appoint as Queen.

Her response was, "I would be fit to be a queen even if I hadn't married you! Why, I am the daughter of Belshazzar, the grandson of Nebuchadnezzar! On the contrary, it is *I* who am of royal descent. You became king on your own, and not because of your noble lineage." Thus, the second verse refers to her as "Queen Vashti" — she thought of herself first as Queen, and only then as Vashti, Ahasuerus' wife.

From the *Vilna Gaon*'s interpretation, it is evident that the women's feast was Vashti's way of emphasizing her eminence; she held it specifically in Ahasuerus' royal chamber in order to drive home the point that the kingdom was hers as much as it was his. Squabbles of this sort were common between them, and they set the stage for the miracles that would later take place through Queen Esther.

2. בַּיָּמִים הָהֵם כְּשֶׁבֶת הַמֶּלֶךְ אֲחַשְׁוֵרוֹשׁ עַל כִּסֵּא מַלְכוּתוֹ אֲשֶׁר בְּשׁוּשַׁן הַבִּירָה — In those days, when King Ahasuerus sat on his royal throne which was in Shushan the Capital.

According to *Rashi,* the verse refers to the period when Ahasuerus crushed several insurgencies with bloody battles and successfully consolidated his kingdom. The verse serves as strong proof for the Sages' statement, "Tranquility for the wicked is harmful to them and harmful to the world" (*Sanhedrin* 71b), for we see that as soon as peace reigned in Ahasuerus' kingdom, he began to plot and carry out evil deeds. It was

בְּשׁוּשַׁ֖ן הַבִּירָֽה׃ ג בִּשְׁנַ֤ת שָׁלוֹשׁ֙ לְמָלְכ֔וֹ עָשָׂ֣ה מִשְׁתֶּ֔ה
לְכָל־שָׂרָ֖יו וַעֲבָדָ֑יו חֵ֣יל ׀ פָּרַ֣ס וּמָדַ֗י הַֽפַּרְתְּמִ֛ים
ד וְשָׂרֵ֥י הַמְּדִינ֖וֹת לְפָנָֽיו׃ בְּהַרְאֹת֗וֹ אֶת־עֹ֙שֶׁר֙ כְּב֣וֹד

---

during this peaceful era that he killed Vashti, thereby fulfilling the first clause, "Tranquility for the wicked *is harmful to them.*" Thereafter, he decreed that beautiful maidens be apprehended and brought to him by force (see 2:1-4), thereby fulfilling the Sages' second clause, ". . .*and harmful to the world.*"

❦ ❦ ❦

This verse sets the stage for Ahasuerus' tribulations and, correspondingly, the Jewish People's redemption. His decline followed the pattern described by R' Elazar Hakappar, who said, "Jealousy, desire and honor take a man out of the world" (*Pirkei Avos* 4:21). "The world" refers to one's portion in both this world and the next.

According to the *Vilna Gaon,* Ahasuerus was the first king to declare the city of Shushan the capital of the Persian Empire. This is alluded to by the words, "when *King Ahasuerus* sat on his royal throne *which was in Shushan the Capital*" — the verse stresses that the location of Ahasuerus' throne was unique. Until this time Babylonia had been the nerve center of the kingdom, and understandably, that is where previous kings had placed their thrones. Ahasuerus' irrational decision to move the capital was prompted by jealousy, for he had always admired King Solomon's magnificent throne, but he had been miraculously prevented from sitting upon it.[1] Thus, he ordered the finest craftsmen in the kingdom — who happened to live in Shushan — to construct an exact replica of Solomon's throne. In time, the throne was completed, but, lo and behold, it was too heavy to be moved to Babylonia. But Ahasuerus would not be denied his wishes: He decided that if the throne could not be moved to the capital, he would just have to move the capital to the throne!

The declaration of a new capital called for an official inauguration, and this is why Ahasuerus held the lavish feast described in the following verses. During the feast, Ahasuerus' physical desires were aroused, as the Sages said, "One group said, 'The women of Medea are the most beautiful!', and others said, 'The women of Persia are the most beautiful!' Ahasuerus said to them, 'The vessel [referring to Vashti, his wife] that I use is not Medean nor Persian, but Casdean! Do you wish to see her?' They said, 'Yes, but only on condition that she appears before us unclothed!' " (*Megillah* 12b).

---

1. The engraved animals adorning the throne miraculously came to life and prevented him from mounting the throne (*Targum, Esther Rabbah 1:12*).

Capital, [3] *in the third year of his reign, he made a feast for all his officials and his servants; the army of Persia and Media, the nobles and officials of the provinces being present;* [4] *when he displayed the riches of his*

Feeling that his honor was on the line, Ahasuerus ordered Vashti to appear unclothed before his guests, and thereby prove his assertion that Casdean women are more beautiful than Medeans or Persians. When Vashti refused, Ahasuerus became incensed, and he condemned her to death. When he finally came to his senses, he missed Vashti's beauty, and felt great sorrow over having killed her.

Thus, we see that Ahasuerus' jealousy led to desire and honor, and as a result, he lost his portion in this world — that is, his wife.

❦ ❦ ❦

The Talmud states, "Rabbah bar Ofron began his exposition of the *Megillah* from the following verse: 'I shall set My throne in Elam, and I shall destroy from there the king and [his] ministers' (*Jeremiah* 49:38) — 'the king' alludes to Vashti, '[his] ministers' refers to Haman and his ten sons" (*Megillah* 10b). From this we learn that Hashem set His throne in Shushan in order to punish the wicked. According to *Megillas Setarim* (s.v. בִּמְלֹאות הַיָּמִים), Hashem, in His mercy, set His throne in Shushan also in order to guard the righteous from succumbing to sin.

This principle can be better understood through the following analogy, which the *Ramban* (*Leviticus* 19:25) uses to explain why there is a greater obligation to observe Hashem's commandment in the Land of Israel than elsewhere: If someone were to deface the King's palace, his punishment would certainly be more severe than that of someone who merely defaced the street. So too, explains the Rambam, the Land of Israel is Hashem's palace.[1]

---

1. The following story illustrates this point:

The late *Sadigurer Rebbe* used to leave home early in the morning without disclosing his destination to anyone. The Rebbe's mysterious behavior aroused the curiosity of his personal attendant, and one day he decided to follow the Rebbe. What the man saw left him speechless — the eminent Rebbe discreetly walked a few blocks away from his home, picked up a broom, and began sweeping the street! Overcome with bewilderment, the man ran over to the Rebbe and asked for an explanation.

The Rebbe told him that during the Second World War, the Nazis had forced him to sweep the street in order to humiliate him and break his spirit. At that time, he comforted himself with the thought that since the entire world belongs to Hashem, sweeping the streets was a great honor, for it was *Hashem*'s street that he was sweeping. He then made a vow that if his life would be spared, he would sweep the streets of *Eretz Yisrael,* Hashem's palace. "Now you know why I am sweeping the street," the Rebbe concluded, returning joyfully to his task.

מַלְכוּתוֹ וְאֶת־יְקָר תִּפְאֶרֶת גְּדוּלָּתוֹ יָמִים רַבִּים
ה שְׁמוֹנִים וּמְאַת יוֹם: וּבִמְלוֹאת | הַיָּמִים הָאֵלֶּה עָשָׂה
הַמֶּלֶךְ לְכָל־הָעָם הַנִּמְצְאִים בְּשׁוּשַׁן הַבִּירָה
לְמִגָּדוֹל וְעַד־קָטָן מִשְׁתֶּה שִׁבְעַת יָמִים בַּחֲצַר גִּנַּת
ו בִּיתַן הַמֶּלֶךְ: חוּר | כַּרְפַּס וּתְכֵלֶת אָחוּז בְּחַבְלֵי־בוּץ
וְאַרְגָּמָן עַל־גְּלִילֵי כֶסֶף וְעַמּוּדֵי שֵׁשׁ מִטּוֹת | זָהָב
ז וָכֶסֶף עַל רִצְפַת בַּהַט־וָשֵׁשׁ וְדַר וְסֹחָרֶת: וְהַשְׁקוֹת

The same idea applies to Rabbah bar Ofron's statement — by "setting His throne" in Shushan, Hashem brought more severe judgment to bear upon the wicked, for suddenly Shushan became "His palace."

A similar theme emerges from the verse, "There was a Jewish man (אִישׁ יְהוּדִי) in Shushan the Capital whose name was Mordechai. . ." (2:5). Why does the verse mention Mordechai's religion before his name? The more usual construction would be, "Mordechai the Jew was in Shushan. . ."

The answer is that the verse alludes to the Sages' statement, "Only a person who has renounced belief in idolatry is called a Jew (אִישׁ יְהוּדִי)" (*Megillah* 13a).[1] We learn that Mordechai was an אִישׁ יְהוּדִי, a truly righteous individual. By placing Mordechai in Shushan, Hashem "prepared the cure in advance of the illness," for the very presence of a person of Mordechai's stature in Shushan brought severe judgment to bear upon the wicked.

According to *Rashi,* this is the same principle that prompted Lot to reject the angel's advice to flee to the hills, as it says, "Please, no! My Lord. . .I cannot escape to the mountain lest the evil attach itself to me and I die" (*Genesis* 19:19). *Rashi* explains that Lot felt safe living among the citizens of Sodom because he knew that in comparison to them he was a righteous man who was worthy to be saved in times of heavenly judgment. On the other hand, if he would have fled to the hills where Avraham lived, he would surely have been regarded as a wicked man. Consequently, severe heavenly judgment would have been brought to bear upon him, and he would have soon died.[1]

This would also explain why Esther advised Mordechai to convene the *Sanhedrin* (High Court of Torah Justice) and teach Torah to his disciples specifically beside the Palace Gate (see *Targum* 5:9). She understood that by bringing the wisdom of the Torah within close proximity of the wicked,

---

1. The *Maharsha* explains that the word יהודי contains the four letters of God's Name (י־ה־ו־ה).

2. In light of this concept, we can well understand why the woman of Zarephath said to Elijah upon the death of her son, "What harm have I done you, man of God, that you should come here to *recall my sin and cause the death of my son*" (*I Kings* 17:18).

glorious kingdom and the splendor of his excellent
majesty for many days — a hundred and eighty
days. 5 *And when these days were fulfilled, the King*
made a week-long feast for all the people who were
present in Shushan the Capital, great and small
alike, in the court of the garden of the King's palace.
6 *There were hangings of white, fine cotton and blue*
wool, held with cords of fine linen and purple wool,
upon silver rods and marble pillars; the couches of
gold and silver were on a pavement of green and
white, and shell and onyx marble. 7 *The drinks were*

---

severe heavenly judgment would be brought to bear upon them, for they could no longer claim in their defense that they had not had the opportunity to see the beauty of Torah.

4. יָמִים רַבִּים שְׁמוֹנִים וּמְאַת יוֹם — For many days — a hundred and eighty days.

Why does the verse state, "a hundred and eighty days," rather than, "six months"? It is in order to teach that there were no interruptions between the meals served in the feast, and hence, the 180 days of rejoicing felt like a single day. This is the intention of the Sages' statement, "a hundred and eighty days — the last day was as the first day" (*Esther Rabbah* 2:3). From this we learn two things: The extent of Ahasuerus' wealth, and the guests' gargantuan appetite for physical pleasure, for even after 180 days of uninterrupted feasting, they were still not revolted by the sight of food!

6. חוּר כַּרְפַּס וּתְכֵלֶת אָחוּז בְּחַבְלֵי־בוּץ וְאַרְגָּמָן — There were hangings of white, fine cotton and blue wool, held with cords of fine linen and purple wool.

Mordechai and Esther described the lavishness of the banquet in great detail in order to vindicate the Jews who succumbed to sin. This concept is mentioned in the Talmud, where the Sages ask "What do the words וְדִי זָהָב (*Deuteronomy* 1:1) mean? The school of R. Yannai said: Moses said before God, 'Master of the Universe! The silver and gold (זָהָב) that You gave so generously to the Israelites, to the point that they said, "Enough!" is what caused them to sin [by worshiping the golden calf]' " (*Berachos* 32).

Similarly, by describing the opulence of the banquet in great detail, Mordechai and Esther conveyed that Ahasuerus' sole intention was to cause the Jews to sin. Thus, they essentially said to Hashem, "It is *Ahasuerus* who should be held liable for their sin, not the Jews."

בִּכְלֵי זָהָב וְכֵלִים מִכֵּלִים שׁוֹנִים וְיֵין מַלְכוּת רָב
ח כְּיַד הַמֶּלֶךְ: וְהַשְּׁתִיָּה כַדָּת אֵין אֹנֵס כִּי־כֵן | יִסַּד
הַמֶּלֶךְ עַל כָּל־רַב בֵּיתוֹ לַעֲשׂוֹת כִּרְצוֹן אִישׁ־
ט וָאִישׁ: גַּם וַשְׁתִּי הַמַּלְכָּה עָשְׂתָה מִשְׁתֵּה
נָשִׁים בֵּית הַמַּלְכוּת אֲשֶׁר לַמֶּלֶךְ אֲחַשְׁוֵרוֹשׁ:

---

7. וְהַשְׁקוֹת בִּכְלֵי זָהָב וְכֵלִים מִכֵּלִים שׁוֹנִים — The drinks were served in golden goblets — no two goblets alike.

According to the Sages (*Megillah* 11a), Ahasuerus brought out the holy vessels of the Temple and used them during the feast. However, the Sages do not explain why Ahasuerus was not punished immediately for this sacrilege, as was Belshazzar when he committed the same sin years earlier.[1]

The answer is that Ahasuerus' sin was mitigated by the fact that there were Torah scholars in attendance at the feast. The Sages teach that Ahasuerus invited the Men of the Great Assembly to the celebration, and that Mordechai himself was the official wine steward (*Rashi* on *Megillah* 12a, s.v. כרצון מרדכי והמן). According to Rashi (*Exodus* 18:12), "when a person benefits from a meal attended by Torah scholars, it is as if he had benefited from the splendor of the Divine Presence."[2] Thus, we see that there was an aspect of holiness to this feast, for just as eating sacrificial meat or *terumah* is an integral component of the Temple service, so too, partaking of a meal attended by Torah scholars is equivalent to bringing a sacrifice upon the Altar. It was this hidden aspect of Temple service that mitigated Ahasuerus' sin, for at his feast the vessels were not used for a *completely* mundane purpose. In contrast, when Belshazzar used the vessels no Torah scholars had been present, and as a consequence he was judged more severely.

This also explains why Ahasuerus did not use the vessels of the Temple during the first 180-day feast, to which the Jews of Shushan were not invited, but only during the seven-day meal that was attended by all the citizens of Shushan, including the Jews. Ahasuerus was well aware of the

---

1. The Sages say that the reason Vashti (Belshazzar's daughter) lost her life is because a heavenly voice declared, "Your predecessors were destroyed because of those vessels, and now you dare repeat their sin?!" (*Megillah* 12). By taking out the holy vessels Ahasuerus awakened memories of the Temple's destruction. Unwittingly, he kindled heavenly judgment against Vashti, who was a descendant of Nebuchadnezzar, the man who destroyed the Temple, and of Belshazzar, who had made profane use of the vessels in previous years.

2. *Pachad Yitzchak* explains that just as the pleasure one derives from the splendor of the Divine Presence is a *mitzvah* (*Rambam, Sefer HaMitzvos*), so too, the pleasure one derives from eating together with Torah scholars is a *mitzvah.*

served in golden goblets — no two goblets alike — and royal wine in abundance, according to the bounty of the King. [8] *And the drinking was according to the law, without coercion, for so the King had ordered all the officers of his house that they should do according to every man's pleasure.*

[9] *Vashti the Queen also made a feast for the women in the royal house of King Ahasuerus.*

---

fact that Belshazzar had been punished for using the vessels, and he certainly did not wish to share his fate. He reasoned that the presence of Torah scholars would protect him from incurring Hashem's wrath.[1]

9. גַּם וַשְׁתִּי הַמַּלְכָּה עָשְׂתָה מִשְׁתֵּה נָשִׁים — Vashti the Queen also made a feast for the women.

Sfas Emes finds it strange that the Jewish People's redemption — which began with Vashti's death — originated from the very same feast that they were held accountable for attending (see *Megillah* 12). The explanation he offers is that once the Jews repented for their sins, Hashem regarded their intentional transgressions as meritorious deeds, as the Sages said, "Repentance is great, for when a person repents sincerely his intentional sins are transformed into merits" (*Yoma* 86b). Hence, Hashem transformed Ahasuerus' feast into the prelude of the Jewish People's redemption.

In a similar vein, the *Rokeach* says that the reason Esther instructed the Jewish People to fast for three days and three nights was in order to rectify their sin of attending Ahasuerus' feast. The feast continued for seven days, but six fasts were sufficient to atone for the sin because the Jews did not attend the feast on Shabbos for fear of desecrating the holy day. On weekdays they attended only during the day, but left the palace as soon as it became dark. Thus, in all, they were present at only six meals, for which they atoned by fasting three days and three nights.

The Jewish People's absence on Shabbos indicates that although they did succumb to sin, they still feared God. This explains why Vashti was sentenced to death specifically on the seventh day of the feast, which fell on Shabbos: The Jews' absence on that day demonstrated that while the

---

1. This theme is also apparent in the verse, "And Aaron and all the elders of Israel came to eat bread with the father-in-law of Moses before God" (*Exodus* 18:13). *Rashi* asks, "And where was Moses? He was waiting upon them and serving them." Many people find *Rashi's* answer difficult, for the Talmud states, "If a king releases others from the obligation to honor him, the obligation to honor him is nevertheless still in place" (*Kiddushin* 32b). If so, how could Moses (who had the status of King of Israel) have served Jethro and the elders? The answer is that serving food to a Torah scholar is not a mundane act, for it is likened to offering a sacrifice upon the Altar.

י בַּיּוֹם הַשְּׁבִיעִי כְּטוֹב לֵב־הַמֶּלֶךְ בַּיָּיִן אָמַר לִמְהוּמָן
בִּזְּתָא חַרְבוֹנָא בִּגְתָא וַאֲבַגְתָא זֵתַר וְכַרְכַּס שִׁבְעַת
הַסָּרִיסִים הַמְשָׁרְתִים אֶת־פְּנֵי הַמֶּלֶךְ אֲחַשְׁוֵרוֹשׁ׃
יא לְהָבִיא אֶת־וַשְׁתִּי הַמַּלְכָּה לִפְנֵי הַמֶּלֶךְ בְּכֶתֶר
מַלְכוּת לְהַרְאוֹת הָעַמִּים וְהַשָּׂרִים אֶת־יָפְיָהּ כִּי־

---

destruction of the Temple had weakened their faith, they still feared Hashem. Hashem knew that had the Temple not been destroyed, their fear of God would have been even more intense, as the verse states, "And you shall eat before HASHEM, your God, in the place that He will choose to rest His Name . . . so that you will learn to *fear* HASHEM, your God, all the days" (*Deuteronomy* 14:23). Thus, Hashem's anger was kindled against Vashti because she was a descendant of Nebuchadnezzar, the wicked man who had ordered the Temple destroyed, and as a result, she was executed on that very day.[1]

10. בַּיּוֹם הַשְּׁבִיעִי כְּטוֹב לֵב־הַמֶּלֶךְ בַּיָּיִן — On the seventh day, when the heart of the King was merry with wine.

Literally, every occurrence of the word הַמֶּלֶךְ ("the King") is a reference to Ahasuerus. The Sages, however, say that it alludes to Hashem, the King of Kings. We will now explain how to understand this verse according to the Sages' interpretation.

The Talmud (*Megillah* 12a) says: Rabbi Shimon bar Yochai's disciples asked him, "Why did the enemies of Israel [a euphemism for 'the Jewish People'] deserve extermination?"

He said to them, "You give an answer."

They said, "Because they derived pleasure from the feast of that wicked man [i.e., Ahasuerus]."

"If so, let [only the Jews] of Shushan be killed, but not the [Jews] in the entire world."

They said to him, "So you tell us [why]."

He said to them, "It was because they bowed down to an image."

They countered, "Was there partiality in this affair?" [Since idolatry is punishable by death, why were the Jews spared?]

---

1. When the First Temple was destroyed, the enemy troops entered the Temple complex on the seventh day of *Av* (*Taanis* 29a), which fell on Friday. The next day, on Shabbos, the eighth of *Av*, they ate and drank in celebration of their victory. On Sunday, the ninth of *Av*, they set fire to the Temple.

Evidently, Ahasuerus' feast on Shabbos resonated with the Babylonian soldiers' feasting inside the Temple complex approximately 70 years earlier, which also took place on Shabbos. Consequently, heavenly judgment was kindled during Ahasuerus' feast, and Vashti — Nebuchadnezzar's direct descendant — became the immediate target.

[10] *On the seventh day, when the heart of the King*
was merry with wine, he ordered Mehuman,
Bizzetha, Harbona, Bigtha and Abagtha, Zethar,
and Carcas, the seven chamberlains who attend-
ed King Ahasuerus, [11] *to bring Vashti the Queen*
before the King wearing the royal crown, to show
off to the people and the officials her beauty; for

He said to them, "They only *pretended* to [worship] it, and so, God only pretended [to destroy] them."

The fact that the answer of Rabbi Shimon's disciples is recorded in the Talmud indicates that it was in fact correct, and that Rabbi Shimon merely added a missing element to their explanation. Thus, there seems to be a correspondence between the sin of bowing down to the statue and the sin of deriving pleasure from Ahasuerus' feast. In order to understand how these two sins are interrelated, we must first ask another question:

According to *Sanhedrin* 61b, a person who bows down to an idol out of fear, when everyone in the generation is doing the same, does not incur the death penalty. Hence, in light of Rabbi Shimon's answer that the Jews only *pretended* to worship the idol, it remains unclear why the Jews were punished so severely.

The answer must be that God expects more than the minimum from a Jew. The Torah says, "I am HASHEM, your God, Who has taken you out of the land of Egypt, from the house of slavery. You shall not recognize the gods of others in My presence" (*Exodus* 20:2-3). In essence, God said to Israel, "You were once slaves to Pharaoh, and now you are My slaves. Therefore, you must not recognize any other gods." Now, if the Jewish People were no more than Hashem's slaves, then merely *pretending* to worship another god would not technically be considered a transgression. However, the relationship between God and the Jewish People runs deeper. It is likened to that of Father and son, as the verse says in reference to the reception of the Torah at Mount Sinai, "You are *children* to God your Lord" (*Deuteronomy* 14:1). Obviously, one expects much more devotion from one's own son than from one's servant. Thus, although the Jewish People did not commit a transgression against their *Master* by bowing down to the image in Ahasuerus' day, they did offend their *Father*. They ought to have shown a willingness to give up their lives rather than bow down to an idol, regardless of whether this was permitted or prohibited according to the strict letter of the law. This shortcoming is precisely what Mordechai came to rectify, as the verse says, "Mordechai did not bow down and prostrate himself" (3:5). Regarding this verse, *Tosafos* (*Sanhedrin* 61b) says, "He was permitted to [bow down], but for the

יב טוֹבַת מַרְאֶה הִיא: וַתְּמָאֵן הַמַּלְכָּה וַשְׁתִּי לָבוֹא
בִּדְבַר הַמֶּלֶךְ אֲשֶׁר בְּיַד הַסָּרִיסִים וַיִּקְצֹף הַמֶּלֶךְ
יג מְאֹד וַחֲמָתוֹ בָּעֲרָה בוֹ: וַיֹּאמֶר

---

sanctification of Hashem's Name, he neither bowed down nor prostrated himself."

According to *Pachad Yitzchak*, the Jewish People's rejection of the Father-son relationship between themselves and Hashem was what prompted them to attend Ahasuerus' feast. Years earlier, Jeremiah the Prophet had foreseen that the exiled Jews living in Babylonia would be returned to the Land of Israel after 70 years in exile (*Megillah* 11b; *Jeremiah* 29:10). However, some Jews doubted Jeremiah's prophecy. They wondered, "After a husband divorces his wife, or a master frees his slave, do they still owe anything to each other?" (*Sanhedrin* 105a). They believed that by expelling the Jews from the Holy Land, God had effectively broken all ties with them and revoked all His assurances, including the promise to redeem them after 70 years of exile.

Ahasuerus was well aware of both Jeremiah's prophecy and the skeptics' viewpoint, and he anxiously waited until the end of the 70-year period to see who would be proven correct. However, unbeknownst to Ahasuerus, his calculations were flawed, and he ushered in the 70th year of the Israelites' exile prematurely. An exuberant Ahasuerus decided to celebrate the date that, as far as he knew, marked Hashem's final rejection of the Jewish People. This is one of the reasons why he held the lavish feast described in the *Megillah* (*Megillah* 11b). The Jews who attended the feast were well aware of his intentions, yet nevertheless participated. By doing so, they effectively renounced the Father-son relationship that had been formed between Hashem and the Jewish People at Mount Sinai.

Thus, we see that both sins — bowing down to the image, and partaking of Ahasuerus' feast — symbolized the Jewish People's renouncement of their unique relationship with Hashem. In the end, they atoned for their sin by rejoicing over their close relationship with Hashem and reaccepting the Torah wholeheartedly, and thereby reestablished the Father-son bond with the Almighty.

With this introduction, we may now interpret the word הַמֶּלֶךְ as referring not to Ahasuerus, but to Hashem:

"On the seventh day" alludes to Shabbos, the day the Torah was given to the Jewish People;[1] "when the heart of the King was merry with wine" alludes to the reception of the Torah at Mount Sinai, when Hashem rejoiced

---

1. As the Sages say, "all agree that the Torah was given to Israel on Shabbos" (*Shabbos* 86b).

2. As in the verse, "He brought me to the wine chamber" (*Song of Songs* 2:4). According to

1/12 *she was beautiful to look upon.* [12] *But Queen Vashti refused to come at the King's commandment conveyed by the chamberlains; the King therefore became very incensed and his anger burned in him.*

---

over the Torah, which is likened to wine.[2] When the Jews joined Ahasuerus' celebration, Hashem recalled the unique Father-son relationship that existed between Himself and the Jewish People. He looked upon the Jews and perceived that they had renounced it, and consequently severe judgment was brought to bear upon them.

12. וַתְּמָאֵן הַמַּלְכָּה וַשְׁתִּי לָבוֹא בִּדְבַר הַמֶּלֶךְ — But Queen Vashti refused to come at the King's commandment.

The Sages ask, "Why did she [Vashti] not come? R' Yose bar Chanina said: 'This teaches that she had broken out with leprosy' " (*Megillah* 12b).

This explanation is difficult, though, for if Vashti indeed had a legitimate reason for not coming, why did the King become so angry at her?

The answer is provided by *Rambam*. He says that Vashti's leprosy was imperceptible to the women who were present at her feast. They could not understand why she refused to comply with the King's commandment, and therefore interpreted her disrespectful conduct as open rebelliousness.

Vashti was punished in kind for her sins. In return for forcing the Jewish girls to undress and thereby *revealing* their shame (see *Rashi*), Vashti's own source of shame — her leprosy — was *concealed* from her friends, and was perceptible only to her. This punishment led to her execution, for had Vashti's friends been aware of her condition, they would have informed Ahasuerus, and it stands to reason that he would not have reacted so angrily when she failed to obey his command. Thus, her punishment was in keeping with the spirit of וְנַהֲפוֹךְ הוּא ("it was turned about"; 9:1), an underlying theme that runs throughout the story of Purim — she was killed because her source of shame remained *concealed.*

בִּדְבַר הַמֶּלֶךְ אֲשֶׁר בְּיַד הַסָּרִיסִים — At the King's commandment conveyed by the chamberlains.

The King sent Vashti a written order in the manner of a royal decree, and had it formally delivered by his own chamberlains in order to give it the stamp of officialdom. He took these precautions because after all the squabbles he had had with her (see notes on 1:1), he feared that she might refuse to comply with his command.

Rashi, this refers to the Tabernacle, where the Jewish People received a more detailed explanation of the Torah. See also 1:2.

הַמֶּ֫לֶךְ לַחֲכָמִ֖ים יֹדְעֵ֣י הָעִתִּ֑ים כִּי־כֵן֙ דְּבַ֣ר הַמֶּ֔לֶךְ
יד לִפְנֵ֕י כָּל־יֹדְעֵ֖י דָּ֥ת וָדִֽין׃ וְהַקָּרֹ֣ב אֵלָ֗יו כַּרְשְׁנָ֤א שֵׁתָר֙

Vashti's indifference toward this legal document stamped with the King's own seal played a major role in the Jewish People's redemption: Years later, when Haman sent the royal decree calling for the destruction of the Jews to all the King's provinces, the people remembered Vashti's disparaging attitude towards official documents bearing the King's seal. Thus, Haman's royal decree did not make a very great impact upon the populace, and many people blithely ignored it.

13. וַיֹּאמֶר הַמֶּלֶךְ לַחֲכָמִים יֹדְעֵי הָעִתִּים כִּי־כֵן דְּבַר הַמֶּלֶךְ לִפְנֵי כָּל־יֹדְעֵי דָּת וָדִין — Then the King conferred with the Sages who knew the times for such was the King's procedure [to turn] to all who knew law and judgment.

The Talmud asks, "Who were 'the Sages'? The Rabbis. [What does] 'who knew the times' [mean]? That they knew how to calculate the intercalation of leap years and set the months" (*Megillah* 12b).

This means that Ahasuerus asked the Rabbis to judge Vashti for her insubordination. This is very strange. Did he not know that the Rabbis hated her with a passion? Why, she was the descendant of Nebuchadnezzar, who had led the destruction of the Holy Temple and exiled the Sages from the Land of Israel! It was she who had tortured the Jewish girls on Shabbos, as the Talmud relates. If so, why did he ask the Jewish Sages, of all people, to judge his wife?

The answer is that even the wicked Ahasuerus recognized the ability of the Rabbis to put aside their grievances and judge a person with absolutely impartiality. For the Rabbis know that true judgment emanates from Hashem, and that a judge must emulate His ways and overlook the dictates of his own emotions.

❧ ❧ ❧

"Law" (דִּין) refers to the legislative laws of a country, whereas "judgment" (דָּת) refers to accepted rules of etiquette. Vashti's insubordinate behavior violated both: By calling Ahasuerus "her father's stableboy" (see *Megillah* 12b), she humiliated the King and thereby committed the crime of rebelling against the authority of the monarch; by refusing to comply with her husband's command, she broke with the accepted social norm that a wife obey her husband.[1]

This explains the wording of 1:15, which says, "as to what should be done,

---

1. As the Sages said, "Who is a proper wife? She who complies with her husband's will" (*Nedarim* 66b).

[13] *Then the King conferred with the Sages who*
knew the times (for such was the King's pro-
cedure [to turn] to all who knew law and judgment.
[14] *Those closest to him were Carshena, Shethar,*

---

legally (כְּדָת), to Queen Vashti for not obeying the bidding of the King Ahasuerus conveyed by the chamberlains." In truth, Ahasuerus still loved Vashti. In order to help her evade capital punishment, he accused her only of having broken the rules of etiquette (דָּת), but not of having humiliated the King, a criminal act punishable by death.

However, at this point Memuchan (alias Haman) intervened. He conceded that under normal circumstances, someone guilty of merely violating social norms would not deserve the death penalty. Nevertheless, he argued, the serious repercussions of Vashti's crime had yet to be felt. Shortly, word of her disgraceful conduct would filter out to the populace, and in no time at all every woman in the kingdom would follow the Queen's example and begin belittling her husband! He insisted that only by sentencing Vashti to death could this sociological catastrophe be stemmed. Furthermore, Haman demanded that a new law be legislated to the effect that any infraction of etiquette with far-reaching negative repercussions to society incur capital punishment.

Haman's persuasiveness swayed the kingdom's legislative body, as it says, "This proposal pleased the King and the officials, and the King did according to the word of Memuchan" (1:21). The law now stated that an infraction of etiquette which the King and his ministers deemed dangerous to the welfare of society could be punishable by death.

Years later, this very law which Haman himself helped institute proved to be his nemesis: The *Megillah* says, "When the King returned from the palace garden to the banquet room, Haman was prostrated on the couch upon which Esther was; so the King exclaimed: 'Would he actually assault the Queen while I'm in the house?' " (7:8). Haman's violation of the rules of etiquette endangered the welfare of society as a whole, since his behavior would lead the populace to believe that the King consented to licentious behavior. Thus, it could not go unpunished, and as Haman himself had so strenuously insisted years earlier, nothing less than execution could stem such a sociological catastrophe!

14. וְהַקָּרֹב אֵלָיו כַּרְשְׁנָא שֵׁתָר אַדְמָתָא תַרְשִׁישׁ מֶרֶס מַרְסְנָא מְמוּכָן — Those closest to him were Carshena, Shethar, Admatha, Tarshish, Meres, Marsena and Memuchan.

The Talmud states, "R' Levi said: This entire verse alludes to sacrificial offerings: Carshena (כַּרְשְׁנָא) — the ministering angels said before the Holy One, Blessed is He, 'Master of the Universe! Did they [the gentiles] offer

אַדְמָ֥תָא תַרְשִׁ֖ישׁ מֶ֥רֶס מַרְסְנָ֖א מְמוּכָ֑ן שִׁבְעַ֞ת
שָׂרֵ֣י ׀ פָּרַ֣ס וּמָדַ֗י רֹאֵי֙ פְּנֵ֣י הַמֶּ֔לֶךְ הַיֹּשְׁבִ֥ים רִאשֹׁנָ֖ה
טו בַּמַּלְכֽוּת׃ כְּדָת֙ מַה־לַּעֲשׂ֔וֹת בַּמַּלְכָּ֖ה וַשְׁתִּ֑י עַ֣ל ׀
אֲשֶׁ֣ר לֹֽא־עָשְׂתָ֗ה אֶת־מַאֲמַר֙ הַמֶּ֣לֶךְ אֲחַשְׁוֵר֔וֹשׁ
°מְמוּכָ֖ן ק׳ טז בְּיַ֖ד הַסָּרִיסִֽים׃ וַיֹּ֣אמֶר °מומכן
לִפְנֵ֤י הַמֶּ֙לֶךְ֙ וְהַשָּׂרִ֔ים לֹ֤א עַל־הַמֶּ֙לֶךְ֙ לְבַדּ֔וֹ עָוְתָ֖ה
וַשְׁתִּ֣י הַמַּלְכָּ֑ה כִּ֤י עַל־כָּל־הַשָּׂרִים֙ וְעַל־כָּל־הָ֣עַמִּ֔ים
יז אֲשֶׁ֕ר בְּכָל־מְדִינ֖וֹת הַמֶּ֥לֶךְ אֲחַשְׁוֵרֽוֹשׁ׃ כִּֽי־יֵצֵ֤א
דְבַר־הַמַּלְכָּה֙ עַל־כָּל־הַנָּשִׁ֔ים לְהַבְז֥וֹת בַּעְלֵיהֶ֖ן
בְּעֵינֵיהֶ֑ן בְּאָמְרָ֗ם הַמֶּ֣לֶךְ אֲחַשְׁוֵר֡וֹשׁ אָמַ֞ר לְהָבִ֨יא
יח אֶת־וַשְׁתִּ֧י הַמַּלְכָּ֛ה לְפָנָ֖יו וְלֹא־בָֽאָה׃ וְֽ֠הַיּוֹם הַזֶּ֜ה
תֹּאמַ֣רְנָה ׀ שָׂר֣וֹת פָּֽרַס־וּמָדַ֗י אֲשֶׁ֤ר שָֽׁמְעוּ֙ אֶת־
דְּבַ֣ר הַמַּלְכָּ֔ה לְכֹ֖ל שָׂרֵ֣י הַמֶּ֑לֶךְ וּכְדַ֖י בִּזָּי֥וֹן וָקָֽצֶף׃

---

before You one-year-old lambs (כָּרִים בְּנֵי שָׁנָה), as did Israel?' Shethar (שֵׁתָר) — 'Did they offer before You two turtledoves (שְׁתֵּי תוֹרִים) [as did Israel]?'. . . Memuchan (מְמוּכָן) — 'Did they set a table (הֵכִינוּ שֻׁלְחָן) before You [as did Israel]?' " (*Megillah* 12b).

Immediately, one wonders why the ministering angels associated Memuchan (i.e., Haman) specifically with the Table (*Shulchan*) that stood in the Temple.

The answer is that the angels alluded to Haman's outstanding character trait. Just as a righteous man who is greater than the rest of his generation possesses an outstanding trait that sets him apart from the others, so too, an evil man who excels in his wickedness possesses an outstanding trait. This principle is also evident in the Pesach Haggadah — it is the wicked son who appears immediately after the wise son. This teaches that the worst villains have the potential to become the most pious individuals, and that the only difference between these two extremes is that the righteous individual channels his outstanding traits towards the service of God, whereas the wicked man utilizes them to perform evil.

Clearly, Haman's outstanding trait was perseverance. Unlike most people, Haman's enthusiasm did not wax and wane. He persisted unrelentingly toward his goal, regardless of the circumstances. The Table that stood in the Temple alludes to this trait, for the verse says, "On the Table shall you place show-bread before Me, *always*" (*Exodus* 25:30). Thus, the angels contrasted

Admatha, Tarshish, Meres, Marsena and Memu-
chan, the seven officers of Persia and Media, who
had access to the King, and who sat first in the
kingdom —) 15 *as to what should be done, legally, to*
Queen Vashti for not obeying the bidding of the King
Ahasuerus conveyed by the chamberlains.
16 *Memuchan declared before the King and the*
officials: "It is not only the King whom Vashti the
Queen has wronged, but also all the officials and all
the people in all the provinces of King Ahasuerus.
17 *For this deed of the Queen will come to the at-*
tention of all women, making their husbands con-
temptible in their eyes, by saying: 'King Ahasuerus
commanded Vashti the Queen to be brought before
him but she did not come!' 18 *And this day the*
princesses of Persia and Media who have heard of
the Queen's deed will cite it to all the King's offi-
cials, and there will be much contempt and wrath.

---

the Jewish People's perseverance in the service of God to Haman's perseverance in propagating evil.[1]

It follows then that Mordechai, who led the struggle against Haman, also possessed this trait. This is corroborated by the *Megillah*, which tells us, "*Every day* Mordechai used to walk about in front of the court of the harem to find out about Esther's well-being and what would become of her" (2:11). This went on for *nine years* without fail — nothing in the world could deter Mordechai from finding out about Esther's well-being.

The world was created through corresponding opposites which are symbiotically related to each other, as the verse says, "God made one opposite the other" (*Ecclesiastes* 7:14). This is the intention behind the Sages' interpretation of the verse " 'Instead of the thorn shall rise a cypress, instead of the nettle shall rise a myrtle' (*Isaiah* 55:13) — instead of Haman shall rise Mordechai." Both men possessed similar traits, but Mordechai used them to serve God, whereas Haman used them to further evil.

---

1. The Sages said, "Haman's descendants taught Torah in Bnei Brak" (*Sanhedrin* 96b). According to the *Midrash Talpios*, this is a reference to R' Shmuel bar Shilas, about whom the Talmud says, "He did not leave his disciples for thirteen years; even when he left them for a short time, he did not take his mind off them" (*Bava Basra* 8b). R' Shmuel bar Shilas employed the trait of perseverance — which he inherited from his ancestor, Haman — in order to serve Hashem.

א/יט־כב יט אִם־עַל־הַמֶּלֶךְ טוֹב יֵצֵא דְבַר־מַלְכוּת מִלְּפָנָיו
וְיִכָּתֵב בְּדָתֵי פָרַס־וּמָדַי וְלֹא יַעֲבוֹר אֲשֶׁר לֹא־
תָבוֹא וַשְׁתִּי לִפְנֵי הַמֶּלֶךְ אֲחַשְׁוֵרוֹשׁ וּמַלְכוּתָהּ
כ יִתֵּן הַמֶּלֶךְ לִרְעוּתָהּ הַטּוֹבָה מִמֶּנָּה׃ וְנִשְׁמַע פִּתְגָם
הַמֶּלֶךְ אֲשֶׁר־יַעֲשֶׂה בְּכָל־מַלְכוּתוֹ כִּי רַבָּה הִיא
וְכָל־הַנָּשִׁים יִתְּנוּ יְקָר לְבַעְלֵיהֶן לְמִגָּדוֹל וְעַד־
כא קָטָן׃ וַיִּיטַב הַדָּבָר בְּעֵינֵי הַמֶּלֶךְ וְהַשָּׂרִים וַיַּעַשׂ
כב הַמֶּלֶךְ כִּדְבַר מְמוּכָן׃ וַיִּשְׁלַח סְפָרִים אֶל־
כָּל־מְדִינוֹת הַמֶּלֶךְ אֶל־מְדִינָה וּמְדִינָה כִּכְתָבָהּ
וְאֶל־עַם וָעָם כִּלְשׁוֹנוֹ לִהְיוֹת כָּל־אִישׁ שֹׂרֵר בְּבֵיתוֹ

---

22. וַיִּשְׁלַח סְפָרִים אֶל־כָּל־מְדִינוֹת הַמֶּלֶךְ . . . לִהְיוֹת כָּל־אִישׁ שֹׂרֵר בְּבֵיתוֹ וּמְדַבֵּר כִּלְשׁוֹן עַמּוֹ — And he sent letters to all the King's provinces . . . to the effect that every man should rule in his own home, and speak the language of his own people.

As mentioned earlier (1:1), every single verse in the *Megillah* amplifies the magnitude of the miracles which took place. However, one may rightly wonder, "What relevance could this verse possibly have to the miracles of Purim?" The answer is as follows:

During the Babylonian exile, many Jews sinned by marrying gentile women (see *Sanhedrin* 21b, *Rashi* ad loc.). In his commentary on the *Megillah*, *R' Yonasan Eibeshitz* writes that these gentile women converted, but their motivation was only in order to marry their Jewish partners. As with all gentiles who convert for the sake of ulterior motives, these women were legally not Jewish.

Now, it stands to reason that these Babylonian women spoke their mother tongue with their children, and that they taught them their pagan beliefs. Haman's decree, however, dramatically changed the lifestyle of these intermarried couples. Since the law now stipulated that "every man should rule in his own home and speak the language of his own people," the gentile women had no choice but to speak to their children in the Israelite tongue, and to bring them up according to the statutes of the Torah.

This explains how no one surmised that Esther was Jewish even though it was well known that she had grown up in Mordechai's home, and that they had been married for years: Since intermarriage had become so common, the fact that Esther was married to Mordechai did not necessarily indicate

[19] *If it pleases the King, let there go forth a royal
edict from him, and let it be written into the laws
of the Persians and the Medes, that it be not revoked, that Vashti never again appear before King
Ahasuerus; and let the King confer her royal estate
upon another who is better than she.* [20] *Then,
when the King's decree which he shall proclaim
shall be resounded throughout all his kingdom
— great though it be — all the wives will show
respect to their husbands, great and small alike."*
[21] *This proposal pleased the King and the officials,
and the King did according to the word of
Memuchan;* [22] *and he sent letters to all the King's
provinces, to each province in its own script,
and to each people in its own language, to the effect
that every man should rule in his own home,*

---

that she was Jewish. Thus, we see that the sinners who married gentile women unwittingly set the scene for the miracle of Purim, for were it not for their sin, Esther's nationality would have swiftly been discovered, and she would never have been appointed Queen.[1]

Further, Haman was miraculously provided with positive "proof" that Esther was *not* Jewish:

The Talmud relates that Haman rejoiced greatly when his lot fell on the month of *Adar* (*Megillah* 13b). It would seem that he rejoiced because he knew that Moses had died during *Adar,* and he suspected that Mordechai was a spiritual descendant of Moses.[2] Thus, he surmised that the casting of the lot indicated that Mordechai would also die on that month. At the same time the lot also eliminated whatever suspicions he had about Esther's nationality, for it made him draw an absolute parallel between Moses and Mordechai — just as Moses had married a gentile woman, Mordechai must also have married a gentile woman. Relieved, he concluded that Queen Esther was not of Jewish origin.

---

1. This supports the opinion of my grandfather, *R' Yechezkel Levinstein*, who would say that even a wicked man's deeds fulfill Hashem's will.

2. According to the *Arizal,* Mordechai indeed possessed fragments of Moses' soul (see *Shem MiShmuel p. 176*). With this understanding, we can better appreciate the wording of *Midrash Rabbah* (*Noach* 38): "Moses was destined to be the *redeemer*, and Mordechai was destined for *redemption*." All redeemers contain a fragment of the soul of Moses, who was the paradigm of all redeemers, and Mordechai was destined to be the man who would bring about the Jewish People's redemption. See commentary to 10:3.

א וּמְדַבֵּר כִּלְשׁוֹן עַמּוֹ׃ אַחַר הַדְּבָרִים
הָאֵלֶּה כְּשֹׁךְ חֲמַת הַמֶּלֶךְ אֲחַשְׁוֵרוֹשׁ זָכַר אֶת־וַשְׁתִּי
ב וְאֵת אֲשֶׁר־עָשָׂתָה וְאֵת אֲשֶׁר־נִגְזַר עָלֶיהָ׃ וַיֹּאמְרוּ
נַעֲרֵי־הַמֶּלֶךְ מְשָׁרְתָיו יְבַקְשׁוּ לַמֶּלֶךְ נְעָרוֹת
ג בְּתוּלוֹת טוֹבוֹת מַרְאֶה׃ וְיַפְקֵד הַמֶּלֶךְ פְּקִידִים
בְּכָל־מְדִינוֹת מַלְכוּתוֹ וְיִקְבְּצוּ אֶת־כָּל־נַעֲרָה־
בְתוּלָה טוֹבַת מַרְאֶה אֶל־שׁוּשַׁן הַבִּירָה אֶל־בֵּית
הַנָּשִׁים אֶל־יַד הֵגֶא סְרִיס הַמֶּלֶךְ שֹׁמֵר הַנָּשִׁים

II

1. אַחַר הַדְּבָרִים הָאֵלֶּה כְּשֹׁךְ חֲמַת הַמֶּלֶךְ אֲחַשְׁוֵרוֹשׁ זָכַר אֶת־וַשְׁתִּי וְאֵת אֲשֶׁר־עָשָׂתָה וְאֵת אֲשֶׁר־נִגְזַר עָלֶיהָ — After these things, when the wrath of King Ahasuerus subsided, he remembered Vashti, and what she had done, and what had been decreed against her.

In reference to this verse, the Sages said, "[He remembered — i.e. realized — that] what she had done is what was decreed against her" (*Megillah* 12b). This teaches that even the evil Ahasuerus recognized that Vashti had been punished in kind for her sin — she was unclothed and executed on Shabbos because she would force young Jewish women to undress and do work on Shabbos.

Nonetheless, this realization did not leave a lasting impression on Ahasuerus, for the very next verse states, "Then the King's pages said: 'Let there be sought for the King beautiful young maidens. . .' " (2:2). The Sages applied to Ahasuerus the proverb, "Every clever man acts knowledgeably, whereas the fool exposes [his] stupidity" (*Proverbs* 13:16), because instead of being jolted back to his senses by the exactness of Vashti's punishment, he accepted the advice of his pages, and he promptly returned to his vain pursuits. This reaffirms the *Chovos Halevavos'* principle that "the evil force is capable of hindering and confusing one's wisdom" (*Chovos Halevavos*, *Shaar Cheshbon Hanefesh*, 10). If this is said about the righteous, then how much more so does it apply to wicked individuals such as Ahasuerus!

The same idea is reflected in my grandfather *R' Yechezkel Levinstein*'s work *Yad Yechezkel* on the verse, " 'Look, I am going to die, so of what use to me is a birthright?' " (*Genesis* 25:32): Although the Sages say that the very mention of a man's death can stir him to repent for his sins (*Berachos* 5b), this principle does not apply to the wicked, for we see that Esau spurned his birthright even though he was convinced that he would

and speak the language of his own people.

1 *After these things, when the wrath of King*
Ahasuerus subsided, he remembered Vashti,
and what she had done, and what had been decreed
against her. 2 *Then the King's pages said: "Let there*
be sought for the King beautiful young maidens;
3 *and let the King appoint commissioners in all the*
provinces of his kingdom, that they may gather
together every beautiful young maiden to Shushan
the Capital to the harem, under the charge of Hegai
the King's chamberlain, guardian of the women;

---

soon die. This, too, is the intention of the verse, "For the paths of God are straight — the righteous walk upon them, but sinners stumble upon them" (*Hosea* 14:10).

זָכַר אֶת־וַשְׁתִּי וְאֵת אֲשֶׁר־עָשָׂתָה וְאֵת אֲשֶׁר־נִגְזַר עָלֶיהָ — He remembered Vashti, and what she had done, and what had been decreed against her.

As stated above, the Sages (*Megillah* 12b) say this verse refers to Vashti's execution on Shabbos, the day when she had forced young Jewish women to undress and do work. The Sages' statement implies that she would unclothe them specifically on Shabbos, but not on any other day. What is the reason?

Further, the *Targum* writes that Vashti deserved to die because "she did not give permission to build the Holy Temple." How can this explanation be reconciled with the Sages' opinion that she was punished because of her ill-treatment of Jewish women?

The answer is as follows: *R' Itzele* of Volozhin used to say that both Shabbos and the Holy Temple have something in common — namely, that they both cause holiness to reside upon the Jewish People. This is the reason why even the act of building the Holy Temple does not override the prohibition of building on Shabbos, for Shabbos brings as much holiness upon the Jewish People as the Holy Temple. As the verse says about Shabbos, "It is a sign between Me and you for your generations, to know that I am HASHEM, Who makes you holy" (*Exodus* 31:13).

Vashti was aware of the effect Shabbos had on the Jewish People. It greatly disturbed her, since holiness was the very antithesis of her evil nature. Thus, she set out to nullify the effect of Shabbos by forcing Jewish women to desecrate it through forbidden work. But she did not stop at this. She knew that by merely wearing Shabbos clothes a Jew could fulfill the

ד וְנָתוֹן תַּמְרוּקֵיהֶן: וְהַנַּעֲרָה אֲשֶׁר תִּיטַב בְּעֵינֵי הַמֶּלֶךְ
תִּמְלֹךְ תַּחַת וַשְׁתִּי וַיִּיטַב הַדָּבָר בְּעֵינֵי הַמֶּלֶךְ וַיַּעַשׂ
ה כֵּן: אִישׁ יְהוּדִי הָיָה בְּשׁוּשַׁן הַבִּירָה
וּשְׁמוֹ מָרְדֳּכַי בֶּן יָאִיר בֶּן־שִׁמְעִי בֶּן־קִישׁ אִישׁ יְמִינִי:

---

mitzvah of honoring the Shabbos,[1] and that it would also cause a degree of holiness to reside upon the Jewish People. Thus, she forced the Jewish women to remove their clothes in order to eliminate all vestiges of Shabbos observance.

5. אִישׁ יְהוּדִי הָיָה בְּשׁוּשַׁן הַבִּירָה וּשְׁמוֹ מָרְדֳּכַי בֶּן יָאִיר בֶּן־שִׁמְעִי בֶּן־קִישׁ אִישׁ יְמִינִי — There was a Jewish man in Shushan the Capital whose name was Mordechai, son of Jair, son of Shimei, son of Kish, a Benjaminite.

The Talmud teaches that Moses and Aaron played fundamentally different roles in bringing about the redemption of the Jewish People in Egypt. Moses focused on observance of the law, whereas Aaron emphasized the importance of peace and harmony among fellow Jews (see *Sanhedrin* 6b). Similarly, Mordechai and Esther brought about the redemption of the Jewish People through their individual traits, which were not at all alike.

The outstanding traits of Mordechai and Esther can best be understood through careful study of the following excerpt from the Talmud: "R' Chana bar Bizna said in the name of R' Shimon Chasida: Because Joseph (יוֹסֵף) sanctified the Name of Heaven without anyone's knowledge, one letter of Hashem's name was added to his name (יְהוֹסֵף; see *Psalms* 81:6); because Judah sanctified the Name of Heaven in public, his *entire name* (יְהוּדָה) contains Hashem's name" (*Sotah* 36b).

Mordechai is referred to as אִישׁ יְהוּדִי ("a Jewish man"; 2:5). *Maharal* asks why the verse did not simply say "a Jew" (יְהוּדִי). His answer is that the verse does not only reveal Mordechai's religion, but also that he served Hashem in the same manner as Judah (יְהוּדָה) — namely, by sanctifying the Name of Heaven in public, as the verse says, "And Mordechai tore his clothes and put on sackcloth with ashes. *He went out into the midst of the city*, and cried loudly and bitterly" (4:1).

In contrast, Esther's way was to sanctify the Name of Heaven in private, without anyone's knowledge. Esther's very name reflects this trait — as R' Meir said, the name Esther (אֶסְתֵּר) alludes to the verse, "But I will surely have concealed (וְאָנֹכִי הַסְתֵּר אַסְתִּיר) My face on that day" (*Deuteronomy* 31:18).

---

1. See *Yalkut* (*Ruth*, 604): " '*And don your clothes*' (*Ruth* 3:3) . . .this refers to her Sabbath attire. Rabbi Chanina derives from here that a person must have two garments, one for weekdays and one for Sabbath." See also *Mishnah Berurah* (262:5) that the directive "And you shall honor [the Sabbath]" (*Isaiah* 58:13) refers to donning special clothes.

let their cosmetics be given them. 4 *Then, let the girl*
who pleases the King be queen instead of Vashti."
This advice pleased the King, and he followed it.
5 ***There was a Jewish man in Shushan the***
Capital whose name was Mordechai, son of
Jair, son of Shimei, son of Kish, a Benjaminite,

As we learn from our father *Abraham,* the real test of faith is to fulfill Hashem's will even if this demands that one behave in a manner that runs contrary to one's natural tendencies. *Abraham,* who was the embodiment of lovingkindness, was commanded to slaughter his only son, Isaac, and offer him as a sacrifice to Hashem. This, too, was Esther's test — to overcome her natural tendency to serve Hashem in private, and to sanctify His Name in public.

❧ ❧ ❧

The Talmud says, "R' Shmuel bar Nachmani began his exposition of the *Megillah* with the following verse: 'Instead of the thorn shall rise a cypress, instead of the nettle shall rise a myrtle' (*Isaiah* 55:13).

" 'Instead of the thorn' — instead of Haman the wicked, who made himself an object of worship.

" 'Shall rise a cypress (ברוש)' — this refers to Mordechai, who is called 'the finest (ראש) of all spices.' As it is said, 'And you, take for you the finest spices, pure myrrh' (*Exodus* 30:23). And the *Targum* there renders [pure myrrh] as *mera dachia* (מֵירָא דַכְיָא)" (*Megillah* 10b).

The reason Mordechai's name is associated with a pleasant fragrance is that the sense of smell is the most elevated of all physical senses. Unlike all the others, the sense of smell gives pleasure even to the soul. This is because the soul and the sense of smell share similar qualities: Just as the soul is the innermost aspect of a human being, so too, the sense of smell enables one to detect the hidden, innermost nature of an object. For example, through smell it is possible to discover that a fruit which looks fresh from the outside is in fact rotten on the inside. Because of their similarity, the soul, a spiritual entity, is able to derive pleasure from smell, a physical sense.

Idolatry, on the other hand, is complete falsehood. Its power derives entirely from its exterior appearance, which makes it seem as though it is composed of real substance. At its core, though, it is nothing but a lie.

We can now well understand the statement of the Sages quoted above. In essence, they said, "Instead of Haman, who made himself an object of worship and whose essence was pure falsehood, shall rise Mordechai, who was the finest of fragrances, and whose essence was absolute truth." Like an idol, Haman gave the false impression of being all-powerful, but because his

ו אֲשֶׁר הָגְלָה מִירוּשָׁלַיִם עִם־הַגֹּלָה אֲשֶׁר הָגְלְתָה עִם
יְכָנְיָה מֶלֶךְ־יְהוּדָה אֲשֶׁר הֶגְלָה נְבוּכַדְנֶאצַּר מֶלֶךְ

---

core was falsehood, he swiftly crumbled. Mordechai, on the other hand, was at first unpopular among the Jews (*Megillah* 13a). Many of them opposed his "extremist" views and instigative tactics because he seemed to be harming, not helping, the Jewish People. However, on the inside, Mordechai's intentions were completely pure, as the *Megillah* itself testifies, "he sought the good of his people and was concerned for the welfare of all his posterity" (10:3). Thus, he is likened to a fine fragrance, for despite the negative impression he made on the outside, his true nature was completely pure.

❦ ❦ ❦

In the passage quoted above, the Sages go on to explain the second half of the verse:

" 'Instead of the nettle' — instead of Vashti the wicked, the granddaughter of Nebuchadnezzar the wicked, who burned the . . . House of God.

" 'Shall rise a myrtle (הדס)' — this refers to Esther the righteous, who was named Hadassah (הדסה), as the verse says, 'And he had reared Hadassah' (2:7)."

Shem MiShmuel asks the following question: Since R' Shmuel bar Nachmani began his exposition of the *Megillah* with this verse, he obviously felt that it captures the central theme of the *Megillah*. The first half of the verse indeed alludes to the pivotal point of the Purim story, for Haman's downfall and Mordechai's subsequent rise to power marked the onset of the redemption. The symmetry between Vashti's death and Esther's appointment as Queen is also quite clear, for Esther played a vital role in bringing about the miracle. However, it is unclear why the Sages make mention of Vashti's lineage to Nebuchadnezzar, for it would seem that this fact has no bearing whatsoever to the story of Purim. Ostensibly, even if Vashti had *not* been related to Nebuchadnezzar, her downfall would still have been a significant turning point in the story.

The answer is that Hashem created the world through corresponding opposites which are symbiotically related to each other. They affect each other inversely — when one rises, the other[1] falls. This theme is evident in numerous verses in Scripture. One example is the verse, "The might shall pass from one regime to the other" (*Genesis* 25:23), in reference to which *Rashi* says, "They [Jacob and Esau] will not be equal in stature — when this one rises, the other shall fall."

So too, Esther was the corresponding opposite of Vashti. The Sages tell us that Esther was brought up and educated by Mordechai.[1] Throughout

---

1. See *Chagiga* 15a.

6 *who had been exiled from Jerusalem along with the exiles who had been exiled with Jehoniah, King of Judah, whom Nebuchadnezzar, King of Babylon,*

---

her early years, he imbued her with his great love for the Jewish People, which gave her the strength to risk her life for their sake and say with full conviction, "I will go in to the King though it is unlawful, and if I perish, I perish" (4:16). Vashti, on the other hand, was brought up in the ways of her wicked grandfather, who vented his fierce hatred of the Jewish People by destroying the Holy Temple.

Thus, when Vashti fell, the inverse relationship with her corresponding opposite took effect, and Esther ascended to power.

5. בֶּן יָאִיר בֶּן־שִׁמְעִי בֶּן־קִישׁ אִישׁ יְמִינִי — Son of Jair, son of Shimei, son of Kish, a Benjaminite.

In reference to this verse, the Sages said, " 'Son of Jair (יָאִיר)' — because he lit up (הֵאִיר) the eyes of Israel with his prayers. 'Son of Shimei (שִׁמְעִי)' — because Hashem listened (שָׁמַע) to his prayers. 'Son of Kish (קִישׁ)' — because he knocked (הִקִּישׁ) on the Gates of Mercy, and they opened for him" (*Megillah* 12b).

Shem MiShmuel points out that according to the Sages' interpretation, the clauses of the verse appear in reversed order: The logical sequence of events should have been that Mordechai first knocked on the Gate of Mercy (son of Kish), that Hashem then listened to his prayers (son of Shimei), and thereafter he lit up the eyes of Israel with his prayers (son of Jair).

In order to answer this difficulty, we must first grasp an important concept that was often repeated by R' Yerucham Levovits, the venerable *Mashgiach* of the Mirrer Yeshiva in Europe. He would begin by quoting *Midrash Rabbah* (*Beshalach*, *Parshah* 61:5), which states, "Why did Hashem [frighten] the [Israelites]? Because Hashem desired their prayers. It says, 'Pharoah approached . . . and the Children of Israel cried out to HASHEM' (*Exodus* 14:10). At that moment Hashem said, 'That is why — because I desired to hear your voices.' " From this *Midrash*, R' Yerucham would say, we learn that the essential purpose behind the Splitting of the Sea was to rouse the Jewish people to prayer.

Similarly, the essential purpose behind the adversity that befell the Jews in Shushan was to dispel the spiritual darkness that comes with exile, and to "light up the eyes of Israel" through Mordechai's prayer. Our verse conveys this by placing this clause first. Hence, the answer to *Shem MiShmuel*'s difficulty is that the clauses of the verse are not arranged in logical se- quence, but rather, in order of importance. This idea is often expressed as, "The final outcome of a deed is the first thing in mind" (סוֹף מַעֲשֶׂה בְּמַחֲשָׁבָה תְּחִילָּה).

---

1. See *Megillah* 13.

ז בָּבֶל׃ וַיְהִ֨י אֹמֵ֜ן אֶת־הֲדַסָּ֗ה הִ֤יא אֶסְתֵּר֙ בַּת־דֹּד֔וֹ כִּ֛י אֵ֥ין
לָ֖הּ אָ֣ב וָאֵ֑ם וְהַנַּעֲרָ֤ה יְפַת־תֹּ֙אַר֙ וְטוֹבַ֣ת מַרְאֶ֔ה וּבְמ֤וֹת
ח אָבִ֙יהָ֙ וְאִמָּ֔הּ לְקָחָ֧הּ מָרְדֳּכַ֛י ל֖וֹ לְבַֽת׃ וַיְהִ֗י בְּהִשָּׁמַ֤ע
דְּבַר־הַמֶּ֙לֶךְ֙ וְדָת֔וֹ וּֽבְהִקָּבֵ֛ץ נְעָר֥וֹת רַבּ֛וֹת אֶל־שׁוּשַׁ֥ן
הַבִּירָ֖ה אֶל־יַ֣ד הֵגָ֑י וַתִּלָּקַ֤ח אֶסְתֵּר֙ אֶל־בֵּ֣ית הַמֶּ֔לֶךְ
ט אֶל־יַ֥ד הֵגַ֖י שֹׁמֵ֥ר הַנָּשִֽׁים׃ וַתִּיטַ֨ב הַנַּעֲרָ֣ה בְעֵינָיו֮ וַתִּשָּׂ֣א
חֶ֣סֶד לְפָנָיו֒ וַ֠יְבַהֵל אֶת־תַּמְרוּקֶ֤יהָ וְאֶת־מָנוֹתֶ֙הָ֙ לָתֵ֣ת
לָ֔הּ וְאֵת֙ שֶׁ֣בַע הַנְּעָר֔וֹת הָרְאֻי֥וֹת לָֽתֶת־לָ֖הּ מִבֵּ֣ית
הַמֶּ֑לֶךְ וַיְשַׁנֶּ֧הָ וְאֶת־נַעֲרוֹתֶ֛יהָ לְט֖וֹב בֵּ֥ית הַנָּשִֽׁים׃

---

7. וַיְהִי אֹמֵן אֶת־הֲדַסָּה הִיא אֶסְתֵּר בַּת־דֹּדוֹ כִּי אֵין לָהּ אָב וָאֵם — And he had reared Hadassah, that is, Esther, his uncle's daughter; since she had neither father nor mother.

The Talmud asks, "Where is Esther (אֶסְתֵּר) [mentioned] in the Torah? In the verse, 'But I will surely have concealed My face on that day (וְאָנֹכִי הַסְתֵּר אַסְתִּיר פָּנַי בַּיּוֹם הַהוּא)' (*Deuteronomy* 31:18)" (*Chullin* 139b). This teaches that Esther's name is associated with exile, not redemption. *Shem MiShmuel* points out that associating Esther's name with exile would seem to imply something derogatory about her character, yet everything we know indicates that Esther was beyond reproach.

The answer lies in *Ramban*'s commentary to *Exodus* 4:10. The verse says, "I am not a man of words. . .I am heavy of mouth and heavy of speech." *Ramban* asks why Moses did not beseech Hashem to cure his speech impediment, since it stands to reason that Hashem would have accepted his prayers. *Ramban*'s answer is that Moses did not wish to be cured of his speech impediment. It was a constant reminder to him of the miraculous manner in which his life had been spared,[1] and it prompted him to continuously express gratitude to Hashem for having performed that miracle.

Similarly, Hadassah deliberately chose the name Esther *because* it represents the darkness of exile, when Hashem's love for the Jewish People

---

1. The Midrash (*Shemos Rabbah* 1:31) relates the following incident:

When Moses was an infant, Pharaoh would hug and kiss him, and Moses would take Pharaoh's crown and place it on his own head. Pharaoh's astrologers expressed their fear that this child may grow up to lead the Jews from Egypt and suggested that he be put to death. Jethro, who was among those present, suggested that they test the young boy to see if he understood what he was doing. They brought in a tray with a pile of gems and a pile of coals. As Moses reached for the gems, the angel Gabriel forced his hand onto the coals. Moses took a coal and placed it in his mouth. This was the cause for his speech impediment.

had exiled. [7] *And he had reared Hadassah, that is, Es-*
ther, his uncle's daughter; since she had neither father
nor mother. The girl was finely featured and beautiful,
and when her father and mother had died, Mordechai
adopted her as his daughter. [8] *So it came to pass,*
when the King's bidding and decree were published,
and when many young girls were being brought to-
gether to Shushan the Capital, under the charge of
Hegai, that Esther was taken into the palace, under
the charge of Hegai, guardian of the women. [9] *The*
girl pleased him, and she obtained his kindness; he
hurriedly prepared her cosmetics and her allowance
of delicacies to present her, along with the seven spe-
cial maids from the palace, and he transferred her
and her maidens to the best quarters in the harem.

---

is all the more meaningful.[1] For even though He hides His countenance from the Jewish People He continues to protect them, as it says, "Behold, the Guardian of Israel neither sleeps nor slumbers" (*Psalms* 121:4). Thus, in order to be continually reminded of Hashem's intense love for the Jewish People during the spiritual darkness of exile, Hadassah chose to be called Esther, which in this context means "in hiding."

9. וְאֵת שֶׁבַע הַנְּעָרוֹת הָרְאֻיוֹת לָתֶת־לָהּ מִבֵּית הַמֶּלֶךְ וַיְשַׁנֶּהָ וְאֶת־נַעֲרוֹתֶיהָ לְטוֹב בֵּית הַנָּשִׁים — Along with the seven special maids from the palace, and he transferred her and her maidens to the best quarters in the harem.

The Sages say that each maid came on a set day, and that in this manner Esther kept track of the days of the week (*Megillah* 13a). According to the *Targum*, she assigned them names representing each day. For example, the maid that served Esther on Shabbos was called רְגוֹעִיתָא, which means "rest." One may rightly wonder, however, why she counted the days of the week in

---

1. Hashem's love for the Israelites during exile is not only more meaningful, but actually *greater*: " 'The children of the forlorn wife are greater than those of the espoused wife' (*Isaiah* 54:1). [In reference to this verse,] R' Levi said: 'When [the Temple] stood, [the Jewish People] produced wicked individuals such as Ahaz, Manasseh, and Amon; when it was destroyed, [the Jewish People] produced righteous individuals such as Daniel and his companions, Ezra and his companions. . .' " (*Yalkut*, *Isaiah* 63).

This theme is also evident from the following analogy, with which *Midrash Rabbah* (*Vayeishev* 86:5) elucidates the verse "Hashem was with Joseph" (*Genesis* 39:2): " 'Hashem was with Joseph' implies that He was with Joseph, but *not* with the rest of Jacob's sons. Why?

"It is analogous to a man who was leading 12 beasts bearing barrels of wine. Suddenly, one bolted away and entered the store of a gentile. The man left the other 11 animals in the

י לֹא־הִגִּידָה אֶסְתֵּר אֶת־עַמָּהּ וְאֶת־מוֹלַדְתָּהּ כִּי
יא מָרְדֳּכַי צִוָּה עָלֶיהָ אֲשֶׁר לֹא־תַגִּיד׃ וּבְכָל־יוֹם
וָיוֹם מָרְדֳּכַי מִתְהַלֵּךְ לִפְנֵי חֲצַר בֵּית־הַנָּשִׁים
יב לָדַעַת אֶת־שְׁלוֹם אֶסְתֵּר וּמַה־יֵּעָשֶׂה בָּהּ׃ וּבְהַגִּיעַ

---

this bizarre manner. As far as we know, she was not kept in isolation, so why did she not keep track of the week in the regular manner?

The answer is that Esther wished to perform *mitzvos* at every opportunity.[1] When Esther was assigned seven maids, she decided to use them to fulfill the *mitzvah* of remembering the Shabbos. According to *Ramban* (*Parshas Yisro* 20:8), this *mitzvah* applies during the entire week: "It is a *mitzvah* to always remember the Shabbos every day and never to forget it nor confuse it with another day. . . This is an important tenet of faith in God."

Alternatively, Esther needed this system because, as Queen, she was no longer permitted to do any menial work, including preparing for Shabbos. Consequently, she feared she would forget all about Shabbos, for as the Sages say, "A person does not pay attention to something that has no relevance to him" (*Shevuos* 41b). This reveals the high level of spirituality and fear of God that Esther achieved, and how punctiliously she observed the *mitzvos* of the Torah.

Another possible explanation is that, as noted above (2:1), Vashti caused her Jewish servants to desecrate the Sabbath. Esther's punctilious observance of Sabbath and taking precautions to remember it was yet another astounding turnabout in the Purim story.

11. וּבְכָל־יוֹם וָיוֹם מָרְדֳּכַי מִתְהַלֵּךְ לִפְנֵי חֲצַר בֵּית־הַנָּשִׁים לָדַעַת אֶת־שְׁלוֹם אֶסְתֵּר וּמַה־יֵּעָשֶׂה בָּהּ — Every day Mordechai used to walk about in front of the court of the harem to find out about Esther's well-being and what would become of her.

This was certainly not a very appropriate place for a righteous person of Mordechai's stature to frequent. However, he was obligated to do so by the

---

street and chased after the stray beast. People said to him, 'Why leave 11 beasts unguarded and chase after one?' He answered them, 'Since those are in a public place, there is no danger that the wine they are carrying will be rendered unkosher by a gentile.'

"Similarly, Jacob's other sons were older and under their father's supervision, unlike Joseph, who was young and alone. That is why the verse says, 'Hashem was *with Joseph*.' "

Just as a mother is more concerned about the safety of a child who is away from home than one who is at her side, so too, Hashem shows greater concern for the Jewish People when they are in exile than when they are in their own land.

1. The Gaon R' Mordechai Benet exemplified this trait. For example, whenever he would try a new pen, he would write the word עמלק (Amalek), and then erase it. Through the mundane act of trying out a pen, he also fulfilled the *mitzvah* of erasing the name of Amalek.

10 *Esther had not told of her people or her kindred,*
for Mordechai had instructed her not to tell. 11 *Every*
day Mordechai used to walk about in front of
the court of the harem to find out about Esther's
well-being and what would become of her.

---

obligation to behave properly toward his fellow man (בֵּין אָדָם לַחֲבֵרוֹ), as well as by his obligation to God (בֵּין אָדָם לַמָּקוֹם). As Esther's husband, he had an obligation to "find out about Esther's well-being," in keeping with the laws between man and his fellow. He also had an obligation to see "what would become of her" — that is, to perceive what role she would play in the unfolding of Hashem's master plan — in keeping with the laws between man and God. For according to *Rashi*, Mordechai was one of the two righteous individuals in all of Jewish history to whom it was revealed that redemption would soon take place (the other was King David). Mordechai reasoned to himself, "It cannot be that such a righteous woman will be taken by a gentile [for no reason]. Rather, it must be that she will eventually rise and redeem Israel!"

Thus, Mordechai continued to walk before the court of the harem every single day, without fail, *for nine years*. It stands to reason that the court of the King's harem was an extremely promiscuous place, creating an atmosphere that was the very antithesis of as pious a man as Mordechai. Nonetheless, he did not let this deter him from visiting frequently because he firmly believed that Esther would one day bring about Israel's redemption, and that it was part of his duty to his fellow man to keep watch over her. Therefore, despite all the obstacles, doubts, and despair, he tenaciously persisted.

Mordechai exemplified a principle taught by the Alter of Kelm (*Chochmah U'mussar* Section 1, p. 104): Whenever some fundamental tenet of faith or Divine Providence becomes clear to a person, it is Hashem's will that he toil to internalize it, that he build a mental fortress around it, and that he never allow anything in the world to sway him from it.[1]

This was one of Mordechai's most dominant traits. He continued visiting the court of the harem because he was convinced that Esther's abduction to Ahasuerus' palace had been an act of Providence. He kept watch on Esther

---

1. People who have great faith in God always look for Divine Providence. In his work *Ohr Yechezkel*, my grandfather, *R' Yechezkel Levinstein,* states, "If a person contemplates the wonders of Creation and ponders over world events in order to learn the ways of Hashem, he will merit untold blessings." My grandfather himself used to inculcate this principle into his daughters by giving them a coin whenever they would recount an event in which they saw Divine Providence. He used to say that a person who sincerely searches for signs of Divine Providence will eventually succeed, and that he will merit to understand things that remain concealed from the rest of humanity.

תֹּר נַעֲרָה וְנַעֲרָה לָבוֹא ׀ אֶל־הַמֶּלֶךְ אֲחַשְׁוֵרוֹשׁ
מִקֵּץ הֱיוֹת לָהּ כְּדָת הַנָּשִׁים שְׁנֵים עָשָׂר חֹדֶשׁ כִּי
כֵּן יִמְלְאוּ יְמֵי מְרוּקֵיהֶן שִׁשָּׁה חֳדָשִׁים בְּשֶׁמֶן הַמֹּר
וְשִׁשָּׁה חֳדָשִׁים בַּבְּשָׂמִים וּבְתַמְרוּקֵי הַנָּשִׁים׃
יג וּבָזֶה הַנַּעֲרָה בָּאָה אֶל־הַמֶּלֶךְ אֵת כָּל־אֲשֶׁר תֹּאמַר
יִנָּתֵן לָהּ לָבוֹא עִמָּהּ מִבֵּית הַנָּשִׁים עַד־בֵּית
יד הַמֶּלֶךְ׃ בָּעֶרֶב ׀ הִיא בָאָה וּבַבֹּקֶר הִיא שָׁבָה
אֶל־בֵּית הַנָּשִׁים שֵׁנִי אֶל־יַד שַׁעַשְׁגַז סְרִיס הַמֶּלֶךְ
שֹׁמֵר הַפִּילַגְשִׁים לֹא־תָבוֹא עוֹד אֶל־הַמֶּלֶךְ כִּי
טו אִם־חָפֵץ בָּהּ הַמֶּלֶךְ וְנִקְרְאָה בְשֵׁם׃ וּבְהַגִּיעַ תֹּר־
אֶסְתֵּר בַּת־אֲבִיחַיִל ׀ דֹּד מָרְדֳּכַי אֲשֶׁר לָקַח־
לוֹ לְבַת לָבוֹא אֶל־הַמֶּלֶךְ לֹא בִקְשָׁה דָּבָר כִּי
אִם אֶת־אֲשֶׁר יֹאמַר הֵגַי סְרִיס־הַמֶּלֶךְ שֹׁמֵר
הַנָּשִׁים וַתְּהִי אֶסְתֵּר נֹשֵׂאת חֵן בְּעֵינֵי כָּל־רֹאֶיהָ׃

---

because he longed to see how Hashem would bring about the redemption of the Jewish People through her. In the end, after nine years of waiting, Mordechai indeed merited to see Divine Providence,[1] as the verse testifies, "Mordechai learned of all that had been done" (4:1). It was he who merited to rouse the Jewish People to prayer and repentance, and it was on his merit that their prayers were accepted, as the Sages say, " 'Son of Jair (יָאִיר)' — because he lit up (הֵאִיר) the eyes of Israel with his prayers" (*Megillah* 12b).

15. וּבְהַגִּיעַ תֹּר־אֶסְתֵּר בַּת־אֲבִיחַיִל דֹּד מָרְדֳּכַי אֲשֶׁר לָקַח־לוֹ לְבַת לָבוֹא אֶל־הַמֶּלֶךְ. . . — Now when the turn came for Esther, daughter of Abihail the uncle of Mordechai (who had adopted her as his own daughter), to come to the King. . .

It is unclear why the verse repeats Esther's lineage, since it was established earlier in verse 2:7. We must conclude that it is of special relevance at this point in the story. The explanation is as follows:

The verse teaches that Esther, unlike most people, could not be

1. "R' Yaakov bar Acha said: The Holy One, Blessed is He, said [to Mordechai], 'Because you sought the good of one person, as the verse says, ". . .to find out about Esther's well-being" (2:11), you will merit to seek the good of the entire nation, as it says, "For Mordechai the Jew . . . sought the good of his people and was concerned for the welfare of all his posterity" (10:3) ' " (*Midrash Rabbah* 10:13).

12 Now when each girl's turn arrived to come to
King Ahasuerus, after having been treated according
to the manner prescribed for women for twelve
months (for so was the prescribed length of their
anointing accomplished: six months with oil of
myrrh, and six months with perfumes and feminine
cosmetics) — 13 thus the girl came to the King; she
was given whatever she requested to accompany
her from the harem to the palace. 14 In the evening
she would come, and the next morning she would
return to the second harem in the custody of
Shaashgaz, the King's chamberlain, guardian of the
concubines. She would never again go to the King
unless the King desired her, and she was summoned
by name.

15 Now when the turn came for Esther, daughter
of Abihail the uncle of Mordechai (who had adopted
her as his own daughter), to come to the King,
she requested nothing beyond what Hegai the
King's chamberlain, guardian of the women, had
advised. Esther would captivate all who saw her.

---

persuaded to reveal a secret. She strictly observed Mordechai's warning against revealing her origins, as a later verse (20) says, "Esther still told nothing of her kindred or her people, as Mordechai had instructed her; for Esther continued to obey Mordechai, just as when she was raised by him" (2:20).One cannot help but wonder what made Esther so unique.

Our verse provides the answer: First, she was the scion of a very noble and righteous dynasty, the daughter of Abihail. Second, she was brought up by Mordechai, the most righteous individual of that entire generation. From the words, "he adopted her as his own daughter," the Sages infer that although he took her as his wife, she continued to behave as though she were his daughter who has no individual will of her own, and whose personality is molded by her parents.

וַתְּהִי אֶסְתֵּר נֹשֵׂאת חֵן בְּעֵינֵי כָּל־רֹאֶיהָ — Esther would captivate all who saw her.

In reference to this verse, the Sages say, "This teaches that everyone thought she was a fellow countryman" (*Megillah* 13a). Miraculously, this trait

טז וַתִּלָּקַח אֶסְתֵּר אֶל־הַמֶּלֶךְ אֲחַשְׁוֵרוֹשׁ אֶל־בֵּית
מַלְכוּתוֹ בַּחֹדֶשׁ הָעֲשִׂירִי הוּא־חֹדֶשׁ טֵבֵת בִּשְׁנַת־
יז שֶׁבַע לְמַלְכוּתוֹ׃ וַיֶּאֱהַב הַמֶּלֶךְ אֶת־אֶסְתֵּר מִכָּל־
הַנָּשִׁים וַתִּשָּׂא־חֵן וָחֶסֶד לְפָנָיו מִכָּל־הַבְּתוּלוֹת
וַיָּשֶׂם כֶּתֶר־מַלְכוּת בְּרֹאשָׁהּ וַיַּמְלִיכֶהָ תַּחַת
יח וַשְׁתִּי׃ וַיַּעַשׂ הַמֶּלֶךְ מִשְׁתֶּה גָדוֹל לְכָל־שָׂרָיו וַעֲבָדָיו
אֵת מִשְׁתֵּה אֶסְתֵּר וַהֲנָחָה לַמְּדִינוֹת עָשָׂה
יט וַיִּתֵּן מַשְׂאֵת כְּיַד הַמֶּלֶךְ׃ וּבְהִקָּבֵץ בְּתוּלוֹת שֵׁנִית
כ וּמָרְדֳּכַי יֹשֵׁב בְּשַׁעַר־הַמֶּלֶךְ׃ אֵין אֶסְתֵּר מַגֶּדֶת
מוֹלַדְתָּהּ וְאֶת־עַמָּהּ כַּאֲשֶׁר צִוָּה עָלֶיהָ מָרְדֳּכָי
וְאֶת־מַאֲמַר מָרְדֳּכַי אֶסְתֵּר עֹשָׂה כַּאֲשֶׁר הָיְתָה
כא בְאָמְנָה אִתּוֹ׃ בַּיָּמִים
הָהֵם וּמָרְדֳּכַי יֹשֵׁב בְּשַׁעַר־הַמֶּלֶךְ קָצַף בִּגְתָן
וָתֶרֶשׁ שְׁנֵי־סָרִיסֵי הַמֶּלֶךְ מִשֹּׁמְרֵי הַסַּף וַיְבַקְשׁוּ
כב לִשְׁלֹחַ יָד בַּמֶּלֶךְ אֲחַשְׁוֵרֹשׁ׃ וַיִּוָּדַע הַדָּבָר לְמָרְדֳּכַי

---

enabled her to hide the fact that she was Jewish. On his part, Ahasuerus was convinced she was Persian. When he asked Esther to reveal her nationality, she demurred by saying, "Can you not surmise it from my appearance?" In this manner, Esther avoided lying outright.

20. אֵין אֶסְתֵּר מַגֶּדֶת מוֹלַדְתָּהּ וְאֶת־עַמָּהּ כַּאֲשֶׁר צִוָּה עָלֶיהָ מָרְדֳּכַי וְאֶת־מַאֲמַר מָרְדֳּכַי אֶסְתֵּר עֹשָׂה כַּאֲשֶׁר הָיְתָה בְאָמְנָה אִתּוֹ — Esther still told nothing of her kindred or her people as Mordechai had instructed her; for Esther continued to obey Mordechai, just as when she was raised by him.

Once we are told that Esther risked her life by not revealing her kindred or her people, it seems superfluous to add that she "continued to obey Mordechai just as when she was raised by him." What do these apparently superfluous words convey?

The Sages interpret this to mean that Esther would ask Mordechai to determine whether she was ritually pure or impure. This is truly astounding — even though she was forced to have intimate relations with the wicked Ahasuerus, her enthusiasm for observing the *mitzvah* of family purity did not wane in the least! This attests to Esther's extraordinary level

16 Esther was taken to King Ahasuerus into his
palace in the tenth month, which is the month of
Teves, in the seventh year of his reign. 17 The King
loved Esther more than all the women, and she won
more of his grace and favor than all the other girls; so
that he set the royal crown upon her head, and made
her Queen in place of Vashti. 18 Then the King made
a great banquet for all his officers and his servants —
it was Esther's Banquet — and he proclaimed an
amnesty for the provinces, and gave gifts worthy of
the King.

19 And when the maidens were gathered together
the second time, and Mordechai sat at the King's
gate, 20 (Esther still told nothing of her kindred or her
people as Mordechai had instructed her; for Esther
continued to obey Mordechai, just as when she was
raised by him.)

21 In those days, while Mordechai was sitting at the
King's gate, Bigthan and Teresh, two of the King's
chamberlains of the guardians of the threshold,
became angry and plotted to lay hands on King
Ahasuerus. 22 The plot became known to Mordechai,

---

of piety, for normally continuous exposure to Ahasuerus' spiritual poison would weaken the faith of even the most devout individual. From our verse, however, we learn that Esther's zeal for *mitzvah* observance remained as strong as ever.

The verse also teaches us a more subtle lesson: Normally when a person undertakes an important task, he tends to forget matters of lesser importance.[1] Esther, however, was different — even while in the midst of risking her life and resisting the King's attempts to discover her origins, she did not overlook the observances she had learned in Mordechai's home. (See also commentary to 2:9 above regarding Esther's continued observance of the Sabbath.)

1. *Midrash Rabbah* (*Exodus* 2:3) says: "Hashem does not grant eminence to a man until He tests him with an insignificant matter. Two great people were tested with an insignificant matter, were found worthy, and thereafter, Hashem raised them to eminence — David and Solomon."

ב/כג וַיַּגֵּד לְאֶסְתֵּר הַמַּלְכָּה וַתֹּאמֶר אֶסְתֵּר לַמֶּלֶךְ בְּשֵׁם
כג מָרְדֳּכָי׃ וַיְבֻקַּשׁ הַדָּבָר וַיִּמָּצֵא וַיִּתָּלוּ שְׁנֵיהֶם עַל־עֵץ
ג/א א וַיִּכָּתֵב בְּסֵפֶר דִּבְרֵי הַיָּמִים לִפְנֵי הַמֶּלֶךְ׃ אַחַר ׀
הַדְּבָרִים הָאֵלֶּה גִּדַּל הַמֶּלֶךְ אֲחַשְׁוֵרוֹשׁ אֶת־הָמָן בֶּן־
הַמְּדָתָא הָאֲגָגִי וַיְנַשְּׂאֵהוּ וַיָּשֶׂם אֶת־כִּסְאוֹ מֵעַל כָּל־

---

22. וַיִּוָּדַע הַדָּבָר לְמָרְדֳּכַי וַיַּגֵּד לְאֶסְתֵּר הַמַּלְכָּה וַתֹּאמֶר אֶסְתֵּר לַמֶּלֶךְ בְּשֵׁם מָרְדֳּכָי — The plot became known to Mordechai, who told it to Queen Esther, and Esther informed the King in Mordechai's name.

The *Targum* says that Esther did not only *say* this information in Mordechai's name, but demanded also that it be *written down* in his name.

In truth, Mordechai did not want Esther to mention his name at all. He foresaw that in the future Esther would play a pivotal role in bringing about the redemption of the Jewish People, and he reasoned that it would be in their best interests for Esther to receive all the credit for foiling the assassination attempt against the King.

On her part, though, Esther could not come to terms with taking all the credit. Her modesty and righteousness would simply not allow her to do such a thing. Hence, she insisted that the pages inscribe in the King's ledger that the information which saved the King's life was forwarded by Mordechai. In reference to Esther's decision, the Sages said, "One who says something in the name of the one who [originally] said it brings redemption to the world" (*Pirkei Avos* 6:6). We see from this that as long as a person seeks to do what is right, not only will no harm befall him, but he will actually gain. For Esther's decision became the critical turning point in the unfolding of the miracles, as follows:

Rashi explains that "sleep eluded the King" (6:1) because he was very troubled by Esther's insistence that Haman attend the next day's feast (see 5:8). Ahasuerus suspected that Esther had developed a fondness for Haman, and that the two of them intended to assassinate him. The Sages say that he thought to himself, "If there is a plot against me, surely one of my loyal subjects will reveal it to me!" But then he thought, "Perhaps the reason no loyal subject has come forward to uncover the plot is because I did not reward him sufficiently for a past favor." Thus, he ordered that the royal records be reviewed, and, lo and behold, it was discovered that Mordechai had saved the King's life and had yet to be rewarded! At this point Haman unsuspectingly appeared in the King's court, and from that moment on, his downfall began.

Now, had Esther listened to Mordechai and taken the credit for scuttling the plot against the King, the miracle would not have come about in this manner. The royal record would have revealed that *Esther* had saved the King's

2/23 *who told it to Queen Esther, and Esther informed
the King in Mordechai's name.* [23] *The matter was
investigated and corroborated, and they were both
hanged on a gallows. It was recorded in the book of
chronicles in the King's presence.*

3/1 [1] *After these things King Ahasuerus promoted
Haman, the son of Hammedatha the Agagite,
and advanced him; he set his seat above all the*

---

life, and Ahasuerus would not have had any reason to reward Mordechai. The miracle, however, was destined to occur specifically in this manner.

III

1. — אַחַר הַדְּבָרִים הָאֵלֶּה גִּדַּל הַמֶּלֶךְ אֲחַשְׁוֵרוֹשׁ אֶת־הָמָן בֶּן־הַמְּדָתָא הָאֲגָגִי **After these things King Ahasuerus promoted Haman, the son of Hammedatha the Agagite**

The verse traces Haman's lineage back to Agag, the King of the Amalekites (*I Samuel* 15), who lived over 500 years earlier. This supports *Rambam*'s opinion that Haman's reign of terror was a direct consequence of King Saul's compassion for Agag. Because Saul did not follow Hashem's commandment to kill every last Amalekite including King Agag, Hashem raised Haman to power and thereby fulfilled the verse, "those of whom you leave shall be pins in your eyes and thorns in your sides, and they will harass you" (*Numbers* 33:55). Similarly, *Tanna Devei Eliyahu* (Chapter 20) teaches that "Hashem brought Haman to the world only on the merit of Agag. When Agag was imprisoned, he groaned and cried, saying, 'Woe to me, lest my progeny be cut off from the world forever!' "

At first glance, this selection from *Tanna Devei Eliyahu* is difficult. It implies that Hashem brought Haman to the world in order to *reward* Agag for his heartfelt prayers, but surely "meriting" progeny such as Haman is no reward! The answer is that Hashem did not reward Agag by bringing *Haman* into the world, but rather by bringing Haman's *grandchildren* into the world. As the Sages say, "Some of Haman's grandchildren studied Torah in Bnei Brak" (*Sanhedrin* 96b). (See footnote to 1:14.)

The *Chazon Ish* said that this principle explains why sometimes children of totally non-observant families suddenly become God-fearing people. He attributed this phenomenon to the tears shed by a righteous ancestor who foresaw that his children would leave the ways of the Torah.

With this principle in mind, we have answered another question: Why was Rebecca consoled by the prophet's words, "Two nations are in your womb" (*Genesis* 25:23), since one of the twins she was carrying at the time was Esau, who was to become one of the most wicked men on earth? In

ב הַשָּׂרִים אֲשֶׁר אִתּוֹ׃ וְכָל־עַבְדֵי הַמֶּלֶךְ אֲשֶׁר־
בְּשַׁעַר הַמֶּלֶךְ כֹּרְעִים וּמִשְׁתַּחֲוִים לְהָמָן כִּי־כֵן
צִוָּה־לוֹ הַמֶּלֶךְ וּמָרְדֳּכַי לֹא יִכְרַע וְלֹא יִשְׁתַּחֲוֶה׃

explanation, the Sages said, "They were Antoninus and Rebbi" (*Rashi* on *Genesis* 25:23). The Sages' explanation is difficult to understand. True, Antoninus was a righteous man, but he lived many generations later, only after numerous wicked descendants emerged from Esau's lineage. Could the knowledge that Rebecca would merit a single righteous descendant through Esau be sufficient consolation?

The answer is, yes. Rebecca recognized the great merit of having even one righteous descendant, even if he would emerge many generations later.[1] As the *Ridbaz* used to say when he discovered a new Torah concept, "It would have been worthwhile for my mother to suffer all the pangs of childbirth for just this one concept!"

❦ ❦ ❦

The Sages ask, "After which things? Rava said: Only after the Holy One, Blessed is He, created a remedy for the affliction [did he send the affliction]. For Reish Lakish said, 'The Holy One, Blessed is He, does not smite Israel unless He has created a remedy beforehand, as the verse says, "When I heal Israel, then the iniquity of Ephraim will be revealed" (*Hosea* 7:1). But in the case of the other nations of the world it is not so: [First] He smites them, and only afterwards does He creates a remedy, as the verse says, "And HASHEM will smite Egypt, smiting and healing" (*Isaiah* 19:22)' " (*Megillah* 13b).

The difference between Israel and the nations is that the Jews derive benefit even from Hashem's blows, for they induce the people to repent for their transgressions. As *Rambam* writes regarding the verse, "Then the King said to Haman, 'The silver is given to you, the people also, to do with as you see fit' " (3:11): "When he [Ahasuerus] answered him [Haman], the angels raised their voices and said, 'Our God! If You allow him to carry out his plan, he will destroy the world, and This World shall become desolate!' In order to test Israel, and to let this [adversity] motivate them to repent, God did not answer them."

In contrast, even the cure that Hashem creates for the nations serves as their punishment, for when miracles are performed for the nations' sake, they "pay" for them with whatever merits they may have accumulated. Thus, even

1. The importance of even one righteous descendant is evident from the verse, "He [Moses] *turned this way and that and saw that there was no man*, so he struck the Egyptian and hid him in the sand" (*Exodus* 2:12). *Rashi* explains: "He prophetically saw that no future proselyte would emerge from the Egyptian assailant." We may infer from this that had Moses foreseen that a proselyte would emerge from the Egyptian in the future, he would not have killed him.

officers who were with him. 2 *All the King's servants at the King's gate would bow down and prostrate themselves before Haman, for this is what the King had commanded concerning him. But Mordechai would not bow down nor prostrate himself.*

---

though the miracle may save the nations from utter destruction, it destroys them spiritually by leaving them bereft of merit.

2. וּמָרְדֳּכַי לֹא יִכְרַע וְלֹא יִשְׁתַּחֲוֶה — But Mordechai would not bow down nor prostrate himself.

Sefas Emes points out that according to the rules of grammar, it would have been more correct to use the past tense, וּמָרְדֳּכַי לֹא כָּרַע, instead of the future tense, יִכְרַע. A comment of *Maharal* would resolve this difficulty. *Maharal* writes, Mordechai could have approached the palace from a different direction and avoided encountering Haman altogether. However, Mordechai purposely chose to encounter Haman and defy him by refusing to bow down to him. Thus, the verse does not merely relate a past event, but rather reveals Mordechai's determination to encounter Haman *and not bow to him*, which is better conveyed by the future tense.

Alternatively, Mordechai conveyed to Haman through his tenacious behavior that he would *never* bow down to him, even if he would be coerced to do so in the future. Mordechai's defiance is why he merited to be called יְהוּדִי ("the Jew"). As the Sages said, "He was called יְהוּדִי because he renounced idolatry, for whoever renounces idolatry is called יְהוּדִי"[1] (*Megillah* 13a). The people who frequented the palace gate were shocked by Mordechai's uncompromising attitude, but they secretly wondered whether it was not merely a brave facade that would quickly dissolve at the first threat of violence. In order to test his resolve, the people "told Haman to see whether Mordechai's words would avail, for he had told them that he was a Jew (יְהוּדִי)" (v. 4).

Mordechai's attitude is all the more inspiring in light of the Sages' opinion that bowing down under such circumstances would not have constituted idolatry. Even though he was halachically permitted to bow down, Mordechai refused because it might have *appeared* as though he had bowed down to an idol.

❦ ❦ ❦

---

1. The term יְהוּדִי is derived from the name יְהוּדָה, Judah, the son of Jacob, who we find to have had unusal dedication to the eradication of idolatry. The *Midrash* (*Bereishis Rabbah* 94:3) tells us that although both Joseph and Pharaoh sent wagons to carry Jacob and his sons to Egypt (*Genesis* 45:19, 21), those sent by Pharaoh had idolatrous images carved on their walls and were burned by Judah.

Mordechai echoed merited the appellation *Yehudi* because he echoed this trait of Judah's. Indeed, it was during the time of Mordechai and Esther that the *yetzer hara* of idolatry was eliminated (*Shir HaShirim Rabbah* 7:14).

ג וַיֹּאמְרוּ עַבְדֵי הַמֶּלֶךְ אֲשֶׁר־בְּשַׁעַר הַמֶּלֶךְ לְמָרְדֳּכָי מַדּוּעַ אַתָּה עוֹבֵר אֵת מִצְוַת הַמֶּלֶךְ׃

The *Targum* explains as follows: "Mordechai would not bow down to the statue [of idolatry], nor would he prostrate himself before Haman, because [Haman] had sold himself as a slave to him for a loaf of bread." Similarly, the Sages say, "R' Chisda said: This one [Mordechai] came from a position of wealth and this one [Haman] came from a position of poverty. R' Papa said: And they called [Haman] 'the slave who sold himself for loaves of bread' " (*Megillah* 15a).

Manos Levi (p. 88b) quotes a Midrash that says that Mordechai and Haman had been fellow officers in Ahasuerus' army, each one in charge of a battalion. It once happened that both battalions were dispatched to suppress an uprising in one of the King's provinces. Each battalion was supplied with sufficient rations for three years. In the way of the righteous, Mordechai ate sparingly and carefully rationed the food to his men. In contrast, the wicked Haman ate without restraint and depleted his rations after only one year into the campaign. When his hunger pangs became unbearable, Haman asked Mordechai to lend him food, even at high interest. Mordechai refused to comply with his request, using the pretext that the Torah prohibits charging interest from one's "brother." He explained to Haman that since Amalek's descent is traced back to Esau, who was Jacob's brother, Haman was in effect Mordechai's relation. Mordechai suggested instead that Haman and all his future descendants become Mordechai's slaves, and that they serve him one day each week. Since they did not have any paper on which to write their agreement, they wrote it on Mordechai's shin-plate.

This Midrash presents a few difficulties: First, the law explicitly states that a Jew may not own a slave who refuses to accept the Seven Noachide Laws (see *Yad Chazakah*, *Hilchos Milah*, 1:6, and *Ravad*). Second, since Haman was an Amalekite, Mordechai should have killed him, for the Torah says, "Wipe out the memory of Amalek from under the heaven" (*Deuteronomy* 25:19). Third, even if we say that the Jewish People were subservient to the nations and therefore the obligation to kill Amalekites did not apply, it is difficult to understand how Mordechai could have agreed to allow an Amalekite to become his servant, since even the sight of an Amalekite's *beast* is regarded as propagating the memory of Amalek in the world (see *Rashi* on *Deuteronomy* 25:18).

The first question can be answered in two ways:

According to some authorities, the law prohibiting a Jew from owning a slave who refuses to accept the seven Noachide Laws applies only in *Eretz Yisrael*, but not in foreign lands (see *Magid Mishneh, Yad Chazakah, Hilchos Issurei Biyah,*, 14:9). Thus, since Mordechai did not live in Israel, but in Shushan, this prohibition did not apply to him.

³ So the King's servants at the King's gate said to Mordechai, "Why do you disobey the King's command?"

Other authorities say that every Jew, regardless of where he lives, has an obligation to force a gentile who is under his control to observe the Seven Noachide Laws (*Kesef Mishneh's* interpretation of *Rambam*). However, Mordechai did not have sufficient control over Haman to qualify for this obligation, since Haman served Mordechai only once a week. Thus, Mordechai was permitted to own Haman as a slave.

The answer to the second and third questions is that the *mitzvah* to obliterate the memory of Amalek will only apply in the days of Messiah, when Hashem will give Israel "rest from all your enemies all around, in the Land that HASHEM, your God, gives you as an inheritance to possess it" (ibid.). This explains why Mordechai did not kill Haman but rather bought him as a slave.

❦ ❦ ❦

As mentioned above, Haman sold himself as a slave to Mordechai (*Megillah* 15a). According to both *Rambam* and *Manos Levi,* the contract between the two stipulated that Haman and his descendants would be Mordechai's slave one day a week for all eternity.

In *Yad Chazakah* (*Hilchos Avadim* 9:3), *Rambam* rules that a gentile may sell his children to slavery, as the verse says, "Also from among the children of the residents who live with you, from them you may purchase, from their family that is with you, whom they begot in your land" (*Leviticus* 25:45). This rule applies even if the gentile's children are adults. The *Kesef Mishneh* did not cite a source for the *Rambam*'s ruling. However, it would seem that the Sages' interpretation of our verse is ample proof for *Rambam*, since they teach that Haman *sold his children to slavery* even though some of them were adults.

However, the Sages' interpretation seems to contradict the opinion of *Minchas Chinuch* (*Mitzvah 347*), who rules that one cannot acquire a gentile as a slave through a sales contract, for we see that Mordechai acquired Haman through a contract.

3. וַיֹּאמְרוּ עַבְדֵי הַמֶּלֶךְ אֲשֶׁר־בְּשַׁעַר הַמֶּלֶךְ לְמָרְדֳּכָי מַדּוּעַ אַתָּה עוֹבֵר אֵת מִצְוַת הַמֶּלֶךְ — So the King's servants at the King's gate said to Mordechai, "Why do you disobey the King's command?"

In his commentary on the *Megillah, Rambam* writes that the following dialogue transpired between the King's servants and Mordechai:

"They said to him 'Why did your ancestor bow down to [Haman's] ancestor?' [They challenged Mordechai's refusal to bow down to Haman with the precedent set by Jacob the Patriarch, who bowed down seven times to Esau, Haman's ancestor; see Genesis 33:3-7.]

ד וַיְהִ֗י °באמרם אֵלָיו֙ י֣וֹם וָי֔וֹם וְלֹ֥א שָׁמַ֖ע אֲלֵיהֶ֑ם
וַיַּגִּ֣ידוּ לְהָמָ֗ן לִרְאוֹת֙ הֲיַֽעַמְדוּ֙ דִּבְרֵ֣י מָרְדֳּכַ֔י כִּֽי־הִגִּ֥יד
ה לָהֶ֖ם אֲשֶׁר־ה֥וּא יְהוּדִֽי׃ וַיַּ֣רְא הָמָ֔ן כִּי־אֵ֣ין מָרְדֳּכַ֔י

כְּאָמְרָם ק׳

"He answered, 'He had good reason, since [Esau] was his older brother. However, Hashem honored my direct ancestor Benjamin more than Jacob's other sons,[1] for while they all bowed down to [Esau], he did not, as the verse says, "Leah, too, came forward with her children and they bowed down; and afterwards, Joseph and Rachel came forward and bowed down" (*Genesis* 33:7) — *Joseph and Rachel* may have bowed down, but not my ancestor Benjamin, for he was still in his mother's womb at the time. I, too, am following his example. Therefore, I shall not bow down to [Haman].' "

From this we learn that although Benjamin was in his mother's womb when she bowed down to Esau, her actions did not affect him. This seems to contradict several Talmudic passages which indicate that an unborn fetus shares the halachic status of its mother. For example, the Talmud teaches that if a pregnant cow causes damage to someone's property, the damaged party must be reimbursed for the damages rendered by both the mother and the unborn calf (*Bava Kamma* 47a; *Yad Chazakah, Nizkei Mamon* 9:1). In our case as well we should say that Rachel's actions were also considered Benjamin's actions.

The answer lies in the opinion of the *Tosafos HaRosh* on Tractate *Avodah Zarah* 24a (s.v. וניחוש דילמא רבעה), who rules that although a red cow is disqualified for holy service once a yoke is placed upon it (see *Numbers* 19:2), its unborn calf does not share the same halachic status as its mother. He differentiates between the red cow and the case mentioned above in the following manner: In that case, the unborn calf shares the legal status of the mother because it is directly involved in the act — the calf's weight increases the extent of the damage wrought by its mother. In contrast, placing a yoke upon a pregnant red cow does not have any perceptible effect upon its unborn calf, and therefore, the halachic status of the mother is not transferred to the calf. Similarly, we may answer that when Rachel bowed down to Esau, Benjamin did not directly benefit from that act, and therefore he is not regarded as having bowed down to Esau.

Mordechai's assertion that Benjamin did not bow down is still difficult to understand, though, for the Torah does explicitly state that *all* the brothers — including Benjamin — bowed down to Joseph in Egypt (see *Genesis* 43:28, 44:14). In theory, one could answer that this is not such a strong

---

1. God said to Benjamin, "May HASHEM's beloved dwell securely by Him; He hovers over him all day long; and rests between his shoulders" (*Deuteronomy* 33:12). He also merited that the Holy Temple be built on his hereditary portion (*Menachos* 53a).

4 *Finally, when they said this to him day after
day and he did not heed them, they told Haman, to see whether Mordechai's words would
avail; for he had told them that he was a
Jew.* 5 *When Haman saw that Mordechai did not*

---

difficulty because, after all, it was only Joseph whom the brothers bowed down to, who was definitely not an idol worshiper. This alone is not a substantial argument, however, since in truth the brothers *thought* they were bowing down to Pharaoh's viceroy, whom they thought *was* an idol worshiper. As the Talmud says, "If someone intended to eat pork but [unwittingly] ate lamb, nevertheless, he must ask for forgiveness and atonement" (*Nazir* 23a).

Rather, the answer must be that it is only wrong to bow down to an idol worshiper when one intends to pay him honor. However, there is nothing wrong with bowing down in the gesture of a greeting, or in order to beg him for mercy or request a favor. In fact, Rashi explains that the brothers first bowed down to Joseph in the manner of a greeting, and the second time, they begged him for mercy. In contrast, when Jacob and his wives and children bowed down to Esau, they were paying him homage.

With this principle in mind, we may also resolve a difficulty on *Midrash Rabbah* (*Genesis* 100:2). In reference to the verse, "When Jacob finished instructing his sons" (*Genesis* 49:33), the *Midrash* says, "He instructed them regarding three issues: idolatry, blasphemy, and carrying his corpse to burial." The commentators wonder what prompted Jacob to remind his sons not to commit idolatry and blasphemy, since they constitute two of the Seven Noachide Laws, which were observed in their entirety by every single member of Jacob's household.

The answer is that Jacob was concerned that his actions may have had a negative influence upon his sons: He feared that the sight of him bowing down to Esau would cause his sons to neglect the prohibition against idolatry, and that after hearing him bless Pharaoh (see *Genesis* 47:7-10), they would make light of the prohibition against blasphemy. Thus, before his death, he felt the need to reemphasize to his sons the importance of observing these two commandments.

4. וַיַּגִּידוּ לְהָמָן לִרְאוֹת הֲיַעַמְדוּ דִּבְרֵי מָרְדֳּכַי כִּי־הִגִּיד לָהֶם אֲשֶׁר־הוּא יְהוּדִי — They told Haman, to see whether Mordechai's words would avail; for he had told them that he was a Jew.

Rashi explains that the King's servants wished to see whether Mordechai would stand behind his words. He had explained to them that, being a Jew to whom idolatry is forbidden, he would never bow down to Haman. We might add that they also wondered from where Mordechai drew so much courage, for defying the King's orders was no trivial matter. His answer to them was that the very knowledge that he was fulfilling Hashem's *mitzvos* imbued him with strength of will and courage.

Ne'os Hadeshe illustrates this point beautifully: The verse says, "[The Torah] is not in heaven, [for you] to say, 'Who can ascend to the heaven for us and take it for us, so that we can listen to it and perform it?' " (*Deuteronomy* 30:12). Regarding this verse, the Sages say, "If it *were* in the heavens, you *would* be obligated to ascend after it and learn it!" (*Eiruvin* 55a). The Sages' statement is difficult, for it does not stand to reason that Hashem would expect a human being to accomplish the impossible feat of ascending up to the heavens. *Ne'os Hadeshe* explains that had such a *mitzvah* existed, Hashem would indeed have created reality in such a way as to enable human beings to reach the heavens, for the Torah is the blueprint Hashem looked into when He created the universe.[1] This is precisely what Mordechai answered the King's servants: The very fact that Hashem commanded the Jewish People not to worship idols filled him with confidence and dispelled self-doubts, for if the Creator of the world decreed this *mitzvah,* then it must be possible to fulfill it!

5. וַיַּרְא הָמָן כִּי־אֵין מָרְדֳּכַי כֹּרֵעַ וּמִשְׁתַּחֲוֶה לוֹ וַיִּמָּלֵא הָמָן חֵמָה — When Haman saw that Mordechai did not bow down and prostrate himself before him, then Haman was filled with rage

As mentioned above (commentary to 1:10) the Talmud relates that Rabbi Shimon bar Yochai's disciples asked him, "Why did the enemies of Israel [a euphemism for 'the Jewish People'] deserve extermination?"

He said to them, "You answer."

They said, "Because they derived pleasure from the feast of that wicked man [i.e., Ahasuerus]."

"If so, let [only the Jews] of Shushan be killed, but not the [Jews] in the entire world."

They said to him, "You tell us [why]."

He said to them, "Because they bowed down to an image."

They countered, "Was there partiality in this affair?" [Since idolatry is punishable by death, why were the Jews spared?]

He said to them, "They only *pretended* to [worship] it, and so, God only pretended [to destroy] them" (*Megillah* 12a).

---

1. The Sages say that our father Abraham observed the laws of the Torah even though the Sinaic revelation took place generations later (*Yoma* 28b). R' Yaakov Kaminetsky explained that since the Torah is the blueprint with which Hashem created the universe (*Bereishis Rabbah* 1:2) our father Abraham was able to derive the contents of the Torah from physical reality, much in the same way as an architect can picture the plans of a building by looking at the completed structure.

bow down and prostrate himself before him, then Haman was filled with rage. [6] However, it seemed

---

Now, according to *Sanhedrin* 61b, if a person bows down to an idol out of fear in times when everyone follows this practice, he does not incur the death penalty. Hence, in light of Rabbi Shimon's answer that the Jews only *pretended* to worship the idol, it remains unclear why they were punished so severely.

The answer lies in the following statement of the Sages: "R' Meir said: Why was the Torah given to Israel? Because they are tenacious. . . R' Shimon ben Lakish said: There are three tenacious creatures: Israel among the nations; the dog among animals; and the rooster among fowl" (*Beitzah* 25b).

Near the end of *Parshas Va'eschanan* (*Deuteronomy* 7:7), *Ramban* explains why Hashem specifically chose Israel as His people: "He perceived that the Jewish People were the most suitable to love Him, more than any other nation . . . for the best friend is one who is capable of enduring another's love under all circumstances. Israel were the most suitable of all the nations, as the Sages said, 'There are three tenacious creatures: Israel among the nations. . .' For Israel endure all the trials that befall them — they exclaim,"either to be a Jew, or to be hanged!' " (*Shemos Rabbah* 42:9).

This explains why the Jews in Ahasuerus' time were punished so severely for bowing down to the image: True, according to the strict letter of the law, they did not deserve the death penalty. However, by bowing down to the image, they demonstrated that they were willing to compromise in the service of Hashem, and that they were no longer the tenacious nation of the past. Thus, they uprooted the foundation stone of the covenant that Hashem formed with them at Mount Sinai, when He selected Israel from among all the nations as His chosen people.

Having established this principle, we may now resolve another difficulty:

When Esther expressed her reservations about Mordechai's order that she appear unsummoned before the King and "plead with him for her people" (3:8), Mordechai replied: "Do not imagine that you will be able to escape in the King's palace any more than the rest of the Jews. For if you persist in keeping silent at a time like this, relief and deliverance will come to the Jews from some other place, *while you and your father's house will perish*" (4:13-14). One may rightly wonder why Mordechai pronounced that not only Esther, but also her father's house, would perish due to her sin, since it is a fundamental tenet of faith that "sons shall not be put to death because of fathers — a man should be put to death for his own sin" (*Deuteronomy* 24:16).

ג/ז בְּעֵינָיו לִשְׁלֹחַ יָד בְּמָרְדֳּכַי לְבַדּוֹ כִּי־הִגִּידוּ לוֹ אֶת־
עַם מָרְדֳּכָי וַיְבַקֵּשׁ הָמָן לְהַשְׁמִיד אֶת־כָּל־הַיְּהוּדִים
ז אֲשֶׁר בְּכָל־מַלְכוּת אֲחַשְׁוֵרוֹשׁ עַם מָרְדֳּכָי׃ בַּחֹדֶשׁ
הָרִאשׁוֹן הוּא־חֹדֶשׁ נִיסָן בִּשְׁנַת שְׁתֵּים עֶשְׂרֵה

The answer lies in *Alshich's* opinion that Esther came to rectify the sin of her ancestor, King Saul. Many years earlier, King Saul forfeited the opportunity to fulfill the *mitzvah* to obliterate Amalek from the face of the earth due to his lack of resolve. Instead, he yielded to his subjects, who requested that he spare Amalek's livestock and keep alive the Amalekite king Agag (see *I Samuel* ch. 15).

Esther rectified this sin through her uncompromising courage. As she told Mordechai, "All the King's servants and the people of the King's provinces are well aware that if anyone. . .approaches the King in the inner court without being summoned, there is but one law for him; that he be put to death; except for the person to whom the King shall extend the gold scepter so that he may live. Now I have not been summoned . . . for the past thirty days" (4:11). Nevertheless, she courageously obeyed Mordechai and risked her life on behalf of the Jewish People, and thereby also saved King Saul's lineage from extinction.

With this, we can better appreciate why the miracles of Purim came about through Mordechai. In that generation, judgment was brought to bear upon the Jewish People because they showed a lack of resolve and thereby effectively revoked their covenant with Hashem. Mordechai, with his uncompromising tenacity regarding Torah and *mitzvos,* rectified this sin. On this merit the miracle came about through him.

According to *Chochmah U'mussar,* even a single individual who manifests this trait of uncompromising tenacity can bring about the salvation of the Jewish People.[1] As the verse says, "Phineas, son of Elazar, son of Aaron the Kohen, turned back My wrath from upon the Children of Israel, *when he zealously avenged Me* among them, so I did not consume the Children of Israel in My vengeance" (*Numbers* 25:11) — had Phineas *not* zealously avenged Hashem, the Jewish People would have been utterly destroyed in the plague that ensued, God forbid! Just as Phineas was not deterred from single-handedly slaying Zimri son of Salu, a leader of the Simeonites, in the presence of his fellow tribesmen, nor of slaying Cozbi, an illustrious Midianite princess, so too, Mordechai single-

---

1. My grandfather, *R' Yechezkel Levinstein,* explained the Sages' statement, "The universe was created for a single individual" (*Sanhedrin* 37a) in a similar manner — the entire universe was created for a single individual because he has the capability to rectify the entire Creation.

contemptible to him to lay hands on Mordechai alone, for they had made known to him the people of Mordechai. So Haman sought to destroy all the Jews who were throughout the entire kingdom of Ahasuerus — the people of Mordechai. 7 *In the first month, which is the month of Nissan, in the twelfth year*

---

handedly saved the Jewish People through his tenacious observance of Torah and *mitzvos.*

6. וַיִּבֶז בְּעֵינָיו לִשְׁלֹחַ יָד בְּמָרְדְּכַי לְבַדּוֹ — However, it seemed contemptible to him to lay hands on Mordechai alone.

Midrash Rabbah states, "[Haman] was 'contemptible one, son of a contemptible one' (בזוי בן בזוי). For one verse says, 'Esau showed contempt for the birthright' (*Genesis* 25:34), and here it says, 'it seemed contemptible to him to lay hands on Mordechai alone' (3:6)." Now, were it not for this *Midrash,* the two verses would seem totally unrelated. Let us consider how they are linked.

By selling his birthright for some lentil stew and bread, Esau demonstrated that he lacked all appreciation of the importance of Divine service. He failed to comprehend that a true servant of Hashem is as important as all of Mankind put together. Similarly, Haman found it contemptible to "lay hands on Mordechai *alone*" because he did not fathom the tremendous effect that a single devout individual's holy service can have on the world. Thus, he regarded it as beneath him to smite a single individual. For a man of such eminence, anything short of complete genocide was simply unbecoming.

The same principle is apparent in the Sages' statement, "If the Holy Temple is not rebuilt during a person's lifetime, it is considered as if it had been destroyed during his lifetime" (see *Yoma* 1:1). At first glance this seems strange, since rebuilding the Temple is a communal obligation, and therefore it does not seem appropriate to hold a particular individual responsible for not fulfilling it. We see from this that the Sages understood the power of a single man's holy service. As far as they were concerned, a single righteous individual has the power to tilt the balance of the entire world,[1] and cause all of Mankind to repent and embrace the ways of Hashem.

---

1. The Talmud states: "R' Elazar son of R' Shimon says: Since the world is judged according to the majority [of people], and a single individual is judged according to the majority [of his deeds], happy is the person who performs a *mitzvah,* for he tilts the balance to virtue for himself and for the entire world. On the other hand, if he commits a transgression, woe to him, for he tilts the balance to culpability for himself and for the entire world" (*Kiddushin* 40b). How awesome is the power of a single individual!

ג/ח לַמֶּלֶךְ אֲחַשְׁוֵרוֹשׁ הִפִּיל פּוּר הוּא הַגּוֹרָל לִפְנֵי
הָמָן מִיּוֹם ׀ לְיוֹם וּמֵחֹדֶשׁ לְחֹדֶשׁ שְׁנֵים־עָשָׂר
ח הוּא־חֹדֶשׁ אֲדָר׃ וַיֹּאמֶר הָמָן
לַמֶּלֶךְ אֲחַשְׁוֵרוֹשׁ יֶשְׁנוֹ עַם־אֶחָד מְפֻזָּר וּמְפֹרָד בֵּין

---

7. הִפִּיל פּוּר הוּא הַגּוֹרָל לִפְנֵי הָמָן מִיּוֹם לְיוֹם וּמֵחֹדֶשׁ לְחֹדֶשׁ שְׁנֵים־עָשָׂר הוּא־חֹדֶשׁ אֲדָר — The lot was cast in the presence of Haman from day to day, and from month to month, to the twelfth month, which is the month of Adar.

The *Midrash* (*Esther Rabbah* [7:13]) says: "When the wicked [Haman] saw that the lot did not fall on days, he began to cast it on months. He first cast it on the month of *Nissan,* but the merit of *Pesach* came up. He cast it on the month of *Iyar,* but the merit of *Pesach Sheini* (see *Numbers* 9:11) came up. He cast it on *Sivan,* but the merit of the Torah (given during *Sivan*) came up. He cast it on *Tamuz,* but the merit of the land came up; on *Elul,* but the merit of the completion of the wall came up; on *Tishrei,* but the merit of the *Shofar,* Yom Kippur and the Festivals came up. He cast it on *Marcheshvan,* but the merit of Sarah the Matriarch came up, for she passed away in that month. He cast it on *Kislev,* but the merit of Hanukkah came up. . . Finally he cast it on *Rosh Chodesh Adar,* and no merit came up. At this point the wicked man began to rejoice. . ."

Radal asks why this *Midrash* ascribes the merit of *Marcheshvan* to Sarah's death, since we know that Sarah passed away when she learned that our father Abraham offered their son Isaac as a sacrifice to Hashem (see *Genesis* 22). It would seem that the merit of *Abraham*'s willingness to sacrifice his only son to Hashem would overshadow the merit of Sarah's death. Further, the *Yafeh Anaf* asks why no merit came up on *Rosh Chodesh Adar,* since that is the day when the obligation to bring the half-*shekel* to the Temple is announced (*Mishnah Shekalim* 1:1).

In order to answer both questions, we must go back to the very beginnings of the Purim story — the Jewish People's sin of attending Ahasuerus' feast. According to *Pachad Yitzchak,* Ahasuerus was aware of Jeremiah's prophecy that the Jewish People would be returned to their homeland after 70 years in exile, and he anxiously awaited the approach of the seventieth year to see whether the prophet's words would be fulfilled. However, his calculations were flawed, and unbeknownst to him, he ushered in the seventieth year prematurely. Seeing that his Jewish subjects had not been returned to their land nor the Holy Temple rebuilt, he became ecstatic with joy. In order to celebrate what he considered the annulment of Jeremiah's prophecy, he decided to throw a lavish feast for all the citizens of Shushan, including the Jews. He even went so far as to serve the wine in the vessels of the Holy

of King Ahasuerus, pur (that is, the lot) was cast in
the presence of Haman from day to day, and from
month to month, to the twelfth month, which is the
month of Adar.
8 *Then Haman said to King Ahasuerus, "There is*
one nation scattered abroad and dispersed among

Temple, thereby underscoring his conviction that the Temple would never again be rebuilt.

On their part, many of the exiled Jews living in Babylonia always had nagging doubts about Jeremiah's prophecy. They wondered, "After a husband divorces his wife, or a master frees his slave, do they still owe anything to each other?" (*Sanhedrin* 105a). Deep down, they believed that by casting them into exile, Hashem had effectively broken all ties with them and revoked all His assurances, including the promise to redeem them after 70 years of exile. Ahasuerus' pronouncements that the seventieth year had passed, combined with the absence of any signs of the long-awaited redemption, dashed the Jewish People's hopes. To make matters worse, they attended the feast even though they knew the cause of the celebration. This is why the Sages said that the Jewish People were sentenced to extinction because they derived benefit from Ahasuerus' feast (*Megillah* 12a) — by celebrating the annulment of the prophecy, they disgraced the Prophet's words and showed that the rebuilding of the Holy Temple was not important in their eyes.

With this introduction, we can well understand why our father Abraham's willingness to sacrifice Isaac was not the merit that came up on the month of *Marcheshvan,* and why the announcement of the obligation to bring the half-*shekel*[1] was not the merit of *Rosh Chodesh Adar*: Since both these events are associated with Temple service,[2] they could not have stood as merits to revoke Haman's evil decree, for by attending Ahasuerus' feast the Jewish People essentially broke all links between themselves and the Holy Temple.

8. וַיֹּאמֶר הָמָן לַמֶּלֶךְ אֲחַשְׁוֵרוֹשׁ יֶשְׁנוֹ עַם־אֶחָד — Then Haman said to King Ahasuerus, "There is one nation."

In reference to this verse the Sages said:

"There was no one who knew [how to] slander [as skillfully] as Haman. For

---

1. During the Temple era, the Scriptural obligation (*Exodus* 30:11-16) for every adult male to pay a half-*shekel* tax was announced on *Rosh Chodesh Adar.* In this way, the offerings of the next month, *Nissan,* could be purchased from the new levy, as required (*Mishnah Shekalim* 1:1; see *Megillah* 29b).

2. On the merit of Isaac being offered on the altar, the Jewish people benefited from Abraham's prayer, in which he beseeched Hashem to bring them to Jerusalem three times a year.

ג/ט הָעַמִּ֔ים בְּכֹ֖ל מְדִינ֣וֹת מַלְכוּתֶ֑ךָ וְדָתֵיהֶ֞ם שֹׁנ֣וֹת
מִכָּל־עָ֗ם וְאֶת־דָּתֵ֤י הַמֶּ֙לֶךְ֙ אֵינָ֣ם עֹשִׂ֔ים וְלַמֶּ֥לֶךְ
ט אֵין־שֹׁוֶ֖ה לְהַנִּיחָֽם׃ אִם־עַל־הַמֶּ֣לֶךְ ט֔וֹב יִכָּתֵ֖ב
לְאַבְּדָ֑ם וַעֲשֶׂ֨רֶת אֲלָפִ֜ים כִּכַּר־כֶּ֗סֶף אֶשְׁקוֹל֙ עַל־יְדֵי֙

[Haman] said to [Ahasuerus], 'Come, let us destroy [the Jews].'

"[Ahasuerus] replied to him, 'I am afraid of their God, that He should not do to me as He did to my predecessors.'

"[Haman] said to [Ahasuerus], 'They have been negligent [in their observance] of the *mitzvos* (יָשְׁנוּ מִן הַמִּצְוֹת), [and their God will therefore not punish you for harming them].'

"[Ahasuerus] answered, 'But there are rabbis among them [who do keep the *mitzvos*].'

"[Haman] said to [Ahasuerus], 'They are one nation' [עַם אֶחָד]" (*Megillah* 13b).

Two questions arise: First, why did the knowledge that the Jews are "one nation" dispel Ahasuerus' fear of incurring God's wrath? On the contrary, he should have become even more frightened, since Israel's unity is a merit, not a fault. And second, how did Haman know that the Jewish People had grown neglectful in their observance of *mitzvos*?

What Haman was referring to when he said, "[They are] one nation," is that the Jews treated each other like equals, regardless of age or erudition. In other words, they failed to honor their sages and spiritual leaders. We find that the Jews in the desert were also guilty of this sin in the episode of the spies, as the verse says, "*All of you approached me* and said. . ." (*Deuteronomy* 1:22) — *Rashi* explains that the people approached Moses in a disorderly, disrespectful manner, with the young pushing ahead of the elder, and older people pushing ahead of leaders. At such times, the strength of Israel's spiritual leaders wanes in much the same way as Hashem's strength "wanes" when the Jewish People perform *mitzvos* without enthusiasm (see *Yalkut Shimoni* on *Deuteronomy* 32:18). Divine assistance is withheld from these leaders, and as a result, they prove incapable of inspiring the Jewish People to progress in their spiritual development. The natural consequence of this lack of leadership is a general decline in religious fervor among the populace.

Haman was aware of this phenomenon. Thus, when he perceived the Jews' lack of respect for their leaders, he correctly surmised that they had grown neglectful in their observance of *mitzvos*. For Haman knew that, just as the lifeblood of the body issues forth from the heart, enthusiasm and diligence in the performance of *mitzvos* emanate from Israel's spiritual leadership.

the peoples in all the provinces of your realm. Their laws are different from every other people's. They do not observe even the King's laws; therefore it is not befitting the King to tolerate them. 9 *If it pleases the King, let it be recorded that they be destroyed; and I will pay ten thousand silver talents into the hands of*

---

9. וַעֲשֶׂרֶת אֲלָפִים כִּכַּר־כֶּסֶף אֶשְׁקוֹל — And I will pay ten thousand silver talents.

The Talmud states, "Reish Lakish said: It was clearly known [in advance] before Hashem that Haman was destined to weigh out *shekalim* [i.e., silver coins] in order to destroy the Jews. Therefore, He caused the Jews to precede their *shekalim* to [Haman's] *shekalim*" (*Megillah* 13b). Here, Reish Lakish is consistent with his own opinion that "The Holy One, Blessed is He, does not smite Israel unless He has created a remedy for them beforehand" (ibid.).

The commentaries ask how the Jewish people's *shekalim,* which consisted of only 100 talents, counteracted the effect of Haman's *shekalim,*[1] which were valued at 10,000 talents. *Ben Yehoyada* answers with the verse, "a hundred of you will pursue ten thousand" (*Leviticus* 26:8), which teaches that each Jew is equivalent to 100 gentiles. Thus, by multiplying the Jewish People's 100 talents by 100, we arrive at 10,000 talents.

In his commentary on the *Megillah, Rambam* offers a different explanation: "The Holy One, Blessed is He, prepared the remedy before the blow by giving the Jewish People an obligation on every *Adar,* as the verse says, 'When you take a census of the Children of Israel. . . This shall they give — everyone who passes through the census — a half-*shekel* of the sacred *shekel,* the *shekel* being twenty *geras,* half a *shekel* as a portion to HASHEM' (*Exodus* 30:12-13). Since each *shekel* was 20 *geras,* each Israelite gave a coin worth 10 *geras.* These 10 *geras* counteracted the effect of the 10,000 *shekalim* for which [the Jewish People] were sold."

Unlike *Ben Yehoyada's* premise that the *total* sum of Israel's *shekalim*

---

1. In the section above, we established that the announcement of the obligation to bring the half-*shekel* could not protect the Jewish People from Haman's evil plot because the Jewish People effectively disassociated themselves from the Holy Temple. However, in this section, the working premise is that the Jewish People's half-*shekel did* counteract Haman's evil plot. The resolution to this apparent contradiction is that the Jewish People repented and renewed their bond with the Holy Temple, as is evident from the following Talmudic passage:

"[Haman] asked [Mordechai's] disciples, 'With what [topic of study] are you occupied?' They answered him, 'When the Holy Temple was in existence, one who pledged a *minchah* offering brought a fistful of fine flour and would gain atonement through it.' [Haman] said to them, 'Your fistful of flour has come and pushed aside my ten thousand silver talents. . .' " (*Megillah* 16a).

י עֹשֵׂי הַמְּלָאכָה לְהָבִיא אֶל־גִּנְזֵי הַמֶּלֶךְ: וַיָּסַר
הַמֶּלֶךְ אֶת־טַבַּעְתּוֹ מֵעַל יָדוֹ וַיִּתְּנָהּ לְהָמָן בֶּן־
יא הַמְּדָתָא הָאֲגָגִי צֹרֵר הַיְּהוּדִים: וַיֹּאמֶר הַמֶּלֶךְ לְהָמָן
הַכֶּסֶף נָתוּן לָךְ וְהָעָם לַעֲשׂוֹת בּוֹ כַּטּוֹב בְּעֵינֶיךָ:

---

was needed to neutralize the effect of Haman's 10,000 silver talents, *Rambam* is of the opinion that each Jew's half-*shekel* was sufficiently powerful to achieve this end. The explanation must be as follows:

According to Reish Lakish it was the merit of the Tabernacle — represented by the half-*shekalim* — that neutralized the accusations of Esau's archangel in the heavenly realms. And regarding the Tabernacle, the *Midrash* (*Shemos Rabbah* 33:9) states, "When the Holy One, Blessed is He, instructed Moses [to build] the Tabernacle, Moses said to Him: 'Master of the Universe, are the Jewish People capable of constructing it?' The Holy One, Blessed is He, answered: 'Even a single Israelite is capable of constructing it, as the verse says, "from every man whose heart motivates him you shall take My portion" (*Exodus* 25:2).' " Thus we see that even a single Jew's half-*shekel* has the power to counteract Haman's evil decree.

10. וַיָּסַר הַמֶּלֶךְ אֶת־טַבַּעְתּוֹ מֵעַל יָדוֹ וַיִּתְּנָהּ לְהָמָן בֶּן־הַמְּדָתָא הָאֲגָגִי צֹרֵר הַיְּהוּדִים — So the King took his signet ring from his hand, and gave it to Haman, the son of Hammedatha the Agagite, the enemy of the Jews.

The Sages said: "R. Abba bar Kahana said: The removal of [Ahasuerus'] signet ring did more than the forty-eight prophets and seven prophetesses who prophesied to Israel, for [they were] all unable to return [the Jews] to the path of righteousness, whereas the removal of the signet ring did return [the Jews] to the path of righteousness" (*Megillah* 14a).

In the context of this passage, we may glean a deeper understanding of the cryptic *Midrash* quoted in *Chochmah U'mussar* (Section One, p. 431): Regarding the verse, "God saw that the light was good, and God separated between the light and the darkness" (*Genesis* 1:4), the *Midrash* says, "We would not know which is better — the deeds of the righteous, or the deeds of the wicked. Now that it says, 'God saw that the *light* was good,' we learn that the deeds of the righteous are better."

The *Midrash* entertained the possibility that the deeds of the wicked are preferable because they are more effective than the deeds of the righteous in inducing people to repent for their sins. As the Sages stated above, the Jews who lived in Ahasuerus' day were good examples of this principle — from one moment to the next, the same people who brazenly disregarded the warnings of 48 prophets were suddenly reduced to tears and fervent repentance by the news that Ahasuerus had conferred unlimited authority to Haman. Nevertheless, by stating that "God saw that the *light* was good," the verse determines

those who perform the duties for deposit in the
King's treasuries." 10 *So the King took his signet ring*
from his hand, and gave it to Haman, the son of
Hammedatha the Agagite, the enemy of the Jews.
11 *Then the King said to Haman, "The silver is given*
to you, the people also, to do with as you see fit."

---

that, on the whole, the deeds of the righteous are better. This is because the deeds of the wicked cast darkness upon the world, and cause the faces of the Jewish People to become "as black as the bottom of a pot" (*Megillah* 11a). In contrast, the deeds of the righteous bring light to the world, as it says, "The Jews had light and gladness and joy and honor" (8:16).

❦ ❦ ❦

Some commentaries ask why the verse goes to such lengths to specify Haman's identity. By now, are we not all too familiar with Haman? Furthermore, when Ahasuerus later gives the signet ring to Mordechai (see 8:2), the verse does not specify Mordechai's identity in such great detail.

The answer is that the verse corroborates the opinion of the Sages, who said that Ahasuerus shared Haman's desire to destroy the Jewish People:

"They [Ahasuerus and Haman] could be compared to two people, one of whom had a mound in his field, and the other a pit. The owner of the pit said, 'If only he would sell me that mound!' while the owner of the mound said, 'If only he would sell me that pit!' Some time later, they met each other. The owner of the pit said to the owner of the mound, 'Sell me your mound.' His response was, '[Please,] take it for free!' " (*Megillah* 14a).

The owner of the pit represents Haman, who "bought" the Jewish People from Ahasuerus. This analogy teaches that, like Haman, Ahasuerus also wished to destroy the Jewish People.

Our verse alludes to Ahasuerus' evil intentions by stressing that he intentionally gave his signet ring to none other than Haman, *the son of Hammedatha the Agagite, the enemy of the Jews.* In full knowledge that Haman was a descendant of Amalek, the embodiment of evil and perversion in this world, Ahasuerus gave him full authority over the Jewish People so that he would achieve their common goal — to obliterate Israel from the face of the earth.

11. וַיֹּאמֶר הַמֶּלֶךְ לְהָמָן הַכֶּסֶף נָתוּן לָךְ וְהָעָם לַעֲשׂוֹת בּוֹ כַּטּוֹב בְּעֵינֶיךָ — Then the King said to Haman, "The silver is given to you, the people also, to do with as you see fit."

Tosafos point out that the numerical value of the word הַכֶּסֶף ("the silver") is equal to that of הָעֵץ ("the tree"), alluding to the fact that Haman would be hanged from a tree as a direct consequence of the silver he gave to Ahasuerus (*Megillah* 14b).

ג/יב־טו יב וַיִּקָּרְאוּ סֹפְרֵי הַמֶּלֶךְ בַּחֹדֶשׁ הָרִאשׁוֹן בִּשְׁלוֹשָׁה
עָשָׂר יוֹם בּוֹ וַיִּכָּתֵב כְּכָל־אֲשֶׁר־צִוָּה הָמָן אֶל
אֲחַשְׁדַּרְפְּנֵי־הַמֶּלֶךְ וְאֶל־הַפַּחוֹת אֲשֶׁר | עַל־מְדִינָה
וּמְדִינָה וְאֶל־שָׂרֵי עַם וָעָם מְדִינָה וּמְדִינָה כִּכְתָבָהּ
וְעַם וָעָם כִּלְשׁוֹנוֹ בְּשֵׁם הַמֶּלֶךְ אֲחַשְׁוֵרֹשׁ נִכְתָּב
יג וְנֶחְתָּם בְּטַבַּעַת הַמֶּלֶךְ: וְנִשְׁלוֹחַ סְפָרִים בְּיַד הָרָצִים
אֶל־כָּל־מְדִינוֹת הַמֶּלֶךְ לְהַשְׁמִיד לַהֲרֹג וּלְאַבֵּד אֶת־
כָּל־הַיְּהוּדִים מִנַּעַר וְעַד־זָקֵן טַף וְנָשִׁים בְּיוֹם אֶחָד
בִּשְׁלוֹשָׁה עָשָׂר לְחֹדֶשׁ שְׁנֵים־עָשָׂר הוּא־חֹדֶשׁ אֲדָר
יד וּשְׁלָלָם לָבוֹז: פַּתְשֶׁגֶן הַכְּתָב לְהִנָּתֵן דָּת בְּכָל־מְדִינָה
וּמְדִינָה גָּלוּי לְכָל־הָעַמִּים לִהְיוֹת עֲתִדִים לַיּוֹם הַזֶּה:
טו הָרָצִים יָצְאוּ דְחוּפִים בִּדְבַר הַמֶּלֶךְ וְהַדָּת נִתְּנָה
בְּשׁוּשַׁן הַבִּירָה וְהַמֶּלֶךְ וְהָמָן יָשְׁבוּ לִשְׁתּוֹת וְהָעִיר
ד/א־ב א שׁוּשָׁן נָבוֹכָה: וּמָרְדֳּכַי יָדַע אֶת־כָּל־אֲשֶׁר
נַעֲשָׂה וַיִּקְרַע מָרְדֳּכַי אֶת־בְּגָדָיו וַיִּלְבַּשׁ שַׂק וָאֵפֶר
ב וַיֵּצֵא בְּתוֹךְ הָעִיר וַיִּזְעַק זְעָקָה גְדֹלָה וּמָרָה: וַיָּבוֹא

It would seem that הָעֵץ also alludes to the evil inclination that surrounded the Tree of Knowledge, as the verse says, "And the woman perceived that the tree was good for eating and that it was a delight to the eyes, and that the tree was desirable as a means to wisdom, and she took of its fruit and ate" (*Genesis* 3:6). After Eve's sin, all these attractions gravitated towards silver and gold, and it is for this reason that so many people err and stumble in monetary affairs.[1]

In order to rectify the evil inclination surrounding monetary wealth, the *Sanhedrin* of that generation instituted the *mitzvah* of *Matanos La'eviyonim,* which requires that every Jew give a gift on Purim to at least two needy people. This act of charity has the force to rectify the evil inclination that surrounds monetary wealth.

The *Midrash* (*Shir HaShirim Rabbah* [7:13]) tells us that the *yetzer hara* of

---

1. The Sages said, "What do the words וְדִי זָהָב (*Deuteronomy* 1:1) mean? The school of R' Yannai said: Moses said before God, 'Master of the Universe! The silver and gold (זָהָב) that You gave so generously to the Israelites, to the point that they said, "Enough!" is what caused them to sin [by worshiping the golden calf]' " (*Berachos* 32).

3/12-15 *12 The King's secretaries were summoned on the
thirteenth day of the first month, and everything was
written exactly as Haman had dictated, to the King's
satraps, to the governors of every province, and to
the officials of every people; each province in its own
script, and to each people in its own language; in
King Ahasuerus' name it was written, and it was
sealed with the King's signet ring. 13 Letters were
sent by courier to all the King's provinces, to destroy,
to slay, and to exterminate all Jews, young and old,
children and women, in a single day, the thirteenth
day of the twelfth month, which is the month of
Adar, and to plunder their possessions. 14 The copies
of the document were to be promulgated in every
province, and be published to all peoples, that they
should be ready for that day. 15 The couriers went
forth hurriedly by order of the King, and the edict
was distributed in Shushan the Capital. The King
and Haman sat down to drink, but the city of
Shushan was bewildered.

4/1-2 *1 Mordechai learned of all that had been done;*
and Mordechai tore his clothes and put on
sackcloth with ashes. He went out into the midst
of the city, and cried loudly and bitterly. 2 He came

---

avodah zarah was taken away during the time of Mordechai and Esther. When a specific *yetzer hara* is eliminated, another takes its place. *Chazal* understood that the *yetzer hara* of money would replace that of *avodah zarah.* Thus, they established the *mitzvah* of giving charity on Purim.

IV

1. וּמָרְדֳּכַי יָדַע אֶת־כָּל־אֲשֶׁר נַעֲשָׂה וַיִּקְרַע מָרְדֳּכַי אֶת־בְּגָדָיו וַיִּלְבַּשׁ שַׂק וָאֵפֶר וַיֵּצֵא בְּתוֹךְ הָעִיר וַיִּזְעַק זְעָקָה גְדֹלָה וּמָרָה — Mordechai learned of all that had been done; and Mordechai tore his clothes and put on sackcloth with ashes. He went out into the midst of the city, and cried loudly and bitterly.

The words, "Mordechai learned of all that had been done" convey that he understood the fundamental reason why the evil decree had been instituted against the Jewish People:

ד/ג עַד לִפְנֵי שַׁעַר־הַמֶּלֶךְ כִּי אֵין לָבוֹא אֶל־שַׁעַר
ג הַמֶּלֶךְ בִּלְבוּשׁ שָׂק׃ וּבְכָל־מְדִינָה וּמְדִינָה מְקוֹם
אֲשֶׁר דְּבַר־הַמֶּלֶךְ וְדָתוֹ מַגִּיעַ אֵבֶל גָּדוֹל לַיְּהוּדִים
וְצוֹם וּבְכִי וּמִסְפֵּד שַׂק וָאֵפֶר יֻצַּע לָרַבִּים׃

When Rebecca inquired why her pregnancy was so painful, Hashem answered her, "Two nations are in your womb; two regimes from your insides shall be separated; *the might shall pass from one regime to the other*. . ." (*Genesis* 25:23). *Rashi* explains as follows: "They shall not be equal in stature — when this one rises, the other shall fall." In other words, when the descendants of Jacob rise in spirituality, the descendants of Esau become weak; but should the descendants of Jacob turn away from Divine Service, then the descendants of Esau grow strong. Similarly, the verse states, אִמָּלְאָה הָחֳרָבָה (*Yehezkel* 26:2), and *Rashi* explains, "Sidon was filled only because Jerusalem was destroyed."

Mordechai was aware of all this, and that is why he donned sackcloth. For the *Arizal* points out that the numerical value of the word שַׂק ("sackcloth") is equivalent to 400 which allude to the 400 warriors that escorted Esau when he rode to meet Jacob (see *Genesis* 33:1). These 400 warriors represent the layers of impurity which surround Esau, and according to the *Imrei David* (p. 436), one of the properties of wearing sackcloth is its ability to counteract the negative effects of such impure layers.

Mordechai also sprinkled ashes upon himself, in memory of Isaac, who was placed upon the altar by our father Abraham as an offering to Hashem. Placing these ashes upon his body was a deed equivalent to the prayer that we utter on *Rosh Hashanah*, "May the offering of Isaac be seen before You." *Sifsei Chaim* explains that Hashem only accepts this prayer if the Jewish people subjugate their will before His will and completely negate their ego, for only then can they share in Isaac's selfless act. At that point, Hashem declares about such an individual, "It is as though I asked you to offer yourselves up as a sacrifice for Me, and you complied with My wish." Undoubtedly, this level of devotion can only be achieved by a Jew, and not by Esau or one of his descendants.

The verse also teaches that Mordechai "went out into the midst of the city, and cried loudly and bitterly." He did this in order to counteract Esau's loud cry, as it says, "And Esau raised his voice and wept" (*Genesis* 27:38). This corresponds with the *Yalkut*, which asks, "Why did Mordechai raise his voice? Was he a simpleton? Does the Holy One, Blessed is He, listen only to loud voices, but not to whispers? Why, we know that Hannah only *thought* her prayer in her mind, and even so Hashem heard her request. As the verse says, 'Hannah spoke *to herself*' (*I Samuel* 1:13), yet Eli said to her, 'Go in

4/3 *until the front of the King's gate, for it was forbidden to enter the King's gate clothed with sackcloth.* 3 *(In every province, wherever the King's command and his decree extended, there was great mourning among the Jews, with fasting, and weeping, and wailing; most of them lying in sackcloth and ashes.)*

---

peace, and may the God of Israel grant your *request*' (ibid., 1:17).' Rather, Mordechai cried out, saying, 'Isaac my father! Esau cried out, and you listened to his voice and blessed him! Now we have been sold to be slaughtered by the sword!' "

Alternatively, it is possible that Mordechai's actions were in memory of the three Patriarchs, whose deeds shall always protect the Jewish People from their enemies:

The sackcloth represents Jacob, about whom the *Yalkut Shimoni* says, "Our forefather Jacob made use of the sackcloth (*Bereishis* 37:334); this is why it remained with his descendants throughout the generations." The ashes represent Isaac, as discussed above. Mordechai cried out in memory of our father Abraham, about whom the *Rambam* (*Yad Chazakah*, *Hilchos Avodah Zarah*, 1) says: "He used to cry out in a loud voice to the entire world in order to teach all of Mankind that the universe was created by Hashem. He would go from city to city and kingdom to kingdom to spread this message."

3. אֵבֶל גָּדוֹל לַיְּהוּדִים וְצוֹם וּבְכִי וּמִסְפֵּד שַׂק וָאֵפֶר יֻצַּע לָרַבִּים — There was great mourning among the Jews, with fasting, and weeping, and wailing; most of them lying in sackcloth and ashes.

The verse mentions the six ways in which a Jew should respond in times of adversity — by mourning, fasting, weeping, wailing, and donning sackcloth with ashes. Through these six stratagems, the Jews atoned for the six occasions when they attended Ahasuerus' feast (see notes on 1:9).

In the Hebrew text, the six words are written in the singular, although the verse speaks of many individuals This teaches that the Jews of that generation attained a degree of unity reminiscent of that reached by the Jewish People at the foot of Mount Sinai when they received the Torah. Regarding that event, it says, "Israel encamped there, opposite the mountain" (*Exodus* 19:2). The verb וַיִּחַן ("encamped") is written in the singular, in contrast to the verbs which appear in earlier verses. This teaches that the multitude of people encamped as though they were a single person with a single desire (*Rashi*).

According to the *Ne'os Hadeshe* (p. 270), the Jewish People's unity was a major catalyst in bringing about the miracles of Purim. It was regarded

ד °ותבואינה נַעֲרוֹת אֶסְתֵּר וְסָרִיסֶיהָ וַיַּגִּידוּ לָהּ
וַתִּתְחַלְחַל הַמַּלְכָּה מְאֹד וַתִּשְׁלַח בְּגָדִים לְהַלְבִּישׁ
ה אֶת־מָרְדֳּכַי וּלְהָסִיר שַׂקּוֹ מֵעָלָיו וְלֹא קִבֵּל׃ וַתִּקְרָא

°וַתָּבוֹאנָה ק׳

---

as such a great merit, that they were able to defeat the Amalekites without the unifying influence of a monarch, since Amalek feeds on discord and disunity, and the only way to overcome him is through unity and synergy.

Thus, our verse uses the singular, for all the Jews throughout Ahasuerus' vast kingdom joined together and mourned over their shared grief and fasted in unison. In this sense, there were not *various* fasts throughout the kingdom, but only one great communal fast.

Through these six expressions of submission and grief, the Jewish People merited to receive the six orders of the Oral Law. As *Sfas Emes* writes, "*Megillas Esther* marks the beginning of the compilation of the Oral Law, for it contains the last miracles recorded in Scripture. It is referred to as a *sefer* (book) as well as an *iggeres* (document) because it is composed of both Written and Oral Torah. This is why the Sages were in disagreement whether it renders one's hands impure [as does a *sefer* of Written Torah]. It is at this time that the compilation of Oral Law began."

The Talmud states that in order to acquire the gift of Torah, one must undergo a measure of hardship (*Berachos* 5a). The Jewish People satisfied this condition through their six expressions of grief. In reward, they received the six orders of *Mishnah*.

They also filled in the missing letter *vav* (which has a numerical value of 6) from the term קִיְּמוּ וְקִבְּלֻ ("the Jews confirmed and undertook upon themselves"; 9:27). The Sages explain that this missing *vav* alludes to the fact that the Jewish People did not accept the Torah wholeheartedly at Mount Sinai — Hashem had to hold the mountain over them and threaten to destroy them before they agreed to accept the Torah (see *Shabbos* 88a). The *Midrash Tanchuma* (*Parshas Noach* 3:3) explains that they initially refused because they found the Oral Law extremely difficult to understand. On Purim, the Jewish People reaccepted the Oral Law with a full heart, and thereby "filled in" the missing *vav*.

❧ ❧ ❧

In *Midrash Esther* it is written: " 'There was a great mourning among the Jews.' Now, I ask you, is there such a thing as a *great* mourning and a *small* mourning? Rather, it is the way of the world that the pain felt by a mourner gradually subsides as the days pass. It is strongest on the first day, but the pain gradually subsides over the next 12 months of mourning. In contrast, the mourning referred to by our verse *increased*

4/4 [4] *And Esther's maids and chamberlains came and told her about it, and the Queen was greatly distressed; she sent garments to clothe Mordechai so that he might take off his sackcloth, but he would not accept them.*

---

with the passing of time, for as each day elapsed, the [Jews] sighed, 'One day less to live.' "[1]

1-4. **וַיִּקְרַע מָרְדֳּכַי אֶת־בְּגָדָיו וַיִּלְבַּשׁ שַׂק וָאֵפֶר וַיֵּצֵא בְּתוֹךְ הָעִיר וַיִּזְעַק זְעָקָה גְדוֹלָה וּמָרָה: וַיָּבוֹא עַד לִפְנֵי שַׁעַר־הַמֶּלֶךְ כִּי אֵין לָבוֹא אֶל־שַׁעַר הַמֶּלֶךְ בִּלְבוּשׁ שָׂק: וּבְכָל־מְדִינָה וּמְדִינָה מְקוֹם אֲשֶׁר דְּבַר־הַמֶּלֶךְ וְדָתוֹ מַגִּיעַ אֵבֶל גָּדוֹל לַיְּהוּדִים וְצוֹם וּבְכִי וּמִסְפֵּד שַׂק וָאֵפֶר יֻצַּע לָרַבִּים: וַתָּבוֹאנָה נַעֲרוֹת אֶסְתֵּר וְסָרִיסֶיהָ וַיַּגִּידוּ לָהּ וַתִּתְחַלְחַל הַמַּלְכָּה מְאֹד וַתִּשְׁלַח בְּגָדִים לְהַלְבִּישׁ אֶת־מָרְדֳּכַי וּלְהָסִיר שַׂקּוֹ מֵעָלָיו וְלֹא קִבֵּל.** — **Mordechai tore his clothes and put on sackcloth with ashes. He went out into the midst of the city, and cried loudly and bitterly. He came until the front of the King's gate, for it was forbidden to enter the King's gate clothed with sackcloth. In every province, wherever the King's command and his decree extended, there was great mourning among the Jews, with fasting and weeping and wailing; most of them lying in sackcloth and ashes. And Esther's maids and chamberlains came and told her about it, and the Queen was greatly distressed; she sent garments to clothe Mordechai so that he might take off his sackcloth, but he would not accept them.**

At first glance, a question arises about the sequence of these verses: Verse 3 should be adjacent to verse 1, for both describe the relation of mourning to Haman's decree. As for verse 2, it should appear immediately before verse 4, since Mordechai arrived at the King's gate and Esther's servants then informed her of his arrival.

The answer is that the *Megillah* subtly conveys the influence Mordechai had on the people of his generation. Before Mordechai's leadership, the Jewish community in Babylonia employed different methods to rescind evil decrees instituted against them by the King: They would entice influential ministers with bribes so that they would speak favorably of the Jews before the King and convince him to revoke the evil decrees. Mordechai, however, loathed these methods. He preferred to turn directly to Hashem through prayer and fasting and beseech only Him, the Master of the Universe, to redeem His people. Following Mordechai's example, the Jews in every

---

1. Perhaps this is the intention behind the blessing which people give to an infant at his *bris*: וְזֶה הַקָּטָן גָּדוֹל יִהְיֶה, *May this little one become great.* They hope that with each passing day the youngster will progress in his spiritual development and attain greater and greater degrees of holiness.

province began fasting and fervently praying to Hashem for salvation, as we learn from verse 3.[1]

The juxtaposition of the verses teaches us that Mordechai understood that if he would interrupt his mourning for even one moment by changing into his everyday clothes to approach the palace gate, he would not merit heavenly assistance. His influence would not have spread throughout the Jewish world, and fasting and repentance would not have been embraced by so many Jews. He understood well the concept of a צַדִּיק[2] יְסוֹד עוֹלָם (*Mishlei* 10:25; literally, "a righteous individual is the foundation of the world"). He realized that his deeds could influence the entire world to repent and return to the ways of God. As R' Israel Salanter purportedly said to his disciples, "As a result of your own observing the laws of Shabbos with more devotion, a Jew in Paris will not light a cigarette on Shabbos."

All this is conveyed by the order of the verses: Verse 1 describes Mordechai's unique approach to revoke evil decrees; verse 2 illustrates the intensity of his mourning, and how he would not let anything in the world distract him from his grief; verse 3 teaches the outcome of Mordechai's awesome commitment.

This explanation also corresponds with *Rashi*'s commentary on the verse, "Mordechai returned to the King's gate" (6:12). *Rashi* explains that immediately after being led upon the King's horse by Haman, Mordechai donned his sackcloth and resumed his mourning. Once again, the *Megillah* underscores Mordechai's unwillingness to be distracted from his mourning for even one moment more than absolutely necessary. In reward for his single-mindedness, Mordechai merited that his prayers be heard and accepted by Hashem.

4. וַתִּשְׁלַח בְּגָדִים לְהַלְבִּישׁ אֶת־מָרְדֳּכַי וּלְהָסִיר שַׂקּוֹ מֵעָלָיו וְלֹא קִבֵּל — She sent garments to clothe Mordechai so that he might take off his sackcloth, but he would not accept them.

Obviously, Mordechai did not lack clothing. Why, then, did Esther send him clothes?

---

1. In the context of this interpretation, we may answer *Pachad Yitzchak*'s question of why verse 1 does not specify what Mordechai "cried out," a term which usually stands for prayer. According to this interpretation, this would be the only instance in Scripture where we are informed that an individual prayed, but are not told what he said.

The answer is that here "he cried out" is to be taken literally — he expressed his grief in a bitter scream in the hope that this would induce the Jews to pray with all their hearts to Hashem. This explanation coincides with the Sages' statement, "Jacob caused his brother Esau to cry out, so Esau's descendant, Haman, caused Mordechai, a descendant of Jacob, to give an anguished shout in Shushan" (*Yalkut, Toldos* 115).

2. See *Yoma* 38b: "R. Yochanan said: 'The world exists even in the merit of a single righteous person.' "

The answer is that she wished to speak with Mordechai privately, but dressed as he was in sackcloth, he would not be permitted to enter the palace. She reasoned that it would be better to speak to him directly rather than sending coded messages back and forth (according to the *Yalkut,* this is how they communicated).

This seems quite a reasonable request. If so, why did Mordechai refuse?

Once again, the answer is that he did not want to interrupt his mourning for even one moment. He feared that if he would wear presentable clothes, he would not feel the same degree of grief as while wearing the sackcloth, for a person's exterior appearance has a dramatic effect upon his state of mind. From this we learn to what extent a person must go to share in the pain of the Jewish People — he must worry that even the slightest change in his life will cause him to become indifferent to the pain of his fellow Jews.

Alternatively, this verse teaches a different lesson:

Evil decrees are instituted against the Jewish People for one of two reasons: Either due to the nations' inherent anti-Semitic feelings, or as a consequence of waning enthusiasm for Torah and *mitzvos* on the part of the Jewish People. The difference between these two types of decrees is that, with the first kind, attempts to revoke it through conventional channels — e.g., bribing influential ministers — can theoretically bear fruit. Decrees of the second type, however, can only be revoked if the Jewish People revitalize their devotion to Torah and dedicate themselves with renewed vigor to the observance of *mitzvos.* Once they do this, the nations themselves will revoke the evil decree.

Esther thought that the decree against the Jewish People stemmed from Ahasuerus' profound anti-Semitic feelings. As always, when the nations are at peace, their hatred towards the Jewish People surfaces, and they turn their attention towards venting it as painfully as possible. Thus, she sent Mordechai clothes in order that he enter the palace and begin lobbying influential ministers to convince the King to revoke the decree.

Mordechai, however, knew that the evil decree was of the second kind, as the Sages said, " 'Through laziness the ceiling collapses, and through idleness of the hands the house leaks' (*Ecclesiastes* 10:18) — because of the laziness of the Jews, who did not engage in Torah study, the enemy of the Holy One, Blessed is He, [euphemistically referring to G-d] became 'poor' (as it were)" (*Megillah* 11a).

5. וַתִּקְרָא אֶסְתֵּר לַהֲתָךְ מִסָּרִיסֵי הַמֶּלֶךְ אֲשֶׁר הֶעֱמִיד לְפָנֶיהָ — Then Esther summoned Hathach, one of the King's chamberlains whom he had appointed to attend her.

Both the Talmud (*Megillah* 15a) and the *Targum* teach that Hathach was

ו וַתְּצַוֵּהוּ עַל־מָרְדֳּכָי לָדַעַת מַה־זֶּה וְעַל־מַה־זֶּה׃ וַיֵּצֵא
הֲתָךְ אֶל־מָרְדֳּכָי אֶל־רְחוֹב הָעִיר אֲשֶׁר לִפְנֵי שַׁעַר־
ז הַמֶּלֶךְ׃ וַיַּגֶּד־לוֹ מָרְדֳּכַי אֵת כָּל־אֲשֶׁר קָרָהוּ וְאֵת ׀
פָּרָשַׁת הַכֶּסֶף אֲשֶׁר אָמַר הָמָן לִשְׁקוֹל עַל־גִּנְזֵי הַמֶּלֶךְ
°בַּיְּהוּדִים ק׳ ח °ביהודיים לְאַבְּדָם׃ וְאֶת־פַּתְשֶׁגֶן כְּתָב־הַדָּת אֲשֶׁר־
נִתַּן בְּשׁוּשָׁן לְהַשְׁמִידָם נָתַן לוֹ לְהַרְאוֹת אֶת־אֶסְתֵּר

---

actually Daniel. The Divine Providence in this is truly astounding — even though King Ahasuerus did not know Esther's nationality, he himself selected none other than the righteous Daniel to be her servant!

7. וַיַּגֶּד־לוֹ מָרְדֳּכַי אֵת כָּל־אֲשֶׁר קָרָהוּ — And Mordechai told him of all that had happened to him

The *Yalkut* explains that Mordechai and Esther communicated through code words. For example, the word קָרָהוּ (lit., "had *happened* to him") was an allusion to the verse אֲשֶׁר קָרְךָ בַּדֶּרֶךְ ("that he [Amalek] *happened* upon you on the way"; *Deuteronomy* 25:18). Thus, Mordechai conveyed to Esther that a descendant of Amalek had risen against the Jewish People.

At first glance, this does not seem such a vital piece of information. After all, one might wonder, does it really make a difference who was behind this evil decree? Once it was instituted, it would seem that the most important matter on everyone's mind should have been how to have it annulled.

The answer is that Mordechai understood that evil decrees instituted against the Jewish People are always in correspondence with their sins. Each transgression draws a particular type of negative force in its wake. Hence, in order to determine what sin the Jewish People are being held accountable for at any given time, one need only consider the dominant characteristic of the nation threatening them, for their enemies are nothing more than a reflection of their transgressions.

Mordechai knew that Amalek can only strike Israel when their enthusiasm for Torah observance wanes. As the *Mechilta* says in reference to the verse, "Amalek came and battled Israel in *Rephidim* (רְפִידִם)" (*Exodus* 17:8), "Amalek came because Israel *loosened their grip on the Torah* (רָפוּ יְדֵיהֶם מִן הַתּוֹרָה)." Similarly, the Sages say, "R' Elazar introduced [his lecture] on this Scriptural portion [the Book of *Esther*] with the following [verse]: 'Through laziness the ceiling collapses, and through idleness of the hands the house leaks' (*Ecclesiastes* 10:18) — because of the laziness of the Jews, who did not engage in Torah [study], the enemy of the Holy One, Blessed is He, became 'poor' " (*Megillah* 11a). The *Maharsha* interprets this to mean that because the Jews neglected the study of Torah, Hashem was rendered "incapable" of saving the Jews from Haman's decree, and in that sense, He is described as "poor."

4/6-8 *and ordered him to go to Mordechai, to learn what
this was about and why.* [6] *So Hathach went out
to Mordechai unto the city square, which was in
front of the King's gate,* [7] *and Mordechai told him
of all that had happened to him, and all about the
sum of money that Haman had promised to pay
to the royal treasuries for the annihilation of the
Jews.* [8] *He also gave him a copy of the text of the
decree which was distributed in Shushan for their
destruction — so that he might show it to Esther*

The ability to induce a lack of enthusiasm is also Amalek's most dominant trait. The Sages point out that Amalek was the first nation to dare attack Israel. Until then, the nations stood in awe of the Israelites, for news of the miracles that Hashem had performed for them in Egypt and at the Sea of Reeds had spread to the four corners of the earth. No nation dared to even consider attacking the Israelites, for they knew that Hashem resided in their midst, and they considered them invincible. Amalek, however, brazenly broke the "barrier" and waged a war against Israel. As the Sages put it, "Amalek jumped into the boiling tub and cooled it off" (*Tanchuma, Va'eschanan* 9).[1]

When Esther learned that the instigator of the evil decree was an Amalekite, she instructed Mordechai to proclaim a three-day fast immediately, even though this would mean that the Jewish People would fast during the Passover Festival.[2] Mordechai replied that he could not comply with her instructions, since *Megillas Taanis* prohibits even the delivering of eulogies any time during the month of *Nissan*; certainly one would be prohibited from declaring public fast days. Instead, he suggested that they postpone the fast until after the Passover Festival. Esther, however, insisted that the fast be proclaimed immediately. She countered that when waging war against Amalek, swiftness and zeal are of prime importance, for only they can counteract Amalek-induced apathy.

Similarly, when Esther originally balked at Mordechai's command to appear unbidden before the King, Mordechai suspected that she had fallen victim to Amalek's sedating spiritual poison. Even though her suggestion that they wait a few more days until Ahasuerus invite her seemed quite

---

1. The commentators say that Amalek's very name denotes its dominant trait: Our Sages tell us that one who reviews his Torah studies 100 times cannot be compared to someone who does so 101 times (*Chagigah* 9:6). A person who stops after 100 times is regarded as "not Hashem's servant," and is still considered to be under Amalek's control. This is because the name "Amalek" (עמלק) can be read as "עמל ק" — "toils to 100 (the numerical value of ק)."

2. See *Yalkut Esther* §4.

וּלְהַגִּיד לָהּ וּלְצַוּוֹת עָלֶיהָ לָבוֹא אֶל־הַמֶּלֶךְ לְהִתְחַנֶּן־
לוֹ וּלְבַקֵּשׁ מִלְּפָנָיו עַל־עַמָּהּ: וַיָּבוֹא הֲתָךְ וַיַּגֵּד לְאֶסְתֵּר ט
אֵת דִּבְרֵי מָרְדֳּכָי: וַתֹּאמֶר אֶסְתֵּר לַהֲתָךְ וַתְּצַוֵּהוּ י
אֶל־מָרְדֳּכָי: כָּל־עַבְדֵי הַמֶּלֶךְ וְעַם מְדִינוֹת הַמֶּלֶךְ יא
יוֹדְעִים אֲשֶׁר כָּל־אִישׁ וְאִשָּׁה אֲשֶׁר־יָבוֹא אֶל־הַמֶּלֶךְ
אֶל־הֶחָצֵר הַפְּנִימִית אֲשֶׁר לֹא־יִקָּרֵא אַחַת דָּתוֹ
לְהָמִית לְבַד מֵאֲשֶׁר יוֹשִׁיט־לוֹ הַמֶּלֶךְ אֶת־שַׁרְבִיט
הַזָּהָב וְחָיָה וַאֲנִי לֹא נִקְרֵאתִי לָבוֹא אֶל־הַמֶּלֶךְ זֶה
שְׁלוֹשִׁים יוֹם: וַיַּגִּידוּ לְמָרְדֳּכָי אֵת דִּבְרֵי אֶסְתֵּר: יב

---

reasonable, Mordechai knew that in the battle against Amalek, swiftness is imperative. In order to rouse Esther to action, he sent her back the harsh message, "Do not imagine that you will be able to escape in the King's palace any more than the rest of the Jews. For if you persist in keeping silent at a time like this. . .you and your father's house will perish" (vs. 13-14).

8. וּלְבַקֵּשׁ מִלְּפָנָיו עַל־עַמָּהּ — And to plead with him for her people.

Midrash Rabbah (*Exodus* 30:4) states: "Esther gave up her life for the sake of Israel. Therefore, they were named after her, as it says, 'to plead with him for *her people.*'" Simply understood, the *Midrash* refers to Esther's decision to appear unbidden before the King, an act potentially punishable by death.

It is also possible that the *Midrash* refers to the verse, "let my life be granted to me as my request (בִּשְׁאֵלָתִי) and my people as my petition (בְּבַקָּשָׁתִי)" (7:3). The Hebrew word שְׁאֵלָה ("request") conveys asking for something which one could do without, whereas בַּקָּשָׁה implies asking for a favor of crucial importance. Esther in effect said to Ahasuerus, "I would appreciate it if you would save my life, but I *implore* you to spare my people." For this, she merited to have the Jewish People named after her.

12. וַיַּגִּידוּ לְמָרְדֳּכָי אֵת דִּבְרֵי אֶסְתֵּר — They related Esther's words to Mordechai.

The Sages teach that Esther's loyal messenger — Hathach — was in fact Daniel. Our verse, however, says, "*they* related Esther's words to Mordechai," which implies that Hathach did not relay this particular message. The Sages infer from this that this one time, Hathach refused to carry out his duties. *Rashi* explains that Hathach did not wish to relay the bad news that Esther refused to follow Mordechai's command to appear unbidden before King Ahasuerus. Consequently, Esther was forced to find a different messenger. In conclusion, the Sages said, "From here [we learn] that [when sent

and inform her, bidding her to go to the King, to appeal to him, and to plead with him for her people.

[9] *Hathach came and told Esther what Mordechai had said.* [10] *Then Esther told Hathach to return to Mordechai with this message:* [11] *"All the King's servants and the people of the King's provinces are well aware that if anyone, man or woman, approaches the King in the inner court without being summoned, there is but one law for him: that he be put to death; except for the person to whom the King shall extend the gold scepter so that he may live. Now I have not been summoned to come to the King for the past thirty days."*

[12] *They related Esther's words to Mordechai.*

---

on a mission], one should not report back with bad news" (*Megillah* 15a).

At this point, two questions arise:

1. If Daniel sincerely felt that Esther had behaved incorrectly by refusing to obey Mordechai, why did he not rebuke her? As *Rambam* writes, "If a person sees his fellow commit a sin or behave in a negative manner, it is a *mitzvah* for him to return his fellow to rectitude and inform him that he is causing himself great harm through his deeds, as the verse says, 'You shall reprove your fellow' " (*Yad Chazakah*, *Hilchos De'os* 6:7).
2. Mordechai sent Esther the return message, "Do not imagine that you will be able to escape in the King's palace any more than the rest of the Jews. For if you persist in keeping silent at a time like this, relief and deliverance will come to the Jews from some other place, and you and your father's house will perish" (vs. 13-14). Why did he send her such scathing words of reproof, and why send such a message through a third party? As *Rambam* writes, "Someone who rebukes his fellow must do so in private, and speak calmly and in a gentle manner. He must explain that his only intention in speaking is to benefit him and help him earn a portion in the world to come."

The answer to both questions is that Esther had solid halachic grounds for refusing to comply with Mordechai's instructions. The law of the land dictated that anyone who approached the King without being summoned was liable to be put to death, which meant that Esther would have placed her life in great danger by obeying Mordechai's command. And even though the lives of millions of Jews were at stake, a person is not halachically obligated to risk his life for the sake of others.[1]

---

1. *Pischei Teshuvah* cites differing opinions regarding whether a person is obligated to place himself in a *potentially* dangerous situation in order to save other Jews from certain death

יג וַיֹּאמֶר מָרְדֳּכַי לְהָשִׁיב אֶל־אֶסְתֵּר אַל־תְּדַמִּי
יד בְנַפְשֵׁךְ לְהִמָּלֵט בֵּית־הַמֶּלֶךְ מִכָּל־הַיְּהוּדִים: כִּי אִם־

Thus, Daniel (Hathach) did not rebuke Esther, because halachically she had done nothing wrong. In fact, even Mordechai did not rebuke her. Mordechai merely revealed to Esther the deeper reason why she, of all people, had been appointed to such an influential position. As *Alshich* explains, Esther's purpose was to rectify the sin of her ancestor, King Saul. Because of the transgression he had committed many years earlier (see *I Samuel* 15), King Saul and his household were sentenced to death and extinction. According to *Yalkut Shimoni*, the only reason King David did not kill Shimi ben Gera — a member of Saul's clan (see *II Samuel* 16:5, 19:22-23) — is because he foresaw that Mordechai and Esther would emerge from his offspring. In light of this, Mordechai pointed out to Esther that even though she had no *halachic* obligation to place her life in danger for the sake of the Jewish People, she *did* have an obligation to risk her life in order to rectify King Saul's sin, for which his entire lineage faced extinction. As Mordechai put it, "And who knows whether it was just for such a time as this that you attained the royal position!" (v. 14).

A closer look at the sins of King Saul and Shimi ben Gera will reveal how Esther's deeds rectified them:

It has been asked how King Saul was able to say to Samuel the Prophet, "I have fulfilled HASHEM's word" (*I Samuel* 15:13), in full knowledge of the fact that he failed to fulfill Samuel's command to "destroy all their possessions; have no mercy on them; put to death the men, the women, the children . . . the oxen and sheep, the camels and the donkeys" (ibid. v. 3). The answer is that Saul thought he had committed an עֲבֵירָה לִשְׁמָהּ — a transgression for the sake of Heaven. He thought that despite the explicit command to slay Amalek's livestock, it would be a greater act of devotion to keep them alive and then sacrifice them as thanksgiving-offerings to Hashem. Samuel reprimanded him for this decision, saying, "Does HASHEM desire burnt-offerings and sacrifices as much as obedience to His command? Behold, obedience is better than offerings, to listen, than the fat of rams" (ibid., v. 22). The greatest expression of gratitude to Hashem is to fulfill His commands.

Regarding Shimi ben Gera, it says, "When King David arrived at Bachurim, a member of Saul's clan — a man named Shimi ben Gera — came out from there, cursing as he came. He threw stones at David and all King David's servants, and at all the troops and the warriors. . .He cursed, 'Get out, get out, you criminal, you villain!' " (*II Samuel* 16:5-7). What prompted Shimi to behave so disrespectfully towards the King? *Yalkut*

(*Yoreh De'ah* 252:2). It seems that *all* opinions would agree that a person is not obligated to place himself in a definite life-threatening situation in order to save other Jews.

[13] *Then Mordechai said to reply to Esther, "Do not imagine that you will be able to escape in the King's palace any more than the rest of the Jews.* [14] *For if*

Shimoni teaches that his real intention was to rebuke King David for not repenting completely for a past infraction. Thus, we see that Shimi ben Gera, too, thought that he was committing an עֲבֵירָה לִשְׁמָהּ — a transgression for the sake of Heaven. His intentions were pure, his only sin being the violent manner in which he rebuked King David (see *Rambam*'s specifications on how rebuke should be given as quoted above).

Similarly, Esther was placed in a situation in which the Jewish People's survival depended on her committing an עֲבֵירָה לִשְׁמָהּ — a transgression for the sake of Heaven. Until this time, Esther had been forced to live with King Ahasuerus, and thus, was not held culpable. However, now Mordechai urged her to approach the King of her own volition and willingly commit a transgression for the sake of saving the Jews' lives. By committing this transgression for the sake of Heaven, Esther saved the Jewish People and also rectified the misdirected "transgressions for the sake of Heaven" committed by her ancestors, King Saul and Shimi ben Gera.

Perhaps this is why, according to the Gemara, the *Megillah* describes the sight of the Divine Spirit enveloping Esther while she approached the King as "Esther donned royalty" (5:1) (*Megillah* 15a) — the Sages mean that Esther's decision to go to the King sustained Saul's Kingdom.

13. וַיֹּאמֶר מָרְדֳּכַי לְהָשִׁיב אֶל־אֶסְתֵּר אַל־תְּדַמִּי בְנַפְשֵׁךְ לְהִמָּלֵט בֵּית־הַמֶּלֶךְ מִכָּל־הַיְּהוּדִים. — Then Mordechai said to reply to Esther: "Do not imagine that you will be able to escape in the King's palace any more than the rest of the Jews."

Mordechai rebuked Esther because her unassuming way of serving Hashem was no longer appropriate for the circumstances at hand. Now the times called for nothing less than public sanctification of Heaven's Name.[1] This is what Mordechai meant when he said to Esther, "if you persist *in keeping silent at a time like this,* relief and deliverance will come to the Jews from some other place, while you and your father's house will perish" (v. 14).

❧ ❧ ❧

1. Similarly, during the Warsaw Ghetto uprising R' Menachem Ziemba ruled that the times called for public sanctification of Hashem's Name by taking up arms against the Nazis. He explained that passively giving up one's life is only considered a sanctification of Hashem's Name when a Jew is given the choice to die or renounce his religion. However, if a Jew is not even given the choice to live, he must not willingly give up his life. Under such circumstances, the way to sanctify Hashem's Name is to remain alive at all costs. He therefore declared it a *mitzvah* to participate in the armed uprising against the Nazis. It would seem that the Jewish People's armed uprising against their enemies in the days of Purim lends support to his decision.

ד/יד הַחֲרֵשׁ תַּחֲרִישִׁי בָּעֵת הַזֹּאת רֶוַח וְהַצָּלָה יַעֲמוֹד
לַיְּהוּדִים מִמָּקוֹם אַחֵר וְאַתְּ וּבֵית־אָבִיךְ תֹּאבֵדוּ
וּמִי יוֹדֵעַ אִם־לְעֵת כָּזֹאת הִגַּעַתְּ לַמַּלְכוּת׃

It is difficult, however, to understand why Mordechai responded to Esther so harshly, since it would seem that she had a valid point in not wanting to risk her life unnecessarily by approaching the King without being summoned. Furthermore, considering that a full month had elapsed since the King had last called Esther, she stood to be summoned before him in the near future. Surely such a short delay would not jeopardize the safety of the Jews, especially in view of the fact that the evil decree against them was only to be enacted in one year's time (see 3:7). However, despite Esther's legitimate arguments, it seems that Mordechai suspected her of turning her back on her people.

It is possible that Mordechai refused to accept Esther's line of reasoning for more esoteric considerations: As the *Alshich* explains, Esther's life-mission was to rectify the sin of King Saul, who disregarded the command of Samuel the Prophet to slay every last Amalekite, including Agag, their king. Instead, Saul captured Agag alive (see *I Samuel* ch. 15). Saul's misplaced compassion gave Agag the opportunity to perpetuate his lineage by having relations with a maidservant during his captivity. For this sin, Saul and his entire household were sentenced to death and extinction.

Aware of Esther's role, Mordechai dismissed her rationale for the following two reasons: First, he feared that if "relief and deliverance would come to the Jews *from some other place,*" and not through Esther, all of King Saul's descendants, including Esther, would perish as Samuel the Prophet had foreseen. Second, Mordechai knew that only swift and decisive action could rectify Saul's hesitance in exterminating the Amalekites. In this context, the words, "*if you persist in keeping silent at a time like this, relief and deliverance will come to the Jews from some other place, while you and your father's house will perish*" (v. 14), take on new meaning.

❦ ❦ ❦

The principle outlined above enables us to better comprehend the Sages' following statement:

" 'She [Esther] stood in the inner court of the King's palace' (5:1) — R' Levi said: As soon as she reached the chamber of idols [on her way through the palace to Ahasuerus], the Divine Presence departed from her. She exclaimed: 'My God, my God, why have You forsaken me?' (*Psalms* 22:2) Could it be that You regard an inadvertent offense as an intentional one, or an offense committed under coercion as one committed willingly? Or perhaps [You have forsaken me] because I called him [Ahasuerus] a dog, as the verse says (ibid. v. 21), 'Rescue my soul from the sword, my only one from the

you persist in keeping silent at a time like this, relief and deliverance will come to the Jews from some other place, while you and your father's house will perish. And who knows whether it was just for such a time as this that you attained the royal position!'"

---

grip of the dog'? " (*Megillah* 15b).

The obvious question is why Esther referred to Ahasuerus as "a dog." Again, the answer lies in Esther's life-mission to rectify King Saul's sin. In order to counterbalance Saul's *compassion* for Agag, Esther consciously mustered up *hatred* for Ahasuerus by calling him "a dog,"[1] thus equating him to Amalek.

❦ ❦ ❦

As in so many instances, here the words of Scripture once again reveal the honesty and straightforwardness of the Torah: Since Esther herself wrote the *Megillah,* [2] she could easily have omitted Mordechai's scathing reproof and recorded for posterity only her noble response, "Go, assemble all the Jews. . ." (v. 16). However, because she understood the invaluable and eternal lessons which Mordechai's words conveyed, she faithfully recounted the dialogue in its entirety. Furthermore, she recognized the value of moral rebuke, about which the *Midrash* says, "Love which is not accompanied by moral rebuke is not [true] love. Reish Lakish said: Moral rebuke promotes peace" (*Midrash Rabbah, Vayeira* 54).

14. כִּי אִם־הַחֲרֵשׁ תַּחֲרִישִׁי בָּעֵת הַזֹּאת רֶוַח וְהַצָּלָה יַעֲמוֹד לַיְּהוּדִים מִמָּקוֹם אַחֵר וְאַתְּ וּבֵית־אָבִיךְ תֹּאבֵדוּ וּמִי יוֹדֵעַ אִם־לְעֵת כָּזֹאת הִגַּעַתְּ לַמַּלְכוּת —
For if you persist in keeping silent at a time like this, relief and deliverance will come to the Jews from some other place, while you and your father's

---

1. Although Ahasuerus himself was not of Amalekite descent, the motivating force behind his decree originated from Amalek. As *Pachad Yitzchak* explains, Amalek is not merely a nation, but also a metaphysical entity which is at the root of every evil deed. It is referred to as "a dog" because it shares something in common with that animal — just as the dog displays great chutzpah by behaving as though it were man's equal, so too, Amalek displays great chutzpah by equating itself to the greatest men on earth. Thus, Esther called Ahasuerus "a dog" — she discerned the hidden presence of Amalek behind Ahasuerus' deeds, and she addressed that metaphysical entity directly.

The fact that Ahasuerus was possessed by the spirit of Amalek is evident from the Sages' following statement: "Rava said: What is [the meaning of] '*when King Ahasuerus sat*'? (1:2). [כְּשֶׁבֶת can mean "when he sat" as well as "when he rested."] It means 'when his mind was put at ease.' [Ahasuerus] said: Belshazzar [the former king of Babylonia] calculated [the seventy years of exile,] but erred [in his calculation], whereas I calculated and have not erred" (*Megillah* 11b). Ahasuerus had the audacity to think that he knew better than Jeremiah the Prophet, who foresaw that the Jewish people would return to their homeland after 70 years in exile. Such a degree of chutzpah can be ascribed to no other nation but Amalek.

2. As the verse says, "Then Queen Esther. . .*wrote with full authority* to ratify this second letter of Purim" (9:29).

 טו־טז וַתֹּאמֶר אֶסְתֵּר לְהָשִׁיב אֶל־מָרְדֳּכָי: לֵךְ כְּנוֹס
אֶת־כָּל־הַיְּהוּדִים הַנִּמְצְאִים בְּשׁוּשָׁן וְצוּמוּ עָלַי
וְאַל־תֹּאכְלוּ וְאַל־תִּשְׁתּוּ שְׁלֹשֶׁת יָמִים לַיְלָה

---

house will perish. And who knows whether it was just for such a time as this that you attained the royal position!"

The verse says, "Rebuke frightens an understanding person more than one hundred blows [frightens] a fool" (*Proverbs* 17:10).

"An understanding person" may be applied to Esther, for we see that in the end she faithfully obeyed Mordechai and risked her life by appearing unsummoned before Ahasuerus. Even though Esther's instincts told her to wait a few days until the King called for her, she suppressed her feelings in deference to Mordechai's wisdom. This, despite knowing that by voluntarily appearing before the King and having intimate relations with him, she would forever be prohibited to Mordechai, her rightful husband. Nevertheless, Esther exercised "understanding" and followed the bidding of Mordechai, the Torah leader of the generation.

Indeed, it was her willingness to accept Mordechai's words of reproof and take refuge in the Almighty that earned her the merit to survive the perilous entry into the King's court. This principle is evident in the *Alter of Kelm's* letter to his son, in which he said: "My precious son, I rejoiced greatly over your acceptance of my rebuke. Do not worry at all, for the Almighty will assist you. [As we say in *Shemoneh Esrei,*] 'Let us not suffer humiliation, for in You we trust.' [And as we say at the conclusion of the *Megillah* reading,] 'They who seek You shall not stumble, and they who take refuge in You shall never suffer humiliation' — this implies that if a person does *not* discipline himself to take refuge in the Almighty, he is destined to suffer humiliation forever more."

"A fool" (in *Proverbs* 17:10) alludes to King Ahasuerus, who knew the evil fate that had befallen every one of Israel's past enemies, yet foolishly joined Haman in his plot to exterminate the Jewish People.

Ahasuerus' knowledge of the misfortune which befell his predecessors is evident from his dialogue with Haman: "Rava said: There was no one who knew how to slander [as skillfully] as Haman. He said [to Ahasuerus], 'Come, let us destroy [the Jews].'

[Ahasuerus] replied, 'I am afraid of their God, *that He should not do to me as He did to my predecessors.*'

[Haman] replied, 'They have been negligent [in their observance] of *mitzvos,* [and their God will therefore not punish you for harming them]' " (*Megillah* 13b).

Ahasuerus revealed his foolishness by failing to learn from the "one hundred blows" which befell his evil predecessors, who, like him, were also

[15] *Then Esther said to reply to Mordechai:* [16] *"Go,
assemble all the Jews to be found in Shushan, and
fast for me. Do not eat or drink for three days, night*

---

bent on exterminating the Jewish People. Instead, he mindlessly allowed himself to be swayed by Haman's ridiculous argument.

Similarly, the Sages (*Megillah* 12) interpreted the verse, "After these things, when the wrath of King Ahasuerus subsided, he remembered Vashti, and what she had done, and what had been decreed against her" (2:1), to mean that Ahasuerus clearly recognized that Vashti was punished in kind for her sin — just as she would force Jewish women to undress and work on Shabbos, so too, she was unclothed and executed on Shabbos. Nonetheless, this realization did not leave a lasting impression on Ahasuerus, for the very next verse states, "Then the King's pages said: Let there be sought for the King *beautiful* young maidens. . ." (2:2). Foolishly, he returned to his vain pursuits — acting on the advice of his pages, he selected the next Queen solely on the basis of her outward looks and not for her virtues. Once again, Ahasuerus revealed his stupidity by failing to learn a lesson from his own "one hundred blows."

This is also what the Sages meant when they said that Ahasuerus remained as wicked when the story of Esther ended as he had been when it first began (*Megillah* 11a). Even though Ahasuerus witnessed Haman's good fortune suddenly and inexplicably decline, and the Jewish People miraculously redeemed from the hands of their enemies, he failed to learn his lesson.

16. לֵךְ כְּנוֹס אֶת־כָּל־הַיְּהוּדִים הַנִּמְצְאִים בְּשׁוּשָׁן וְצוּמוּ עָלַי וְאַל־תֹּאכְלוּ וְאַל־תִּשְׁתּוּ — "Go, assemble all the Jews to be found in Shushan, and fast for me. Do not eat or drink.

According to *Yalkut Shimoni,* the term, "the Jews to be found in Shushan," refers specifically to the Jews who attended Ahasuerus' feast. The *Midrash* also says, "[Why does the verse say,] 'fast for me. *Do not eat or drink. . .*'? Can a person fast and eat simultaneously? Rather, [Esther in effect said to the Jewish People,] 'You must fast for having derived pleasure from Ahasuerus' feast.' "

In light of this explanation it remains unclear why Esther herself fasted, since we may safely assume that *she* did not attend Ahasuerus' feast. Surely she followed Mordechai's opinion, who, alone among the Torah scholars of that generation, discouraged the Jews from attending the royal feast (*Midrash Megillas Esther* 7:18).[1]

---

1. Mordechai said, "Do not attend the feast lest you provide the Satan with a valid accusation against you" (*Midrash Megillas Esther* 7:18).

At first glance, one could simply answer that she fasted in order not to set herself apart from her brethren, in fulfillment of the *mishnah,* "Do not set yourself apart from the rest of the congregation" (*Pirkei Avos* 2:5). However, if this were the reason she fasted, the verse should have said, "fast for me, and do not eat or drink for three days, night or day, *and* I, with my maids, will fast also." By omitting the connective *vav* (וְ — "and I") between the first and second clause, the verse suggests that she did not fast for the same reason as the rest of the Jewish People.

Rather, the answer lies in *Pachad Yitzchak*'s interpretation of the following Talmudic passage:

"[The verse says,] 'Moses brought the people forth from the camp toward God, *and they stood at the bottom of the mountain*' (*Exodus* 19:17). R' Avdimi bar Chama bar Chassa said: This teaches that the Holy One, Blessed is He, held the mountain over them [the Jewish People] as though it were a barrel and said to them, 'If you accept the Torah, good. But if you do not, that place shall become your graveyard.' R' Acha bar Yaakov said: From this, there is a very strong plea of annulment of [the acceptance of] the Torah (because it was under duress)" (*Shabbos* 88a).

Unlike those who interpret R' Acha bar Yaakov's statement to mean that the Jewish People could *theoretically* have rejected the Torah on the basis of the coercive manner in which it was given to them, *Ramban* is of the opinion that the Jewish People actually *did* reject the Torah once. It happened when they were exiled from the Land of Israel. As the verse recounts, the Jewish People said, "We shall be like the nations, like the families of the land, worshiping wood and stone" (*Ezekiel* 20:32).

Pachad Yitzchak poses a difficulty: If so, why did the Sages ascribe Haman's evil decree to the Jewish People's sin of deriving pleasure from Ahasuerus' feast, since their rebellious assertion cited above seems a much greater sin?

He answers by redefining the transgression of attending the King's feast: The Jewish People who attended the feast were not guilty of eating unkosher food — on the contrary, Mordechai himself made certain that the food and drink served to the Jews met the strictest standards of *kashrus.* Rather, they were held accountable for joining Ahasuerus in celebrating the passing of the 70th year of the Israelites' exile. As we have mentioned earlier (see 3:7), Jeremiah the Prophet foresaw that the exiled Jews living in Babylonia would be returned to the Land of Israel after 70 years in exile (*Megillah* 11b; *Jeremiah* 29:10). Ahasuerus knew of Jeremiah's prophecy, and he anxiously waited until the end of the 70-year period to see whether it would be fulfilled. However, unbeknownst to Ahasuerus, his calculations were flawed, and he ushered in the 70th year of the Israelites' exile prematurely. Exuberantly, Ahasuerus made a feast in celebration of this day, which he thought marked the end of the Jewish People's eternal relationship with Hashem. Now, he thought, the Jews are no longer God's "Chosen People."

Let us now return to our original question: If Esther did not attend Ahasuerus' feast, why did she fast?

The answer is that Mordechai detected a weakness in Esther's faith in the eternal relationship between Hashem and the Jewish People. This is evident from his words of reproof to her, in which he emphasized that the Jewish people would endure forever regardless of her actions: "Do not imagine that you will be able to escape in the King's palace any more than the rest of the Jews. For if you persist in keeping silent at a time like this, *relief and deliverance will come to the Jews from some other place,* while you and your father's house will perish" (v. 13-14).

Esther took Mordechai's words to heart. After much introspection, she realized that he was correct; deep down, she harbored doubts concerning the eternity of the Jewish People, albeit to a much lesser degree than those Jews who attended Ahasuerus' feast. Acknowledging her "sin," she reasoned that she had as much of an obligation to fast as they did. However, in order to draw a clear distinction between Esther's almost imperceptible weakness of faith and the forthright transgression committed by the Jews who attended the King's feast, the verse omitted the connective *vav* (ו — "and") between the first and second clause.[1]

When the Jews repented for their sins and merited to be redeemed, the *Megillah* says, "The Jews confirmed and undertook upon themselves (קִיְּמוּ וְקִבְּלֻ), and their posterity, and upon all who might join them, to observe these two days. . .each year" (9:27). The Sages said in reference to this verse, "Rava said: In the days of Ahasuerus, they [the Jewish People] confirmed (קִיְּמוּ) what they once undertook (קִבְּלֻ) upon themselves" (*Shabbos* 88a). *Rashi* explains that the Jews living in Ahasuerus' day reaccepted the Torah through their profound appreciation for the miracles which Hashem performed for their sake. It would seem that simultaneously, they also invalidated the "ability to plea annulment of the Torah" which was possible since the revelation at Mount Sinai.

Ramban adds, "[The miracles of Purim] were more dear to them than the redemption in Egypt." As a result, they also merited the promise that "these days of Purim shall never cease among the Jews, nor shall their remembrance perish from their descendants" (9:28). The Sages interpret this verse to mean that in the future, of all the Festivals, Purim alone shall remain. It is indeed appropriate that the redemption of Purim, which

1. This also explains how Esther surmised that Haman's evil decree came as a result of the Jews' sin of attending Ahasuerus' feast, for all Mordechai told her was that an Amalekite was behind the evil decree — Esther knew that heavenly punishment is always in kind with the sinner's transgression. She was also aware that Amalek's principal goal is to persuade the entire world that the Jewish People are no different than any other nation. Thus, she reasoned that if Amalek was behind the evil decree, it must mean that the Jews' faith in the eternity and uniqueness of the Jewish People was weak, and that this was why they had attended Ahasuerus' feast. As soon as she came to this conclusion, she declared the three-day fast in order to rectify this sin.

ד/טז וָיוֹם גַּם־אֲנִי וְנַעֲרֹתַי אָצוּם כֵּן וּבְכֵן אָבוֹא אֶל־הַמֶּלֶךְ אֲשֶׁר לֹא־כַדָּת וְכַאֲשֶׁר אָבַדְתִּי אָבָדְתִּי׃

---

confirmed the eternal existence of the Jewish People, be commemorated for eternity.

❧ ❧ ❧

What is the meaning of the words, וְצוּמוּ עָלַי, "fast *for me*"?

According to the *Chida,* the word עָלַי ("for me") in our verse should be taken in the same way as in the verse, עָלַי קִלְלָתְךָ בְּנִי ("Your curse *be upon me,* my son" (*Genesis* 27:13). At first glance, the correlation between the two occurrences of the word עָלַי is difficult to grasp. In order to understand the *Chida*'s interpretation, let us take a closer look at the verse in *Genesis.*

Rebecca, Jacob's mother, urged him to disguise himself as his elder brother, Esau, and thereby receive the blessing of the first-born from Isaac, their ailing father. Jacob feared being discovered and earning his father's curse instead of his blessing. In order to allay Jacob's fears, Rebecca said to him, עָלַי קִלְלָתְךָ בְּנִי ("Your curse be upon me"). The *Vilna Gaon* explains that the Hebrew word עָלַי is an acronym for עֵשָׂו (Esau), לָבָן (Laban),יוֹסֵף (Joseph). In effect, Jacob's mother revealed to him that he would indeed suffer hardship, but only from these three individuals, and not from Isaac, his father.

The word עָלַי in the *Megillah* may be understood in a similar light. Esther in essence revealed that the three-day fast would atone for three sins, which are alluded to in the acronym עָלַי: The ע stands for עֵשָׂו (Esau), alluding to the sin of deriving pleasure from Ahasuerus' feast — just as Esau said, "Pour into me, now, some of that very red stuff" (*Genesis* 25:30), so too, the Jews followed their evil inclination and ate and drank together with the wicked Ahasuerus. The ל stands for לָבָן (Laban), alluding to the sin of idolatry. Just as Laban believed in idolatry (see ibid. 31:19,30), so too, the Jews in Ahasuerus' day committed idolatry by bowing down to an image (see *Megillah* 12a). The י stands for יוֹסֵף (Joseph), alluding to the sin of marrying gentile women — unlike Joseph, who overcame his physical desires and resisted the enticements of Potiphar's wife (see ibid. 39:7-12), the Jews in Ahasuerus' day succumbed to their desires and married gentile women (see *Ezra* Ch. 9).

It would seem that each day of fasting atoned for a different sin. Thus, the third day of fasting atoned for the sin of intermarriage. It is no coincidence, then, that Esther entered the King's court to voluntarily have relations with him specifically on the third day — she knew that the merit of the Jewish people's fasting and repentance would protect her, as is evident from the verse, "Do not eat or drink for three days. . .*Then I will* go in to the King though it's unlawful." (4:16).

or day; I, with my maids, will fast also. Then I will go in to the King though it's unlawful; and if I perish, I perish."

וּבְכֵן אָבוֹא אֶל־הַמֶּלֶךְ אֲשֶׁר לֹא־כַדָּת וְכַאֲשֶׁר אָבַדְתִּי אָבָדְתִּי — Then I will go in to the King though it's unlawful; and if I perish, I perish."

Rashi paraphrases the last clause to mean, "Just as I have begun to approach destruction, so shall I continue to perish." Esther went to the King with intent to sanctify the Name of Heaven. This coincides with the verse, "I should be sanctified among the Children of Israel" (*Leviticus* 22:32), about which *Rashi* says, "If a Jew is faced with a situation where he is required to give up his life in sanctification of the Name, he should do so without expecting a miracle to occur on his behalf, for if a person should give up his life on condition that a miracle occur, a miracle will not occur." Esther entered the King's court unconditionally, ready to die for her people.

Even so, Esther never lost hope in Hashem's mercy, in keeping with the Talmudic adage, "Even if a sharp sword is upon one's neck, one should not withhold himself from (praying for) mercy" (*Berachos* 10a). For as the *Midrash Shochar Tov* on *Psalms* 22:19 says, when Esther said, "I will go in to the King," the servants in Ahasuerus' palace were overcome with excitement hoping that he would become enraged and kill her! They then began laying claims on her possessions. One said, "When she dies, her clothes belong to me!" and another, "Her jewelry is mine!" Upon hearing this, Esther prayed, "They divide my clothes among themselves, casting lots for my garments. But You, HASHEM, do not be distant; my Strength, hasten to my aid!" (*Psalms* 22:19-20).

On the merit of Esther's prayers and faith in Hashem, her life was spared. As King David said, "Behold, God looks towards those who fear Him, towards those who yearn for His lovingkindness, to save them from death, to sustain them in famine" (33:18-19). On the merit of Esther's self-inflicted "famine" — fasting and prayer — she merited to be saved from death.

❧ ❧ ❧

In reference to this verse the Sages said, "[This means:] Just as I [Esther] was lost from my father's house, so shall I be lost from [Mordechai]" (*Megillah* 15a). *Rashi* explains that by submitting *voluntarily* to Ahasuerus, Esther knew she would be forbidden forever to Mordechai, her legitimate husband (see *Sotah* 2a). However, *Tosafos* asks why Mordechai did not simply divorce Esther — had he done so, he would have been permitted by law to remarry her even though she lived voluntarily with Ahasuerus. *Tosafos* answers that Mordechai feared the mandatory witnesses to a divorce would spread news of the divorce, eventually reaching the King.

Tosafos' explanation is difficult, however, in light of the following words of *Rambam* (in his commentary to *Esther*): "How great was the merit of that generation! Everyone knew that Esther was Mordechai's niece, yet no one informed Ahasuerus . . . This is why they merited to be redeemed.

"We learn this principle from Moses, about whom the verse says, 'He went out the next day and behold! two Hebrew men were fighting. He said to the wicked one, "Why would you strike your fellow?" He replied, "Who appointed you as a dignitary, a ruler, and a judge over us? Do you propose to murder me, as you murdered the Egyptian?" Moses was frightened and he thought, "Indeed, the matter is known!" ' (*Exodus* 2:14). In other words, Moses thought, 'This generation is surely lost; I do not think that in their present state they are worthy of being redeemed.'

"Only when that entire generation perished and there were no more informers who revealed the secrets of fellow Jews to the gentiles did Hashem say to Moses, 'Go, return to Egypt, for all the people who seek your life have died' (ibid., 4:19). Now they were worthy of being redeemed, for they no longer revealed secrets about each other to the Egyptians. . ."

In light of *Rambam's* words, it would appear that Mordechai had no reason to fear that news of Esther's divorce would reach the King. Why then, did he not divorce her as *Tosafos* suggested?

The answer is that Mordechai knew that Torah defines reality, and not vice versa. Thus, since the Torah specifies that witnesses must be present at the divorce proceedings *in order that it become public knowledge* (see *Pnei Yehoshua, Kiddushin; Nesivos Hamishpat* §36), that is exactly what would happen, regardless of the integrity and virtue of Mordechai's generation.[1]

17. וַיַּעֲבֹר מָרְדֳּכָי וַיַּעַשׂ כְּכֹל אֲשֶׁר צִוְּתָה עָלָיו אֶסְתֵּר — Mordechai then left and did exactly as Esther had commanded him.

Given Mordechai and Esther's unequal status — he was her cousin and guardian who had adopted her in her youth — it would have been more appropriate for the verse to say, "Mordechai. . .did exactly as Esther had *requested* of him." Why, then, does the verse use the word *command*? Evidently, in order to underscore the degree of Mordechai's humility, the verse teaches that he fulfilled Esther's request as though she had

1. The following account illustrates this point: A *mohel* (ritual circumcisor) once asked R' Moshe Feinstein about a situation in which a circumcision would be performed without drawing a single drop of blood, and that he wished to know whether such a circumcision would be halachically valid, or whether blood must be drawn some other way. R' Moshe thought for a moment, but then emphatically asserted that *Tosafos* explicitly says that blood would emerge during circumcision. The *mohel* insisted that he is sure that no blood will come out. At this point, R' Moshe became annoyed and said, "If *Tosafos* says that blood comes out, then it must come out!"

4/17 [17] *Mordechai then left and did exactly as Esther had commanded him.*

5/1 [1] *Now it came to pass on the third day, Esther donned royalty and stood in the inner court*

---

commanded him, as though he were a slave, and she, his mistress. Mordechai, the head of the *Sanhedrin,* the supreme Torah council in Israel, humbly complied with Esther's request by assembling the Jews and instructing them to fast on Passover.

V

1. וַיְהִי בַּיּוֹם הַשְּׁלִישִׁי וַתִּלְבַּשׁ אֶסְתֵּר מַלְכוּת — Now it came to pass on the third day, Esther donned royalty.

Regarding this verse the Sages said, "[Scripture] should have said [that Esther donned] *royal garments,* [not *in royalty.* In reply,] R' Elazar said in the name of R' Chanina: This teaches that [Esther] clothed herself in the Divine Spirit, for it is written here, "Esther *donned* (וַתִּלְבַּשׁ)," and elsewhere it is written, 'And the Spirit *clothed* (לָבְשָׁה) Amasai' (*I Chronicles* 12:19) " (*Megillah* 15a).

This explanation is difficult to understand — can a person *wear* the Divine Spirit?

Pachad Yitzchak cites this verse in order to solve an oft-repeated difficulty concerning the story of Purim: The Gemara tells us that the *mitzvah* to exterminate Amalek is only applicable when the Jewish People have appointed a king. This is why the Israelites crossing into the Promised Land were first commanded to appoint a king, and only afterwards to exterminate Amalek (*Sanhedrin* 20a). If so, how could the Jews in Ahasuerus' day have fulfilled the *mitzvah* of exterminating Amalek by slaying Haman and his sons, since at the time they were not under the sovereignty of a Jewish king?

Pachad Yitzchak resolves the difficulty with the words, "Esther clothed herself in royalty" — it teaches that she assumed sovereign control over Israel, thereby empowering the Israelites to exterminate Amalek. However, *Pachad Yitzchak* does not explain what gave Esther the right to independently assume the throne.

According to *Shem MiShmuel,* the essential role of a king is to unite his countrymen.[1] As *Rambam* says about a Jewish king, "His heart was the heart of the entire Jewish People" (*Melachim* 3:6). With this principle, we may answer our question on *Pachad Yitzchak*: Esther did not *literally* assume

---

1. The Holy Temple also has the power to unite the people, as is evident from the verse, "The tribes will assemble at the mount" (*Deuteronomy* 33:19; see *Rashi*).

the throne. Rather, she enveloped herself with the intense love for fellow Jews which a monarch must possess if he is to succeed in uniting the people. This would also explain why our verse says, "she *donned* herself in royalty" — Mishnaic literature speaks of individuals "wearing" a particular trait.[1]

We may now understand what the Sages meant by, "This teaches that [Esther] clothed herself in the Divine Spirit." By Esther "enveloping herself" with love for her fellow Jews, she united the entire Jewish People, and as a consequence, the Divine Spirit resided upon her.[2]

Alternatively, *Nefesh HaChaim* describes a different method by which a person may "clothe himself" in the Divine Spirit. The Talmud states, "R' Chanina said: 'HASHEM, He is the God. There is nothing other than Him' (*Deuteronomy* 4:35), including witchcraft!" (*Chullin* 7b). Citing this passage, *R' Chaim* of *Volozhin* writes:

"In truth, this is a fundamental principle of faith, as well as a method by which to remove and nullify extraneous forces and entities. It can prevent such forces from affecting or gaining control over one's being. [The method is as follows:] An individual should instill into his heart the thought, 'Hashem is the true God, and there is nothing other than Him, no force in the entire universe. Everything is filled with His essential unity, Blessed is His Name.' A person should give absolutely no validity in his heart to any force or entity in the world. Instead, he should subjugate and adhere his **thoughts** exclusively to the true Master of the Universe, Blessed is He. In return, Hashem will prevent any force in the universe from affecting such an individual" (*Nefesh HaChaim, Shaar* 3, Section 12).[3]

R' Chaim adds that an individual who reaches this level of purity will merit miracles which defy the laws of Nature. It would seem, then, that this is what the Sages meant by "Esther clothed herself in the Divine Spirit" — by focusing on the thought that no other power or entity can exist indepen-

---

1. See, for example, *Pirkei Avos* 6:1: "The Torah clothes him in humility and fear of HASHEM."

2. This also explains why Hannah found fault with Eli the Priest at seeing that the Divine Spirit did not reside upon him (see *Berachos* 31b). Ostensibly, it does not seem right to *blame* someone for not meriting the Divine Spirit. However, Hannah in effect said to him, "If you would sincerely love your fellow Jews, you would have merited to have the Divine Spirit reside upon you, and you would not have suspected me of being a drunkard!"

3. Reb Yitzchak Zev Soloveitchik, the *Rav* of Brisk, recounted that as a young man he had been in danger of being conscripted into the Russian army. When he went before the draft board, his father, Rabbi Chaim Soloveitchik, advised him to concentrate intently on these words of *Nefesh HaChaim.* He followed his father's instructions and he was not inducted.

The *Rav* also told of concentrating on this *Nefesh HaChaim* while fleeing with his family from Warsaw to Vilna early in World War II. The Nazis controlled portions of Poland and the roads were full of vigilantes looking for Jews. When the *Rav* became a bit distracted for a moment, a Nazi soldier suddenly appeared — as if from nowhere — and began to harass the Rav and his party. The *Rav* strengthened his concentration and the soldier left them alone and they made their escape.

dently of Hashem, the laws of Nature were suspended, and great miracles transpired.

❦ ❦ ❦

As mentioned above, the Sages said in reference to this verse, "[Scripture] should have said [that Esther donned] *royal garments,* [not *royalty.* In reply] R' Elazar said in the name of R' Chanina: This teaches that [Esther] was clothed in the Divine Spirit, for it is written here 'Esther *donned* (וַתִּלְבַּשׁ),' and elsewhere it is written, 'And the Spirit *clothed* (לָבְשָׁה) Amasai' (*Chronicles* 12:19)" (*Megillah* 15a).

Two questions may be asked at this point: First, why did Esther see the need to "clothe herself in the Divine Spirit" before approaching the impure Ahasuerus? Second, as the *Pachad Yitzchak* asks, why does the verse refer to the Divine Spirit as "royalty"?

The Torah relates (*Exodus* 2:12) that before Moses killed the Egyptian who was striking his fellow Jew, "he saw that there was no man." *Rashi* explains that it was only after he saw through Divine Spirit that no descendant of this Egyptian would convert that he struck the man. Esther, too, was faced with a similar dilemma. On the one hand, she had good reason to ask the King to execute Haman, but on the other hand, she wondered whether righteous descendants would one day come forth from Haman's seed. Thus, with the help of the Divine Spirit which resided upon her,[1] she scanned through Haman's future offspring. She found that, indeed, righteous descendants *would* one day come forth from Haman's lineage — as the Sages said, "Haman's descendants taught Torah in Bnei Brak" (*Gittin* 57b). However, Esther also discerned that the offspring from whom these righteous descendants would come forth had already been born, and that no additional righteous descendants would ever emerge from

---

1. Similarly, when Avishai son of Zeruiah asked King David, "Shouldn't Shimei be put to death for cursing God's anointed one?" the King answered, "Is this your business, sons of Zeruiah, that you should oppose me today? *Should an Israelite be put to death?*" (*II Samuel* 19:22-23). Regarding King David's response, *Yalkut Shimoni* says, "King David perceived through *Divine Spirit* that a great individual would one day emerge from his lineage, and that he would bring about a great salvation [for the Jewish People]. The Holy One, Blessed is He, said to David — who was from the tribe of Judah (יְהוּדָה) — "Today you saved Shimei's life because he will bear a righteous descendant [referring to Mordechai son of Jair son of Shimei. In reward], I will write him down for posterity after your name, as the verse says, 'There was a Jewish man (אִישׁ יְהוּדִי) in Shushan the Capital' (2:5)."

This may also be the answer to our second question — why did the Sages refer to the Divine Spirit as "royalty"? They did so in order to teach that Esther scanned Haman's future lineage in the same manner as King David — "royalty" — scanned Shimei's future lineage. Esther realized that had King David not taken the time to look through Shimei's future descendants, neither she nor Mordechai would have been born. This is why the importance of taking into account a wicked man's future offspring was very much on Esther's mind at all times. Therefore, before proceeding to ask Ahasuerus to execute Haman, she emulated King David and carefully examined Haman's future descendants with the help of the Divine Spirit which enveloped her.

ה/ב בַּחֲצַר בֵּית־הַמֶּלֶךְ הַפְּנִימִית נֹכַח בֵּית הַמֶּלֶךְ
וְהַמֶּלֶךְ יוֹשֵׁב עַל־כִּסֵּא מַלְכוּתוֹ בְּבֵית הַמַּלְכוּת
ב נֹכַח פֶּתַח הַבָּיִת: וַיְהִי כִרְאוֹת הַמֶּלֶךְ אֶת־
אֶסְתֵּר הַמַּלְכָּה עֹמֶדֶת בֶּחָצֵר נָשְׂאָה חֵן בְּעֵינָיו
וַיּוֹשֶׁט הַמֶּלֶךְ לְאֶסְתֵּר אֶת־שַׁרְבִיט הַזָּהָב אֲשֶׁר
בְּיָדוֹ וַתִּקְרַב אֶסְתֵּר וַתִּגַּע בְּרֹאשׁ הַשַּׁרְבִיט:

Haman. Only at this point, when there was clearly no reason to spare Haman's life, did Esther proceed with her plans to persuade the King to execute him. We see, then, why Esther saw the need to "clothe herself with the Divine Spirit" before approaching Ahasuerus.

The answer to our second question lies in *Alshich*'s opinion that Esther came to rectify King Saul's sin (see notes on 4:13). By perceiving that righteous individuals would one day emerge from Haman's lineage, Esther somewhat mitigated Saul's sin of sparing Agag's life. She demonstrated that some good came from this sin, for had Saul followed Samuel's instructions exactly and executed Agag, Haman's descendants who "taught Torah in Bnei Brak" would never have been born. Afterwards, she rectified Saul's sin of showing mercy to Agag by bringing about the death of Haman, Agag's descendant. With this, we may answer our second question: The Sages referred to the Divine Spirit as "royalty" because it played such a central role in enabling Esther to restore the honor of King Saul's royal lineage.[1]

וַתַּעֲמֹד בַּחֲצַר בֵּית־הַמֶּלֶךְ הַפְּנִימִית — And stood in the inner court of the King's palace.

The Sages say: " 'She [Esther] stood in the inner court of the King's palace' (v. 1) — R' Levi said: As soon as she reached the chamber of idols [on her way through the palace to Ahasuerus], the Divine Presence departed from her. She exclaimed: 'My God, my God, why have You forsaken me?

---

1. This also sheds light on the verse, "Benjamin is a predatory wolf; in the morning he will devour prey and in the evening he will distribute spoils" (*Genesis* 49:27). *Rashi* explains that "the morning" alludes to Saul, who rose as Israel's champion in the dawn of Israel's history, when the nation began to flourish. "The evening" alludes to the nation's *evening* of decline, when the people were exiled to Babylonia and Persia. The verse foresaw that Benjamin's offspring would triumph over Israel's enemies and divide the spoils of victory. This alludes to Mordechai and Esther, from the Tribe of Benjamin, who defeated Haman and were awarded his estate.

At first glance, *Rashi*'s interpretation is difficult, for why would King Saul be a source of pride for the Tribe of Benjamin? Did Samuel the Prophet not say to him, "You have rejected God's word, and God has rejected you as King over Israel" (*I Samuel* 15:26)?

However, in light of our explanation, *Rashi*'s interpretation can be understood — King Saul continues to remain a source of pride to the Tribe of Benjamin because Esther rectified his sin and restored the honor of his royal household.

of the King's palace facing the King's house while the King was sitting on his throne in the throne room facing the chamber's entrance. 2 *When the King noticed Queen Esther standing in the court, she won his favor. The King extended to Esther the gold scepter that was in his hand, and Esther approached and touched the tip of the scepter.*

Could it be that You regard an inadvertent offense as an intentional one, or an offense committed under coercion as one committed willingly? Or perhaps [You have forsaken me] because I called him (Ahasuerus) a dog, as the verse (*Psalms* 22:21) says, "Rescue my soul from the sword, my only one from the grip of the dog"?' She [therefore] retracted and called him a lion, as the verse (ibid. v. 22) says, 'Save me from the lion's mouth' " (*Megillah* 15b).

Shem MiShmuel wonders why Esther apparently overlooked the most obvious reason why the Divine Presence departed from her — her physical proximity to idols. It is a well-known principle that objects of idol worship are repugnant to Hashem, and that they repel the Divine Presence. This is why Hashem would not reveal Himself to Moses within the boundaries of Pharaoh's capital, where idol worship was rampant. Instead of this straightforward explanation, Esther grasped for reasons which at face value seem farfetched. For example, what difference would it make to the Divine Presence whether Esther called Ahasuerus a dog or a lion?

The answer is that the way of the righteous is to always wonder whether they have truly fulfilled the obligation incumbent upon them. Hence, whenever setbacks[1] occur, they automatically assume that their own shortcomings are responsible. Esther, too, assumed that it was *she* who had driven away the Divine Presence. It did not even cross her mind that Ahasuerus' idols might have been the reason.

Thus, Esther began scrutinizing her deeds. In her prayer, she had referred to Ahasuerus as "a dog." Recognizing that all forms of affliction are decreed by Hashem, and that in a sense, they are His envoys, Esther wondered whether it had been disrespectful[2] of her to call the King a dog. After all, she thought, it is Hashem who has sent Ahasuerus to terrorize us. Similarly, the commentaries say in regard to the verse "evil and faithful illnesses" (*Deuteronomy* 28:59), "evil illnesses which *faithfully carry out their assign-*

---

1. Similarly, we find that Joseph's brothers, finding themselves suspected by the viceroy of Egypt to be spies, recognized their lot was Divine punishment for their callous treatment of Joseph. That this was their immediate reaction is illustrative of their greatness (*Genesis* 42:21).

2. We find that Hashem ordered Moshe to act respectfully to Pharaoh because of the latter's royal position (*Exodus* 6:13).

ג וַיֹּאמֶר לָהּ הַמֶּלֶךְ מַה־לָּךְ אֶסְתֵּר הַמַּלְכָּה וּמַה־
ד בַּקָּשָׁתֵךְ עַד־חֲצִי הַמַּלְכוּת וְיִנָּתֵן לָךְ׃ וַתֹּאמֶר
אֶסְתֵּר אִם־עַל־הַמֶּלֶךְ טוֹב יָבוֹא הַמֶּלֶךְ וְהָמָן
ה הַיּוֹם אֶל־הַמִּשְׁתֶּה אֲשֶׁר־עָשִׂיתִי לוֹ׃ וַיֹּאמֶר הַמֶּלֶךְ
מַהֲרוּ אֶת־הָמָן לַעֲשׂוֹת אֶת־דְּבַר אֶסְתֵּר וַיָּבֹא
הַמֶּלֶךְ וְהָמָן אֶל־הַמִּשְׁתֶּה אֲשֶׁר־עָשְׂתָה אֶסְתֵּר׃
ו וַיֹּאמֶר הַמֶּלֶךְ לְאֶסְתֵּר בְּמִשְׁתֵּה הַיַּיִן מַה־שְּׁאֵלָתֵךְ
וְיִנָּתֵן לָךְ וּמַה־בַּקָּשָׁתֵךְ עַד־חֲצִי הַמַּלְכוּת וְתֵעָשׂ׃
ז־ח וַתַּעַן אֶסְתֵּר וַתֹּאמַר שְׁאֵלָתִי וּבַקָּשָׁתִי׃ אִם־
מָצָאתִי חֵן בְּעֵינֵי הַמֶּלֶךְ וְאִם־עַל־הַמֶּלֶךְ טוֹב לָתֵת
אֶת־שְׁאֵלָתִי וְלַעֲשׂוֹת אֶת־בַּקָּשָׁתִי יָבוֹא הַמֶּלֶךְ

---

ment" (*Rashi* ad loc.).[1] Therefore, she quickly retracted and referred to Ahasuerus as "a lion," a more dignified beast.

Alternatively, "a dog" refers not to Ahasuerus, but to Haman:

The Sages say that Hashem cursed the dog with a perpetual feeling of hunger. This explains why dogs are constantly eating, and why their bark sounds so similar to the words הב הב (Aramaic for "Give me! Give me!"). Esther referred to Haman as "a dog" with this idea in mind — like a dog, Haman was never satisfied with what he had. This is evident from the verse, "Haman recounted to them the glory of his wealth and his large number of sons, and every instance where the King had promoted him and advanced him above the officials and royal servants. Haman said: 'Moreover, Queen Esther invited no one but myself to accompany the King to the banquet that she prepared, and tomorrow, too, I am invited by her along with the King. *Yet all this means nothing to me* so long as I see that Jew Mordechai sitting at the King's gate" (5:11-13).

However, when she perceived that the Divine Presence suddenly departed, Esther began wondering whether her choice of words had been appropriate. By referring to Haman's insatiable desire for honor — which was further kindled by Mordechai's refusal to bow down before him — Esther grew concerned that she had unwittingly cast blame upon Mordechai for endangering the Jewish People and had thus been disrespectful to him. In those days, this was an extremely delicate subject. There was a strong

---

1. This is why hardship always comes in waves, like birth pangs, periodically intensifying, waning, and then surging again — such an unlikely pattern proves beyod doubt that affliction is an instrument of heavenly judgment, and not merely a natural coincidence.

5/3-8 [3] *The King said to her, "What is it for you, Queen*
Esther? And what is your petition? Even if it be half
the kingdom, it shall be granted you." [4] *Esther said,*
"If it please the King, let the King and Haman come
today to the banquet that I have prepared for him."
[5] *Then the King commanded, "Tell Haman to hurry*
and fulfill Esther's wish." So the King and Haman
came to the banquet that Esther had prepared.
[6] *The King said to Esther during the wine feast,*
"What is your request? It shall be granted you. And
what is your petition? Even if it be half the kingdom,
it shall be fulfilled." [7] *So Esther answered and said,*
"My request and my petition: [8] *If I have won the*
King's favor, and if it pleases the King to grant my
request and to perform my petition — let the King

---

undercurrent of resentment against Mordechai among the Jews, for they blamed him for deliberately provoking Haman. As the Sages said, "The congregation of Israel said, 'Look what a Judahite did to me and what a Benjaminite paid me — [King] David, [who was from the Tribe of Judah,] did not kill Shimi, from whom descended Mordechai, *who provoked Haman,* [thereby causing all our troubles]' " (*Megillah* 13a).

Thus, Esther retracted and called Haman, "a lion," the beast symbolizing Babylonia.[1] In this manner, Esther shifted the blame away from Mordechai and attributed the affliction to the Jewish People's sin of bowing down upon duress to the image in Nebuchadnezzar's day (see *Megillah* 12a). This is what she meant by "Save me from the lion's mouth" — "Save me from the heavenly accusation which emerged from the Jewish People's sin in the days of the lion, Nebuchadnezzar!"

6-8. וַיֹּאמֶר הַמֶּלֶךְ לְאֶסְתֵּר בְּמִשְׁתֵּה הַיַּיִן מַה־שְּׁאֵלָתֵךְ וְיִנָּתֵן לָךְ וּמַה־בַּקָּשָׁתֵךְ . . . וַתַּעַן אֶסְתֵּר וַתֹּאמַר שְׁאֵלָתִי וּבַקָּשָׁתִי: . . . לָתֵת אֶת־שְׁאֵלָתִי וְלַעֲשׂוֹת אֶת־בַּקָּשָׁתִי — The King said to Esther during the wine feast, 'What is your request? It shall be granted to you. And what is your petition? . . .' So Esther answered and said, 'My request and my petition: . . . to grant my request and to perform my petition.

At first glance, the words, "My request and my petition," seem superfluous.

The *Vilna Gaon* explains that the Hebrew word שְׁאֵלָה ("request") conveys a personal appeal, while בַּקָּשָׁה ("petition") implies a plea on behalf of others.

---

1. As the verse says, "The lion has come up from its thicket" (*Jeremiah* 4:7), in reference to Nebuchadnezzar, King of Babylonia.

וְהָמָן אֶל־הַמִּשְׁתֶּה אֲשֶׁר אֶעֱשֶׂה לָהֶם וּמָחָר אֶעֱשֶׂה
ט כִּדְבַר הַמֶּלֶךְ׃ וַיֵּצֵא הָמָן בַּיּוֹם הַהוּא שָׂמֵחַ וְטוֹב
לֵב וְכִרְאוֹת הָמָן אֶת־מָרְדֳּכַי בְּשַׁעַר הַמֶּלֶךְ וְלֹא־
קָם וְלֹא־זָע מִמֶּנּוּ וַיִּמָּלֵא הָמָן עַל־מָרְדֳּכַי חֵמָה׃
י וַיִּתְאַפַּק הָמָן וַיָּבוֹא אֶל־בֵּיתוֹ וַיִּשְׁלַח וַיָּבֵא אֶת־
יא אֹהֲבָיו וְאֶת־זֶרֶשׁ אִשְׁתּוֹ׃ וַיְסַפֵּר לָהֶם הָמָן אֶת־כְּבוֹד

Thus, Ahasuerus did not merely wax poetic when he said, "What is your *request*? It shall be granted to you. And what is your *petition*? Even if it be half the kingdom, it shall be fulfilled." Rather, he informed Esther in no uncertain terms that there were limits to his benevolence. For Esther herself he would do anything, assuring her, "It shall be granted to you." But if she should beseech the King to show kindness towards others, he warned her that he would not surrender more than "half the kingdom."

Upon hearing Ahasuerus' words, Esther in effect answered, "My request *is* my petition!" In other words, she informed Ahasuerus that she saw no difference between the needs of others or her own — both were equally important to her.

She embraced the same trait as Moses, about whom the verse says, "It happened in those days that Moses grew up and went out to his brethren *and observed their burdens*" (*Exodus* 2:11). *Rashi* says this to mean that "Moses saw their suffering and felt their grief." The *Alter of Kelm* explains that Moses empathized with his fellow Jews and vicariously felt their suffering. The word "saw" conveys that Moses contemplated their suffering in his mind, while "felt" conveys that he felt their pain in his heart.

9. וְכִרְאוֹת הָמָן אֶת־מָרְדֳּכַי בְּשַׁעַר הַמֶּלֶךְ וְלֹא־קָם וְלֹא־זָע מִמֶּנּוּ וַיִּמָּלֵא הָמָן עַל־מָרְדֳּכַי חֵמָה — But when Haman noticed Mordechai in the King's gate and that he neither stood up nor stirred before him, Haman was infuriated with Mordechai.

According to the *Targum,* Mordechai infuriated Haman by extending his right leg and showing him the contract both men had signed years earlier, which stated that Haman had agreed to become Mordechai's slave in exchange for a loaf of bread.

My father, זצ״ל,[1] elucidated the *Targum*'s opinion as follows:

Two questions arise: First, it seems that in this verse the *Megillah* attempts to degrade Haman by describing his uncontrollable wrath. However, in light of the *Targum*'s commentary, one can hardly blame Haman for losing his

---

1. R' Efraim Mordechai Ginsburg, Rosh HaYeshivah of the Mirrer Yeshiva in America from 1948 until his passing on 15 Av 5720 (1960).

and Haman come to the banquet that I shall prepare
for them, and tomorrow I will do the King's bidding."
9 *That day Haman went out joyful and exuberant.*
But when Haman noticed Mordechai in the King's
gate and that he neither stood up nor stirred be-
fore him, Haman was infuriated with Mordechai.
10 *Nevertheless, Haman restrained himself and went*
home. He sent for his friends and his wife, Zeresh,
11 *and Haman recounted to them the glory of his*

---

temper — only someone as humble as Moses could have subdued his anger in the face of such an affront! Second, why did Mordechai provoke Haman? As the *Targum* relates, Haman proved his viciousness all too convincingly by slaying Hathach — who was actually Daniel — shortly before the encounter with Mordechai. On what basis, then, did Mordechai intentionally risk his life by annoying the murderous Haman?

The answer is that Mordechai did not extend his leg in order to show the contract to Haman, but rather to look at it himself. Mordechai certainly would not have waved the red flag before the bull. Rather, Mordechai felt it necessary to read the contract in order to strengthen his own resolve. By rereading Haman's bill of sale, Mordechai put things back into perspective and helped him avoid being intimidated by Haman's regal bearing. Nevertheless, when Haman saw Mordechai looking at the contract, he became furious. Once again, we see the extent of Haman's wickedness!

9-10. וַיִּמָּלֵא הָמָן עַל־מָרְדֳּכַי חֵמָה: וַיִּתְאַפַּק הָמָן וַיָּבוֹא אֶל־בֵּיתוֹ — Haman was infuriated with Mordechai. Nevertheless, Haman restrained himself and went home.

In explanation of the words, "Haman restrained himself," *Rashi* writes, "He overcame his anger because he was afraid of taking unauthorized revenge."

A few questions come to mind: First, how did the wicked Haman manage to restrain himself while his anger burned within him? This is a difficult feat for anyone! Second, what prompted Haman to suddenly fear the repercussions of his violent actions? According to the *Targum,* Haman did not hesitate in murdering Daniel in a fit of anger just a short while earlier. Third, why did Haman think he lacked authorization to slay Mordechai? Had he himself not authored the royal decree calling for the extermination of every last Jew in the kingdom?

The answer is that Haman knew the rule, "When they make a decree and one of them dies, they rescind their decree" (*Taanis* 29a). As *Rashi* explains, "they" refers to a monarch's advisers — when "one of them dies," the surviving advisers interpret their colleague's death as a heavenly sign that they should rescind the decree which they had formulated together. Haman

ה/יב־יד עָשְׁרוֹ וְרֹב בָּנָיו וְאֵת כָּל־אֲשֶׁר גִּדְּלוֹ הַמֶּלֶךְ וְאֵת
יב אֲשֶׁר נִשְּׂאוֹ עַל־הַשָּׂרִים וְעַבְדֵי הַמֶּלֶךְ: וַיֹּאמֶר הָמָן
אַף לֹא־הֵבִיאָה אֶסְתֵּר הַמַּלְכָּה עִם־הַמֶּלֶךְ אֶל־
הַמִּשְׁתֶּה אֲשֶׁר־עָשָׂתָה כִּי אִם־אוֹתִי וְגַם־לְמָחָר אֲנִי
יג קְרוּא־לָהּ עִם־הַמֶּלֶךְ: וְכָל־זֶה אֵינֶנּוּ שֹׁוֶה לִי בְּכָל־
עֵת אֲשֶׁר אֲנִי רֹאֶה אֶת־מָרְדֳּכַי הַיְּהוּדִי יוֹשֵׁב בְּשַׁעַר
יד הַמֶּלֶךְ: וַתֹּאמֶר לוֹ זֶרֶשׁ אִשְׁתּוֹ וְכָל־אֹהֲבָיו יַעֲשׂוּ־עֵץ
גָּבֹהַּ חֲמִשִּׁים אַמָּה וּבַבֹּקֶר ׀ אֱמֹר לַמֶּלֶךְ וְיִתְלוּ אֶת־
מָרְדֳּכַי עָלָיו וּבֹא עִם־הַמֶּלֶךְ אֶל־הַמִּשְׁתֶּה שָׂמֵחַ
ו/א א וַיִּיטַב הַדָּבָר לִפְנֵי הָמָן וַיַּעַשׂ הָעֵץ: בַּלַּיְלָה

---

feared that if he would slay Mordechai — who was one of Ahasuerus' advisers (see *Megillah* 13a) — the other members of the King's council would respond to his death by revoking the decree against the Jews. Thus, drawing strength from his profoundly anti-Semitic feelings, Haman subdued his anger and restrained himself from slaying Mordechai. Instead, the wicked Haman consoled himself with the thought that in time every single Jew — including Mordechai — would perish at his hand.

13. וְכָל־זֶה אֵינֶנּוּ שֹׁוֶה לִי — Yet all this means nothing to me.

Ne'os Deshe points out that the last letters of these words spell out the Divine Name י־ה־ו־ה backwards. According to the *Zohar,* such instances in Scripture always allude to an awakening of heavenly judgment. The lesson our verse teaches is quite clear: When someone who enjoys as much prosperity as Haman still fails to feel content with his station in life, his ingratitude arouses severe heavenly judgment, and the forces of retribution swiftly remove all the goodness which had been bestowed upon him.

In addition, by inverting the words so that the last letters spell the Divine Name י־ה־ו־ה in the correct order — לִי שֹׁוֶה אֵינֶנּוּ זֶה (lit., "To Me, that is of no value" — To Me referring to Hashem) — the verse conveys that all the achievements which Haman listed in the previous two verses meant absolutely nothing to Hashem. This corresponds with the words of Jeremiah the Prophet, who said, "Let not the wise man glory in his wisdom, nor the strong man [glory] in his strength, nor the rich man [glory] in his wealth. Only in this should one glory — becoming wise and knowing Me, for that is My desire, declares HASHEM!" (*Jeremiah* 9:22).[1]

---

1. My friend R' Yosef Friedman pointed out to me another interesting combination of first and last letters: The first verse of *Parshas Tetzaveh* begins with the words, וְאַתָּה תְּצַוֶּה

wealth and of his many sons, and every instance where the King had promoted him and advanced him above the officials and royal servants.
12 *Haman said, "Moreover, Queen Esther invited no one but myself to accompany the King to the banquet that she had prepared, and tomorrow, too, I am invited by her along with the King.*
13 *Yet all this means nothing to me so long as I see that Jew Mordechai sitting at the King's gate."*
14 *Then his wife, Zeresh, and all his friends said to him, "Let a gallows be made, fifty cubits high; and tomorrow morning tell the King and have them hang Mordechai on it. Then, in good spirits, accompany the King to the banquet." This suggestion pleased Haman, and he had the gallows erected.*

---

14. וּבַבֹּקֶר אֱמֹר לַמֶּלֶךְ — And tomorrow morning tell the King.

Shem MiShmuel points out that Haman's advisors did not say to him "*request* of the King," but rather "*tell* the King." Faithfully, Haman followed their advice, as the verse says, "Haman had just come into the outer court *to tell* the King to hang Mordechai on the gallows he had prepared for him" (6:4).

The manner in which Haman addressed the King shows what great power Ahasuerus granted him when he "took his signet ring from his hand and gave it to Haman. . . Then the King said to Haman: 'The silver is given to you, the people also, to do with as you see fit' " (ibid., 3:10-11). It seems that it was only out of courtesy that Haman came that fateful morning to inform the King of his plans to hang Mordechai.

Correspondingly, when the Jews were redeemed and the roles were reversed — in keeping with the spirit of וְנַהֲפוֹךְ הוּא — Mordechai took over Haman's post as the King's viceroy, and like his predecessor, he too was granted unlimited authority. However, unlike Haman, who took advantage of his power to *harm* the Jews without prior consultation with the King, Mordechai used his unlimited authority to *assist* the Jews.

וַיִּיטַב הַדָּבָר לִפְנֵי הָמָן וַיַּעַשׂ הָעֵץ — This suggestion pleased Haman, and he had the gallows erected.

Midrash Rabbah teaches that after Haman erected the gallows he went to look for Mordechai. He found Mordechai in the study hall, teaching Torah to

---

אֶת־בְּנֵי יִשְׂרָאֵל וְיִקְחוּ — "Now you shall command the Children of Israel that they shall take" (*Exodus* 27:20). The last letters of these last four words spell out תלוי ("hanged"), and the first letters, אב וי' ("the father and the ten"). This alludes to Haman (אב) and his ten (י) children, who were hung on Purim, which usually coincides with *Parshas Tetzaveh.*

Jewish children clad in sackcloth. According to the *Midrash,* Mordechai and the Jewish children awakened Hashem's mercy. Hashem rose from the Throne of Judgment, sat on the Throne of Mercy, and tore the documents upon which the evil decrees against the Jewish People had been inscribed.

This *Midrash* seems to imply that the children's Torah study awakened Hashem's mercy to a greater degree than the Torah study of that generation's leading sages. Since this concept is difficult to grasp, we shall elaborate. But first, let us closely examine the following Talmudic passage.

The Sages said, " 'The Jews had light and gladness and joy and glory' (8:16). R' Yehudah said: 'Light' refers to Torah, as the verse says, 'For the commandment is a lamp, and Torah is light' (*Proverbs* 6:23). 'Gladness' refers to the holiday, as the verse says, 'You shall be glad on your holiday' (*Deuteronomy* 16:14). 'Joy' refers to circumcision, as the verse says, 'I rejoice over Your word' (*Psalms* 119:162). 'Glory' refers to *tefillin,* as the verse says, 'All the nations of the world will see that the Name of God is called upon you, and they will be in awe of you' (*Deuteronomy* 28:10)' " (*Megillah* 16b).

One cannot help but wonder why the verse did not explicitly say, "The Jews had *Torah* and a holiday and circumcision and *tefillin.*" Why use the allusion of "light," which requires a correlation to the verse, "Torah is light," to be understood?

The clarification to all the above questions lies in the following *Midrash*:

"The verse says, 'If it pleases the King, let it be recorded that they [the Jewish People] be destroyed' (3:9). Reish Lakish said: When Haman said to Ahasuerus, 'Let's exterminate the Jewish people,' Ahasuerus replied, 'You cannot defeat them, for their God does not abandon them. Just look at what He did to previous kings [who attempted to destroy them]!' Haman answered, 'The God Who drowned Pharaoh in the sea and performed miracles and wonders for Israel has grown old. He is totally incapable of doing such things on their behalf again!' Upon hearing this, Ahasuerus accepted Haman's argument, and they agreed to exterminate the Jewish People" (*Midrash Rabbah* 7:13).

Regarding this *Midrash, Darkei Mussar* asks how Haman and Ahasuerus — who apparently believed in the miracles which Hashem performed for Israel in the past — could have been so foolish as to think that Hashem "grew old." Did they not know that Hashem is not a corporeal being, and therefore, not subject to such physical limitations as the infirmities of old age?

The answer is as follows: As noted earlier, the Sages said, "R' Elazar introduced [his lecture on] this Scriptural portion [the Book of *Esther*] with the following verse: 'Through laziness the ceiling collapses, and through idleness of the hands the house leaks' (*Ecclesiastes* 10:18) — because of the laziness of the Jews who did not engage in [study of] Torah, the enemy of the Holy One, Blessed is He [referring to the Holy One], 'became weakened' " (*Megillah* 11a). As *Rashi* explains, due to the Jews' sin of neglecting the study of Torah, Hashem was rendered "incapable" of saving the Jews from

Haman's decree, and in that sense He is described here as "poor."

We learn from this an astounding principle: If it were possible to say it, Hashem's strength waxes and wanes in accordance with Israel's deeds — when the Jewish People study Torah diligently, Hashem's strength increases, but when they fulfill this *mitzvah* unenthusiastically,[1] Hashem's strength diminishes.[2]

This, then, is what Haman meant when he said that Israel's God has "grown old" — as a consequence of the Jews' lack of enthusiasm in observing *mitzvos,* Hashem was rendered "incapable" of protecting them, and in this sense, He resembled an old and frail man.

With this understanding, we may address the questions raised above:

Why did the verse say, "The Jews had *light,* " instead of simply saying, "The Jews had *Torah*"? The answer is that the Jews had not been guilty of completely neglecting Torah study, or for that matter, any other *mitzvah.* Rather, their shortcoming was their lack of *enthusiasm* for *mitzvos.* It was the inner light of the *mitzvah* which they lacked, the spark of excitement and fervor for doing Hashem's will. The miracles which Hashem performed for Israel stoked the smoldering embers within each Jew and evoked a new fervor for the performance of *mitzvos,* reawakening the "light" of Torah study, the "gladness" of the *Yom Tov* holidays, the "joy" of circumcision, the "glory" of *tefillin.*

Why was the Torah study of the Jewish children greater than that of the generation's leading Torah sages? Because children do everything with enthusiasm. When they learn Torah, they drink it in thirstily and are never sated with the knowledge they have gained. This explains why Mordechai chose to spend those fateful hours teaching Torah to the Jewish children instead of studying with his more learned colleagues: He knew that the Jewish People's shortcoming was their lack of enthusiasm for the observance of *mitzvos,* and he correctly concluded that he stood the best chance of rectifying it by teaching Torah to the responsive Jewish children.

Indeed, Mordechai and the Jewish children succeeded in rectifying Israel's shortcoming. The Jewish People's dormant zeal for *mitzvos* was rekindled by the cataclysmic miracles which followed, reaching previously unattained spiritual heights. This is reflected in the fact that the Scroll of Esther is the only *megillah* which is read twice, once at night and once during the day, presenting them with this *mitzvah* as reward for their new acquired zeal for

---

1. This is how *Darkei Mussar* interprets the Sages' account of Haman's statement to Ahasuerus, "They [the Jewish People] have been negligent [in their observance] of the *mitzvos*" (*Megillah* 13b) — not that the Jews neglected the observance of the *mitzvos* altogether, but that they performed the *mitzvos* without enthusiasm.

2. Similarly, regarding the verse, "HASHEM is your protection (צִלְּךָ) at your right hand" (*Psalms* 121:5), the *Midrash* says: "The word צִלְּךָ ('your protection,' or more literally, 'your *shade*') teaches that Hashem is like Israel's shadow." In other words, Hashem's willingness to protect the Jewish People varies in exact ratio to their level of enthusiasm in observing His *mitzvos.*

הַהוּא נָדְדָה שְׁנַת הַמֶּלֶךְ וַיֹּאמֶר לְהָבִיא אֶת־סֵפֶר
הַזִּכְרֹנוֹת דִּבְרֵי הַיָּמִים וַיִּהְיוּ נִקְרָאִים לִפְנֵי הַמֶּלֶךְ׃
ב וַיִּמָּצֵא כָתוּב אֲשֶׁר הִגִּיד מָרְדֳּכַי עַל־בִּגְתָנָא וָתֶרֶשׁ
שְׁנֵי סָרִיסֵי הַמֶּלֶךְ מִשֹּׁמְרֵי הַסַּף אֲשֶׁר בִּקְשׁוּ לִשְׁלֹחַ
ג יָד בַּמֶּלֶךְ אֲחַשְׁוֵרוֹשׁ׃ וַיֹּאמֶר הַמֶּלֶךְ מַה־נַּעֲשָׂה יְקָר
וּגְדוּלָּה לְמָרְדֳּכַי עַל־זֶה וַיֹּאמְרוּ נַעֲרֵי הַמֶּלֶךְ
ד מְשָׁרְתָיו לֹא־נַעֲשָׂה עִמּוֹ דָּבָר׃ וַיֹּאמֶר הַמֶּלֶךְ מִי
בֶחָצֵר וְהָמָן בָּא לַחֲצַר בֵּית־הַמֶּלֶךְ הַחִיצוֹנָה
לֵאמֹר לַמֶּלֶךְ לִתְלוֹת אֶת־מָרְדֳּכַי עַל־הָעֵץ אֲשֶׁר־
ה הֵכִין לוֹ׃ וַיֹּאמְרוּ נַעֲרֵי הַמֶּלֶךְ אֵלָיו הִנֵּה הָמָן עֹמֵד
ו בֶּחָצֵר וַיֹּאמֶר הַמֶּלֶךְ יָבוֹא׃ וַיָּבוֹא הָמָן וַיֹּאמֶר לוֹ
הַמֶּלֶךְ מַה־לַּעֲשׂוֹת בָּאִישׁ אֲשֶׁר הַמֶּלֶךְ חָפֵץ בִּיקָרוֹ
וַיֹּאמֶר הָמָן בְּלִבּוֹ לְמִי יַחְפֹּץ הַמֶּלֶךְ לַעֲשׂוֹת יְקָר
ז יוֹתֵר מִמֶּנִּי׃ וַיֹּאמֶר הָמָן אֶל־הַמֶּלֶךְ אִישׁ אֲשֶׁר
ח הַמֶּלֶךְ חָפֵץ בִּיקָרוֹ׃ יָבִיאוּ לְבוּשׁ מַלְכוּת אֲשֶׁר

---

mitzvos. As the Sages said, "A person is obligated to read the *Megillah* on the night of Purim and repeat it on the day, as the verse says, 'So that my soul might sing to You and not be stilled, HASHEM my God, forever will I thank You' (*Psalms* 30:13)" (*Megillah* 4a).

With this principle, we may also answer *Shem MiShmuel*'s question regarding the following Talmudic passage: "R' Shmuel bar Nachmani introduced [his lecture on] this Scriptural portion [the Book of *Esther*] with the verse, 'Instead of the thorn, a cypress shall rise, and instead of the nettle, a myrtle shall rise' (*Isaiah* 55:13). 'Instead of the thorn' — instead of the wicked Haman. . .'a cypress shall rise,' referring to Mordechai. 'Instead of the nettle' — instead of the wicked Vashti, *granddaughter of the wicked Nebuchadnezzar, who burnt the resting place of the House of God. . .* 'a myrtle shall rise,' referring to Esther" (*Megillah* 10b). *Shem MiShmuel* asks why the Sages saw it necessary to specify Vashti's relationship with Nebuchadnezzar, for even if she had not been that wicked man's granddaughter, the verse could still be understood as alluding to her demise and Esther's subsequent succession to the throne.

The answer may be that the Sages mentioned Nebuchadnezzar's name in order to teach that the same sin which brought about the evil decree in

6/1-8 1 *That night sleep eluded the King so he ordered*
that the record book, the chronicles, be brought
and be read before the King. 2 *There it was found*
recorded that Mordechai had denounced Bigthana
and Teresh, two of the King's chamberlains of the
guardians of the threshold, who had plotted to lay
hands on King Ahasuerus. 3 *"What honor or dignity*
has been conferred on Mordechai for this?" asked the
King. "Nothing has been done for him," replied the
King's pages. 4 *The King said, "Who is in the court?"*
(Now Haman had just come into the outer court of
the palace to speak to the King about hanging
Mordechai on the gallows he had prepared for him.)
5 *So the King's servants answered him, "It is Haman*
standing in the court." And the King said, "Let him
enter." 6 *When Haman came in the King said unto*
him, "What should be done for the man whom the
King especially wants to honor?" (Now Haman
reasoned to himself, "Whom would the King espe-
cially want to honor besides me?") 7 *So Haman said*
to the King, "For the man whom the King especially
wants to honor, 8 *have them bring a royal robe that*

Ahasuerus' day also brought about the destruction of the First Temple at the hands of Nebuchadnezzar. Once again, the inverse relationship between good and evil made itself apparent: As the Jewish People's flame of enthusiasm for *mitzvos* flickered, the fires of evil correspondingly flared wildly, enabling Nebuchadnezzar to burn the Holy Temple. This is a recurring pattern in every generation — when enthusiasm for spiritual growth wanes, the power of corporeality and evil commensurately grows in strength, and vice versa.

We derive this inverse relationship from the verse, "Amalek came and battled Israel in Rephidim (רְפִידִם)" (*Exodus* 17:8) — the *Baal HaTurim* interprets the word Rephidim as a contraction of רָפוּ יְדֵיהֶם מִן הַמִּצְוֹת, or "they grew lax in the observance of *mitzvos*." This teaches that Amalek draws the necessary strength to wage war against Israel from the Jewish People's own shortcomings — when their enthusiasm for *mitzvos* decreases in intensity, Amalek, their perennial enemy, grows in strength. This underlying pattern corresponds with the esoteric teaching, "impurity and evil both draw their strength from holiness."

לָבַשׁ־בּוֹ הַמֶּלֶךְ וְסוּס אֲשֶׁר רָכַב עָלָיו הַמֶּלֶךְ וַאֲשֶׁר
ט נִתַּן כֶּתֶר מַלְכוּת בְּרֹאשׁוֹ׃ וְנָתוֹן הַלְּבוּשׁ וְהַסּוּס
עַל־יַד־אִישׁ מִשָּׂרֵי הַמֶּלֶךְ הַפַּרְתְּמִים וְהִלְבִּישׁוּ
אֶת־הָאִישׁ אֲשֶׁר הַמֶּלֶךְ חָפֵץ בִּיקָרוֹ וְהִרְכִּיבֻהוּ עַל־
הַסּוּס בִּרְחוֹב הָעִיר וְקָרְאוּ לְפָנָיו כָּכָה יֵעָשֶׂה לָאִישׁ
י אֲשֶׁר הַמֶּלֶךְ חָפֵץ בִּיקָרוֹ׃ וַיֹּאמֶר הַמֶּלֶךְ לְהָמָן
מַהֵר קַח אֶת־הַלְּבוּשׁ וְאֶת־הַסּוּס כַּאֲשֶׁר דִּבַּרְתָּ

VI

10. וַיֹּאמֶר הַמֶּלֶךְ לְהָמָן מַהֵר קַח אֶת־הַלְּבוּשׁ וְאֶת־הַסּוּס כַּאֲשֶׁר דִּבַּרְתָּ — Then the King said to Haman, "Hurry, then, get the robe and the horse as you have said."

The Talmud expounds upon this verse as follows:

"[Haman] said to [Mordechai]: Arise, put on these garments, and ride this horse, for the King wishes you [to do so].

[Mordechai] responded to him: I cannot [do so] until I [first] go to the bathhouse and have my hair cut, for it is not proper to use the garments of the King in this state. [Meanwhile,] Esther sent [an order] and detained all the bathhouse attendants and all the barbers [so that Haman would have to attend to Mordechai personally].

[Haman] went and brought scissors from his house, and was cutting [Mordechai's] hair. While cutting it, [Haman] felt faint and groaned.

[Mordechai] asked [Haman]: Why do you groan?

[Haman] answered him: Should the man who was more valued by the King than all his nobles now become a bathhouse attendant and a barber?

[Mordechai] retorted: Villain! Were you not once the barber in the village of Kartzum?" (*Megillah* 16a).

Haman's closing remark is a perfectly understandable reaction to his turn of fortune. However, Mordechai's somewhat cryptic reply requires clarification.

The explanation is as follows: Regarding the verse, "He [Ishmael] lived in the desert of Paran, *and his mother took a wife for him from the Land of Egypt*" (*Genesis* 21:21), the Sages said, "[Hagar chose a wife for her son Ishmael] from her birthplace — as people say, 'Throw a stick in the air, and it will invariably land on its bottom.'" (*Bereishis Rabbah* 53:15). (That is, things have a tendency to return to their roots.) Similarly, Mordechai in effect said to Haman, "What are you complaining about? In reality, you are not fit to be anything *but* a barber! Your rise to power can be likened to a stick that was flung in the air — just as its nature does not permit it to remain suspended in mid-air for long, so will your true nature prevent

the King has worn and a horse that the King has ridden, one with a royal crown on his head. 9 *Then let the robe and horse be entrusted to one of the King's most noble officers, and let them attire the man whom the King especially wants to honor, and parade him on horseback through the city square proclaiming before him, 'This is what is done for the man whom the King especially wants to honor.' "* 10 *Then the King said to Haman, "Hurry, then, get the robe and the horse as you have said*

---

you from remaining in power for much longer!"

Like monetary wealth, power can also corrupt and make one go astray. Haman fell victim to the vices of power, for had he remained the lowly barber of Kartzum, he most probably would have lived to a ripe old age.

The Talmud goes on to describe Haman's humiliation in greater detail:

"After [Haman] cut [Mordechai's] hair, he dressed him in the [royal] garments. He said to [Mordechai]: Get on [the King's horse] and ride.

[Mordechai] said to him: I am not able to [get on the horse], for my strength is weakened from the days of fasting.

[Haman] bent down and [Mordechai stepped on Haman's back and] climbed up on [the horse]. As he was climbing up, he kicked [Haman].

[Haman] asked him: Is it not written, 'When your enemy falls, do not rejoice'? (*Proverbs* 24:17). [Why, then, did you kick me?]

[Mordechai] answered him: These words were stated concerning a *Jewish* [enemy,] but about [an enemy such as] you it is written, 'And you shall tread upon their high places' (*Deuteronomy* 33:29)" (*Megillah* 16a).

Mordechai's somewhat vindictive behavior requires some explanation, as does Esther's decision to detain all the bathhouse attendants and barbers, thereby increasing Haman's humiliation by forcing him to personally attend to Mordechai.

The answer lies in the *Ramban*'s commentary (*Genesis* 12:6) regarding Abraham the Patriarch's nomadic wanderings in the Land of Canaan. As he explains, the prophets knew that a physical deed was sometimes necessary to bring about the fulfillment of a heavenly decree. For example, this is why Jeremiah commanded Seraiah, "When you finish reading this scroll, tie a stone to it and throw it into the Euphrates and say, 'Thus shall Babylon sink and never rise again. . .' " (*Jeremiah* 51:63-64). So too, Mordechai and Esther knew that their participation was required to trigger the onset of the heavenly decree calling for Haman's downfall. This is why they assumed an active role in increasing Haman's mortification.

❀ ❀ ❀

וַעֲשֵׂה־כֵן לְמָרְדֳּכַי הַיְּהוּדִי הַיּוֹשֵׁב בְּשַׁעַר הַמֶּלֶךְ
יא אַל־תַּפֵּל דָּבָר מִכֹּל אֲשֶׁר דִּבַּרְתָּ׃ וַיִּקַּח הָמָן אֶת־
הַלְּבוּשׁ וְאֶת־הַסּוּס וַיַּלְבֵּשׁ אֶת־מָרְדֳּכָי וַיַּרְכִּיבֵהוּ
בִּרְחוֹב הָעִיר וַיִּקְרָא לְפָנָיו כָּכָה יֵעָשֶׂה לָאִישׁ אֲשֶׁר
יב הַמֶּלֶךְ חָפֵץ בִּיקָרוֹ׃ וַיָּשָׁב מָרְדֳּכַי אֶל־שַׁעַר הַמֶּלֶךְ

Some commentators wonder why Ahasuerus hastened Haman to do his bidding. Since their dialogue took place in the early hours of the morning, Haman still had the entire day at his disposal to fulfill the King's command.

One answer is that Ahasuerus hated the Jews as much as Haman, as is evident from the Talmudic passage cited earlier on our comments to 1:1. Therefore, after specifying Mordechai's reward, Ahasuerus demanded that his command be carried out quickly lest he change his mind due to his hatred of Jews, which would not be very becoming of a king.

Alternatively, Ahasuerus was suddenly overcome with compassion for Haman, his faithful adviser. Wishing to spare him a measure of shame, the King urged Haman to fulfill the command promptly in the early hours of the morning while the streets were still empty. Mordechai and Esther, however, frustrated this plan. While Mordechai deliberately delayed Haman with all kinds of excuses, such as his need for a bath and a haircut before riding the King's horse, Esther ordered that all bathhouse attendants and barbers be detained. Consequently, by the time Haman finished bathing Mordechai and trimming his hair, the streets were teeming with people.

It was no coincidence that the redemption of the Jewish People began with Mordechai riding the King's horse and being led about the city dressed in royal garments. As *Yalkut Shimoni* explains, Haman's evil decree came in consequence of the selling of Joseph — just as Jacob's ten sons sold their brother Joseph while they sat down to eat their meal (see *Genesis* 37:25), so too, Ahasuerus "sold" the Jewish People to Haman while they sat and drank. By causing Mordechai to be led around the city upon the King's horse, Hashem signaled to the Jews that the sin of selling Joseph had finally been forgiven, for also regarding Joseph the verse says, "[Pharaoh] had [Joseph] dressed in garments of fine linen. . . He also had him ride in his second royal chariot, and they proclaimed before him, 'Avrech!' " (*Genesis* 41:42-43).

וַעֲשֵׂה־כֵן לְמָרְדֳּכַי הַיְּהוּדִי הַיּוֹשֵׁב בְּשַׁעַר הַמֶּלֶךְ אַל־תַּפֵּל דָּבָר מִכֹּל אֲשֶׁר דִּבַּרְתָּ — And do all this for Mordechai the Jew, who sits at the King's gate. Do not omit a single detail that you have suggested!"

The Sages explain why Ahasuerus gave Haman such a detailed description of Mordechai, and why he warned Haman not to "*omit a single detail*":

"[Haman] asked [Ahasuerus]: Who is Mordechai?

and do all this for Mordechai the Jew, who sits at the
King's gate. Do not omit a single detail that you have
suggested!" 11 *So Haman took the robe and the*
horse and attired Mordechai, and led him through
the city square proclaiming before him, "This is what
is done for the man whom the King especially wants
to honor."
12 *Mordechai returned to the King's gate; but*

[Ahasuerus] answered: The Jew.

[Haman] responded: But there are many Mordechais among the Jews!

[Ahasuerus] answered: The one who sits by the King's gate.

[Haman, upon realizing his blunder,] said: It is sufficient for him [to be given] a village or a river [from which he can collect taxes].

[Ahasuerus] answered: [Good idea!] Give him this as well! [Ahasuerus' last reply is alluded to by the words,] '*Do not omit a single detail that you have suggested*' " (*Megillah* 16a).

It is interesting to note that Ahasuerus said, "the one who sits by *the King's* gate," and not "the one who sits by the gate of *my* palace" or "of *my* house." Why does the verse use the third person?

The answer is that the verse alludes to a deeper concept: Figuratively, Mordechai sat by the gate of *Hashem,* the King of kings. As the *Baal Shem Tov* explains, a person is where his thoughts are. Thus, since Mordechai's mind was always preoccupied with beseeching Hashem and knocking on the Gates of Mercy on behalf of the Jewish People,[1] the verse describes him as "the one who sits by *the King's* gate."

11. וַיִּקַּח הָמָן אֶת־הַלְּבוּשׁ וְאֶת־הַסּוּס וַיַּלְבֵּשׁ אֶת־מָרְדֳּכָי — So Haman took the robe and the horse and attired Mordechai.

As noted above, the Sages say that when Mordechai requested a bath and a haircut before riding the King's horse, Esther quickly ordered that all the bathhouse attendants and barbers be detained (*Megillah* 16a). In reference to the Sages' statement, the *Vilna Gaon* asks the following question: "This Talmudic passage defies comprehension, for how could Esther have possibly detained all of Shushan's bathhouse attendants and barbers? Furthermore, had she done so, she would have revealed her close relationship to Mordechai."

The answer may be that Esther "detained the bathhouse attendants and barbers" by persuading Ahasuerus to declare a compulsory public holiday

---

1. As the Sages said, "[He was called] 'Son of Kish (קִישׁ)' because he knocked (הִקִּישׁ) on the Gates of Mercy, and they opened for him" (*Megillah* 12b).

יג וְהָמָן נִדְחַף אֶל־בֵּיתוֹ אָבֵל וַחֲפוּי רֹאשׁ׃ וַיְסַפֵּר הָמָן
לְזֶרֶשׁ אִשְׁתּוֹ וּלְכָל־אֹהֲבָיו אֵת כָּל־אֲשֶׁר קָרָהוּ

---

in honor of Mordechai's heroism in thwarting the assassination attempt against the King. In this manner, Esther prevented Haman from delegating Mordechai's bath and haircut to bathhouse attendants and barbers, since everyone was on vacation. In addition, she also magnified Mordechai's honor and Haman's humiliation by keeping all the residents of Shushan home, away from work or school, ensuring that no one would miss the upcoming spectacle.

Nevertheless, it remains unclear why Esther was not concerned that she may actually have been *helping* Haman by presenting him with the opportunity to attend to the needs of a Torah scholar. For the Sages said, "R' Yochanan said in the name of R' Shimon bar Yochai: Attending to the needs of Torah is greater than its study, as the verse says, 'Elisha son of Shaphat, who poured water on the hands of Elijah, is here. "The word of God is with him," said Jehoshaphat' (*II Kings* 3:11 — it does not say that [Elisha] *studied* [with Elijah], but that he *poured water* [on Elijah's hands]. This teaches that attending to the needs of Torah [scholars] is greater than its study" (*Berachos* 7b).

The answer is that Haman clearly resented having to attend to Mordechai's personal needs, and he only did so because he had no other choice. Thus, Esther had no reason for concern, for she knew that when a *gentile* performs a *mitzvah*[1] under coercion, he earns no reward.

The Sages said: " '*Haman took the robe and the horse*' and went and found the rabbis sitting before [Mordechai]. He was demonstrating the laws of *kemitzah* to them" (*Megillah* 16a). *Rashi* explains that Mordechai expounded upon the laws of *kemitzah* — the first of the four essential services of a flour offering (see *Leviticus* 2:2) — because that day was the 16th of *Nissan,* when the *Omer* sacrifice would be offered in the Holy Temple. The Talmud then recounts the dialogue that ensued between Haman and Mordechai's disciples:

"[Haman] asked: What topic are you studying?

They answered: When the Holy Temple was in existence, one who pledged a *minchah* offering brought a fistful of fine flour, through which he would gain atonement.

[Haman] said to them: Your fistful of flour has supplanted my ten thousand silver talents" (*Megillah* 16a).

From this exchange it is quite evident that the Holy Temple was the focal point of Haman's hatred. This is corroborated by the *Targum,* who interprets

---

1. When a Jew does a *mitzvah* under coercion he still receives reward (see *Rambam, Laws of Divorce* 2:20).

6/13 *Haman hurried home, despondent and with his*
head covered. 13 *Haman told his wife, Zeresh, and*
all his friends everything that had happened to him,

---

the verse, "After these things" (3:1), to mean that Haman traveled from Shushan to Jerusalem to halt the construction of the Holy Temple. The *Midrash* adds, "Do not think the *mitzvah* of the Omer is insignificant, for it was on the merit of this *mitzvah* that our father Abraham inherited the Land of Canaan, as it says, 'I shall give to you and to your offspring. . .the whole of the Land of Canaan [*on condition*] *that you keep My covenant*' (*Genesis* 17:8-9) — what does the verse mean by, 'My covenant'? The *mitzvah* of the Omer" (*Vayikra Rabbah* 28:6).

This *Midrash* reveals why Mordechai decided to teach his disciples the laws of the Omer at this crucial hour — he knew that by delving into this subject he and his disciples would reawaken the memory of our father Abraham, who inherited the Land of Canaan on the merit of this *mitzvah.* As a result of their diligent study of the Omer laws, Mordechai and his disciples earned the Jewish People sufficient merit to return to Israel, repossess the land, and reconstruct the Holy Temple despite the many obstacles their enemies placed in their way.

Shem MiShmuel, however, rightly points out that the interpretation of the words, "My covenant," in the *midrash* quoted above is unconventional, for this term commonly refers to the *mitzvah* of *milah* (circumcision), not to the Omer.

The answer is that the words, "My covenant," are indeed a reference to the *mitzvah* of *milah.* However, the underlying principle of this *mitzvah* is תְּמִימוּת — wholehearted faith in Hashem. This is evident from the verse, "Walk before Me and become perfect (תָמִים)" (*Genesis* 17:1), which refers to the *mitzvah* of *milah.* The essential theme of the Omer is also wholehearted faith, as we see from the verse, "You shall count for yourselves — from the morrow of the rest day, from the day when you bring the Omer of the waving — seven weeks, *they shall be complete* (תְּמִימֹת תִּהְיֶינָה)" (*Leviticus* 23:15). Perhaps it is this correlation between the *mitzvah* of *milah* and the Omer that R' Yochanan had in mind when he said, "it was on the merit of the *mitzvah* of the Omer that our father Abraham inherited the Land of Canaan."

Hence, we see that if a person exhibits the trait of תְּמִימוּת by humbly accepting whatever Hashem may send his way with love and devotion, he effectively silences all accusations against him in the Heavenly Court. Hashem will surely redeem such an individual from all forms of hardship and adversity.

This is what Haman meant by "Your fistful of flour has come and supplanted my ten thousand silver talents" — even he knew that תְּמִימוּת is the antidote to his Amalekite venom, and he recognized its presence among

ו/יד וַיֹּאמְרוּ לוֹ חֲכָמָיו וְזֶרֶשׁ אִשְׁתּוֹ אִם מִזֶּרַע הַיְּהוּדִים
מָרְדֳּכַי אֲשֶׁר הַחִלּוֹתָ לִנְפֹּל לְפָנָיו לֹא־תוּכַל לוֹ כִּי־
יד נָפוֹל תִּפּוֹל לְפָנָיו׃ עוֹדָם מְדַבְּרִים עִמּוֹ וְסָרִיסֵי הַמֶּלֶךְ
הִגִּיעוּ וַיַּבְהִלוּ לְהָבִיא אֶת־הָמָן אֶל־הַמִּשְׁתֶּה אֲשֶׁר־
ז/א־ד א עָשְׂתָה אֶסְתֵּר׃ וַיָּבֹא הַמֶּלֶךְ וְהָמָן לִשְׁתּוֹת עִם־
ב אֶסְתֵּר הַמַּלְכָּה׃ וַיֹּאמֶר הַמֶּלֶךְ לְאֶסְתֵּר גַּם בַּיּוֹם
הַשֵּׁנִי בְּמִשְׁתֵּה הַיַּיִן מַה־שְּׁאֵלָתֵךְ אֶסְתֵּר הַמַּלְכָּה
וְתִנָּתֵן לָךְ וּמַה־בַּקָּשָׁתֵךְ עַד־חֲצִי הַמַּלְכוּת וְתֵעָשׂ׃
ג וַתַּעַן אֶסְתֵּר הַמַּלְכָּה וַתֹּאמַר אִם־מָצָאתִי חֵן
בְּעֵינֶיךָ הַמֶּלֶךְ וְאִם־עַל־הַמֶּלֶךְ טוֹב תִּנָּתֶן־לִי נַפְשִׁי
ד בִּשְׁאֵלָתִי וְעַמִּי בְּבַקָּשָׁתִי׃ כִּי נִמְכַּרְנוּ אֲנִי וְעַמִּי

Mordechai's disciples. At this point, Haman resigned himself to the fact that his evil plot against the Jews was doomed to fail.

13. וַיֹּאמְרוּ לוֹ חֲכָמָיו וְזֶרֶשׁ אִשְׁתּוֹ אִם מִזֶּרַע הַיְּהוּדִים מָרְדֳּכַי אֲשֶׁר הַחִלּוֹתָ לִנְפֹּל לְפָנָיו לֹא־תוּכַל לוֹ כִּי־נָפוֹל תִּפּוֹל לְפָנָיו — his advisers and his wife, Zeresh, said to him: 'If Mordechai, before whom you have begun to fall, is of Jewish descent, you will not prevail against him, but will undoubtedly fall before him."

I heard the following elucidation in the name of R' Meir Shapiro:

Were Zeresh and the rest of Haman's advisers previously unaware of Mordechai's origins? Surely everyone in Shushan knew that Mordechai was Jewish! What, then, did they mean by "*If* Mordechai. . .is of Jewish descent"? Furthermore, the word זֶרַע (lit. "offspring," translated as "descent") seems superfluous. Would it not have been sufficient to simply say, אִם מֵהַיְּהוּדִים מָרְדֳּכַי, meaning "If Mordechai. . .is Jewish"?

The answer must be that although Haman's advisers knew Mordechai was Jewish, they were doubtful whether he had the ability to influence the younger generation of Jews — the זֶרַע, or "offspring," growing up in Shushan. Haman's wicked advisers knew that effective communication between the older and younger generations was the key to Jewish continuity. Had this rapport between Mordechai and the Jewish youth not existed, Haman would no doubt have succeeded in realizing his evil plot. However, when Haman told his advisers that he had seen Mordechai in the study hall teaching Torah to 22,000 Jewish children, the verdict was unanimous: "You *will not* prevail against him, but will undoubtedly fall before him!"

6/14 *and his advisers and his wife, Zeresh, said to him, "If
Mordechai, before whom you have begun to fall, is
of Jewish descent, you will not prevail against him,
but will undoubtedly fall before him."* 14 *While they
were still talking with him, the King's chamberlains
arrived, and they hurried to bring Haman to the
banquet which Esther had arranged.*

7/1-4 1 *So the King and Haman came to feast with
Queen Esther.* 2 *The King asked Esther again on
the second day at the wine feast, "What is your
request, Queen Esther? — it shall be granted you.
And what is your petition? — Even if it be up to half
the kingdom, it shall be fulfilled."* 3 *So Queen Esther
answered and said, "If I have won Your Majesty's
favor and if it pleases the King, let my life be
granted to me as my request and my people as my
petition.* 4 *For we have been sold, I and my people,*

An alternative answer to R' Meir Shapiro's questions may be the following: Haman's advisers knew Mordechai was Jewish, but they were unsure whether he possessed the quality of spiritual vitality and renewal, suggested by the word זֶרַע (lit. "seed"). This quality insulates a person against the endemic spiritual apathy which may set in on his particular generation, and enables him to strive forward and overcome even the mightiest obstacles. Because an individual possessing this quality does not focus on the negative aspects of life, he remains perpetually young and confident that all his needs are within reach. On the other hand, if a person succumbs to his shortcomings and resigns himself to live in accordance with the moral codes set by his society's lowest common denominator, he may well seem "old and worn out" even if he is young in years.

This is why Zeresh and the other advisers became so concerned when Haman disclosed to them that Mordechai was studying the laws of the Omer. They realized that if Mordechai was capable of devoting his undivided attention to the study of a *mitzvah* which would only be applicable when the Hcly Temple would be rebuilt, it was a sure sign that Mordechai possessed spiritual vitality. In their eyes, Mordechai's actions reflected his unwavering faith in the redemption of Israel and the reconstruction of the Temple despite all the Jewish People's setbacks. Hence, they sadly informed Haman, "You *will not* prevail against him, but will undoubtedly fall before him!"

ז/ה־י לְהַשְׁמִ֥יד לַהֲר֖וֹג וּלְאַבֵּ֑ד וְ֠אִלּוּ לַעֲבָדִ֨ים וְלִשְׁפָח֤וֹת
נִמְכַּ֙רְנוּ֙ הֶחֱרַ֔שְׁתִּי כִּ֣י אֵ֥ין הַצָּ֛ר שֹׁוֶ֖ה בְּנֵ֥זֶק
ה הַמֶּֽלֶךְ׃ וַיֹּ֙אמֶר֙ הַמֶּ֣לֶךְ אֲחַשְׁוֵר֔וֹשׁ וַיֹּ֖אמֶר
לְאֶסְתֵּ֣ר הַמַּלְכָּ֑ה מִ֣י ה֥וּא זֶה֙ וְאֵי־זֶ֣ה ה֔וּא אֲשֶׁר־
ו מְלָא֥וֹ לִבּ֖וֹ לַעֲשׂ֥וֹת כֵּֽן׃ וַתֹּ֣אמֶר אֶסְתֵּ֔ר אִ֚ישׁ צַ֣ר
וְאוֹיֵ֔ב הָמָ֥ן הָרָ֖ע הַזֶּ֑ה וְהָמָ֣ן נִבְעַ֔ת מִלִּפְנֵ֥י הַמֶּ֖לֶךְ
ז וְהַמַּלְכָּֽה׃ וְהַמֶּ֜לֶךְ קָ֤ם בַּחֲמָתוֹ֙ מִמִּשְׁתֵּ֣ה הַיַּ֔יִן אֶל־
גִּנַּ֖ת הַבִּיתָ֑ן וְהָמָ֣ן עָמַ֗ד לְבַקֵּ֤שׁ עַל־נַפְשׁוֹ֙ מֵֽאֶסְתֵּ֣ר
הַמַּלְכָּ֔ה כִּ֣י רָאָ֔ה כִּֽי־כָלְתָ֥ה אֵלָ֛יו הָרָעָ֖ה מֵאֵ֥ת
ח הַמֶּֽלֶךְ׃ וְהַמֶּ֡לֶךְ שָׁב֩ מִגִּנַּ֨ת הַבִּיתָ֜ן אֶל־בֵּ֣ית ׀ מִשְׁתֵּ֣ה
הַיַּ֗יִן וְהָמָן֙ נֹפֵ֔ל עַל־הַמִּטָּה֙ אֲשֶׁ֣ר אֶסְתֵּ֣ר עָלֶ֔יהָ
וַיֹּ֣אמֶר הַמֶּ֔לֶךְ הֲ֠גַם לִכְבּ֧וֹשׁ אֶת־הַמַּלְכָּ֛ה עִמִּ֖י בַּבָּ֑יִת
ט הַדָּבָ֗ר יָצָא֙ מִפִּ֣י הַמֶּ֔לֶךְ וּפְנֵ֥י הָמָ֖ן חָפֽוּ׃ וַיֹּ֣אמֶר
חַ֠רְבוֹנָה אֶחָ֨ד מִן־הַסָּרִיסִ֜ים לִפְנֵ֣י הַמֶּ֗לֶךְ גַּ֣ם הִנֵּה־
הָעֵ֣ץ אֲשֶׁר־עָשָׂ֣ה הָמָ֡ן לְמָרְדֳּכַ֞י אֲשֶׁ֧ר דִּבֶּר־ט֣וֹב עַל־
הַמֶּ֗לֶךְ עֹמֵד֙ בְּבֵ֣ית הָמָ֔ן גָּבֹ֖הַּ חֲמִשִּׁ֣ים אַמָּ֑ה וַיֹּ֥אמֶר
י הַמֶּ֖לֶךְ תְּלֻ֥הוּ עָלָֽיו׃ וַיִּתְלוּ֙ אֶת־הָמָ֔ן עַל־הָעֵ֖ץ אֲשֶׁר־
ח/א א הֵכִ֣ין לְמָרְדֳּכָ֑י וַחֲמַ֥ת הַמֶּ֖לֶךְ שָׁכָֽכָה׃ בַּיּ֣וֹם
הַה֗וּא נָתַ֞ן הַמֶּ֤לֶךְ אֲחַשְׁוֵרוֹשׁ֙ לְאֶסְתֵּ֣ר הַמַּלְכָּ֔ה
אֶת־בֵּ֥ית הָמָ֖ן צֹרֵ֣ר °היהודיים וּמָרְדֳּכַ֗י בָּ֚א °הַיְּהוּדִ֑ים ק׳
לִפְנֵ֣י הַמֶּ֔לֶךְ כִּֽי־הִגִּ֥ידָה אֶסְתֵּ֖ר מַ֥ה הוּא־לָֽהּ׃

VII-VIII

7:10-8:1. וַיִּתְלוּ אֶת־הָמָן. . . בַּיּוֹם הַהוּא נָתַן הַמֶּלֶךְ אֲחַשְׁוֵרוֹשׁ לְאֶסְתֵּר הַמַּלְכָּה אֶת־בֵּית הָמָן צֹרֵר הַיְּהוּדִים — So they hanged Haman. . . That very day, King Ahasuerus gave the estate of Haman, the enemy of the Jews, to Queen Esther.

Why does the *Megillah* emphasize that Ahasuerus gave Haman's estate to Esther on the "very day" that he was hung?

The answer is that killing a minister as powerful as Haman without a just trial was no casual matter, even for King Ahasuerus. It stands to reason that

7/5-10 to be destroyed, slain, and exterminated. Had we
been sold as slaves and servant-girls, I would have
kept quiet, for the adversary is not worthy of the
King's damage."
5 Thereupon, King Ahasuerus exclaimed and said
to Queen Esther, "Who is it? Where is the one who
dared to do this?" 6 And Esther said, "An adversary
and an enemy! This wicked Haman!" Haman trem-
bled in terror before the King and Queen. 7 The King
rose in a rage from the wine feast and went into the
palace garden while Haman remained to beg Queen
Esther for his life, for he saw that the King's evil
determination against him was final. 8 When the
King returned from the palace garden to the banquet
room, Haman was prostrated on the couch upon
which Esther was; so the King exclaimed, "Would he
actually assault the Queen while I'm in the house?"
As soon as the King uttered this, they covered
Haman's face. 9 Then Harbonah, one of the chamberlains in attendance of the King, said, "Furthermore, the fifty-cubit-high gallows which Haman
made for Mordechai — who spoke good for the King
— is standing in Haman's house." And the King
said, "Hang him on it." 10 So they hanged Haman on
the gallows which he had prepared for Mordechai,
and the King's anger abated.

8/1 1 That very day, King Ahasuerus gave the estate of
Haman, the enemy of the Jews, to Queen
Esther. Mordechai presented himself to the King
(for Esther had revealed his relationship to her).

Haman had a wide base of support in the royal council and the populace at large. Ahasuerus knew that his rather impulsive decision to execute Haman would enrage many of his subjects, and he feared that their disenchantment would escalate into a full-blown rebellion. In order to prevent such an eventuality, Ahasuerus spread the word that he had executed Haman for attempting to seduce the Queen.

This piece of disinformation mollified Ahasuerus' disgruntled subjects. They suddenly sympathized with the King, thinking, "Well, a man certainly

ב וַיָּסַר הַמֶּלֶךְ אֶת־טַבַּעְתּוֹ אֲשֶׁר הֶעֱבִיר מֵהָמָן
וַיִּתְּנָהּ לְמָרְדֳּכָי וַתָּשֶׂם אֶסְתֵּר אֶת־מָרְדֳּכַי עַל־בֵּית
ג הָמָן׃ וַתּוֹסֶף אֶסְתֵּר וַתְּדַבֵּר לִפְנֵי הַמֶּלֶךְ וַתִּפֹּל
לִפְנֵי רַגְלָיו וַתֵּבְךְּ וַתִּתְחַנֶּן־לוֹ לְהַעֲבִיר אֶת־רָעַת
הָמָן הָאֲגָגִי וְאֵת מַחֲשַׁבְתּוֹ אֲשֶׁר חָשַׁב עַל־הַיְּהוּדִים׃
ד וַיּוֹשֶׁט הַמֶּלֶךְ לְאֶסְתֵּר אֵת שַׁרְבִט הַזָּהָב וַתָּקָם אֶסְתֵּר
ה וַתַּעֲמֹד לִפְנֵי הַמֶּלֶךְ׃ וַתֹּאמֶר אִם־עַל־הַמֶּלֶךְ טוֹב
וְאִם־מָצָאתִי חֵן לְפָנָיו וְכָשֵׁר הַדָּבָר לִפְנֵי הַמֶּלֶךְ
וְטוֹבָה אֲנִי בְּעֵינָיו יִכָּתֵב לְהָשִׁיב אֶת־הַסְּפָרִים
מַחֲשֶׁבֶת הָמָן בֶּן־הַמְּדָתָא הָאֲגָגִי אֲשֶׁר כָּתַב לְאַבֵּד
ו אֶת־הַיְּהוּדִים אֲשֶׁר בְּכָל־מְדִינוֹת הַמֶּלֶךְ׃ כִּי אֵיכָכָה
אוּכַל וְרָאִיתִי בָּרָעָה אֲשֶׁר־יִמְצָא אֶת־עַמִּי וְאֵיכָכָה
ז אוּכַל וְרָאִיתִי בְּאָבְדַן מוֹלַדְתִּי׃ וַיֹּאמֶר
הַמֶּלֶךְ אֲחַשְׁוֵרֹשׁ לְאֶסְתֵּר הַמַּלְכָּה וּלְמָרְדֳּכַי
הַיְּהוּדִי הִנֵּה בֵית־הָמָן נָתַתִּי לְאֶסְתֵּר וְאֹתוֹ
תָּלוּ עַל־הָעֵץ עַל אֲשֶׁר־שָׁלַח יָדוֹ °ביהודיים׃ °בַּיְּהוּדִים ק׳

---

cannot be expected to act rationally under such circumstances!" To lend further support to his claim, Ahasuerus followed through by instituting an additional penalty against Haman *on the very day* he was hung: He decreed that Haman's estate be transferred to Esther's possession as compensation for making the Queen undergo such a disgraceful ordeal.[1]

❦ ❦ ❦

It would seem that the words, *the enemy of the Jews,* are superfluous. By this point, are we not all too familiar with Haman's sentiments towards the Jewish People?

The answer is that the *Megillah* adds these words in order to convey the exactness of heavenly judgment: Because Haman sinned with his possessions — "I will pay 10,000 silver talents" (3:9) — it was decreed that all his possessions be transferred to Queen Esther, who risked everything, including her own life, for the sake of the Jewish People. And because an earlier

---

1. We find (*Genesis* 2:16) that Abimelech, King of Gerar, gave Sarah gifts as compensation when he returned her to Abraham.

2 *The King slipped off his signet ring, which he had*
removed from Haman, and gave it to Mordechai; and
Esther put Mordechai in charge of Haman's estate.
3 *Esther yet again spoke to the King, collapsed at*
his feet, and cried and begged him to avert the evil
intention of Haman the Agagite, and his scheme
which he had plotted against the Jews. 4 *The King*
extended the gold scepter to Esther, and Esther arose
and stood before the King. 5 *She said, "If it pleases*
the King, and if I have won his favor, and the
proposal seems proper in the King's opinion, and I be
pleasing to him, let a decree be written to counter-
mand those dispatches devised by Haman, the son
of Hammedatha the Agagite, which he wrote order-
ing the destruction of the Jews who are in all the
King's provinces. 6 *For how can I bear to witness the*
disaster which will befall my people! How can I bear
to witness the destruction of my relatives!"
7 *Then King Ahasuerus said to Queen Esther*
and Mordechai the Jew, "Behold, I have given
Haman's estate to Esther, and he has been hanged
on the gallows because he plotted against the Jews.

---

verse said, "So the King took off his signet ring. . .and gave it to Haman . . . *the enemy of the Jews*" (v. 10), here too, when Haman is punished for his sins, the verse shows the exactness of heavenly judgment by once again referring to Haman as "*the enemy of the Jews.*" In heavenly judgment nothing is forgotten, even the smallest mundane item is brought to judgment.[1]

7. הִנֵּה בֵית־הָמָן נָתַתִּי לְאֶסְתֵּר וְאֹתוֹ תָּלוּ עַל־הָעֵץ עַל אֲשֶׁר־שָׁלַח יָדוֹ בַּיְּהוּדִים — "Behold, I have given Haman's estate to Esther, and he has been hanged on the gallows because he plotted against the Jews.

Two questions must be asked: First, since Esther was actually standing before the King, the verse should have used the first person: "Behold, I have given Haman's estate to *you.*" Why did the verse instead use the third person? Second, why did Ahasuerus refer to the Queen simply as Esther?

---

1. It is said that the *Vilna Gaon* once saw an apostate eating bread and unkosher meat. The *Gaon* immediately sent one of his disciples to request of the apostate to wash his hands before taking another bite of bread. The apostate found this request quite amusing. He remarked, "Here I am eating unkosher meat, a Torah-ordained prohibition, and you're

ח וְאַתֶּם כִּתְבוּ עַל־הַיְּהוּדִים כַּטּוֹב בְּעֵינֵיכֶם בְּשֵׁם
הַמֶּלֶךְ וְחִתְמוּ בְּטַבַּעַת הַמֶּלֶךְ כִּי־כְתָב אֲשֶׁר־נִכְתָּב
בְּשֵׁם־הַמֶּלֶךְ וְנַחְתּוֹם בְּטַבַּעַת הַמֶּלֶךְ אֵין לְהָשִׁיב׃
ט וַיִּקָּרְאוּ סֹפְרֵי־הַמֶּלֶךְ בָּעֵת־הַהִיא בַּחֹדֶשׁ הַשְּׁלִישִׁי
הוּא־חֹדֶשׁ סִיוָן בִּשְׁלוֹשָׁה וְעֶשְׂרִים בּוֹ וַיִּכָּתֵב כְּכָל־
אֲשֶׁר־צִוָּה מָרְדֳּכַי אֶל־הַיְּהוּדִים וְאֶל הָאֲחַשְׁדַּרְפְּנִים
וְהַפַּחוֹת וְשָׂרֵי הַמְּדִינוֹת אֲשֶׁר ׀ מֵהֹדּוּ וְעַד־כּוּשׁ
שֶׁבַע וְעֶשְׂרִים וּמֵאָה מְדִינָה מְדִינָה וּמְדִינָה כִּכְתָבָהּ
וְעַם וָעָם כִּלְשֹׁנוֹ וְאֶל־הַיְּהוּדִים כִּכְתָבָם וְכִלְשׁוֹנָם׃

Why did he not use the more dignified title "*Queen* Esther," as in the verse, "That very day, King Ahasuerus gave the estate of Haman. . .to *Queen* Esther" (8:1)? The answer is as follows:

In reference to this verse, the *Manos Levi* cites a *midrash* which says, "Two wealthy individuals came to the world. One was an Israelite, the other, a gentile. Both suffered terrible setbacks due to their great wealth. Korach was the Israelite — he found the gold and silver treasure which Joseph had concealed. Haman was the gentile — he found the treasures of the Judean Kings." *Pirkei D'Rebbi Eliezer* provides more details about Haman's wealth: "Haman took all the treasures of the Judean Kings and all the treasures of the Holy of Holies. Thus, it was fitting that Mordechai retrieve these treasures and rebuild the Holy Temple with them — they came from a holy place, and to a holy place they returned."

Pirkei D'Rebbi Eliezer implies that Esther conferred Haman's estate to Mordechai, who then used it to rebuild the Holy Temple. This was rather daring of Esther, for after all, the King himself had bestowed Haman's estate to her. It is not difficult to imagine how a King would react if he would discover that his Queen casually lends her friends the personal gifts he gives her — he would surely be consumed by rage! How, then, did Esther dare give Haman's estate to Mordechai?

The answer to all the above questions is that Ahasuerus did not give Haman's estate to Esther on the merit of her being the Queen, but on the merit of her being Esther the Jewess. Indeed, we find that the verse here refers to Esther, not "Queen Esther." Ahasuerus ruled that Haman's estate be given to the Jews as indemnity for all the crimes Haman had

---

concerned that I haven't complied with the rabbinical dictate to wash one's hands for bread!?"

The *Gaon* responded, "You will be judged for *every* transgression you commit, including eating bread without washing your hands!"

[8] *You may write concerning the Jews whatever you
desire, in the King's name, and seal it with the royal
signet, for an edict which is written in the King's
name and sealed with the royal signet may not be
revoked."* [9] *So the King's secretaries were summoned at that time, on the twenty-third day of the
third month, that is, the month of Sivan, and it was
written exactly as Mordechai had dictated to the
Jews and to the satraps, the governors and officials
of the provinces from Hodu to Cush, a hundred
and twenty-seven provinces, to each province in its
own script, and each people in its own language,
and to the Jews in their own script and language.*

---

committed against them. As far as the King was concerned, the Jews could do whatever they wished with Haman's estate. Thus, Esther did not act as Queen when she received Haman's estate, but merely as the Jewish People's representative. According to this interpretation, the words "because he plotted against the Jews," refer back to the first clause of the verse — "I have given Haman's estate to Esther ... *because he plotted against the Jews.*"

The exactness of heavenly punishment made itself apparent once again — Haman's estate, which included the treasures seized from the Holy of Holies, came back into the possession of the Jewish People, who then used it to rebuild the Holy Temple. How miraculous! The possessions of the wicked Haman, the Jewish People's fiercest enemy, ended up being used to reconstruct the Holy Temple in Jerusalem!

With this theme in mind, we may better understand *Rashi*'s commentary on the verse, "Benjamin is a predatory wolf; in the morning he will devour prey (עַד) and in the evening he will distribute spoils" (*Genesis* 49:27). *Rashi* explains that "the morning" alludes to Saul, who rose as the Jewish People's champion in the dawn of their history, when the nation began to flourish. "The evening" alludes to the nation's decline, when the people were exiled to Babylonia and Persia. The verse foresaw that Benjamin's offspring would triumph over Israel's enemies and divide the spoils of victory. This alludes to Mordechai and Esther, from the Tribe of Benjamin, who defeated Haman and were awarded his estate.

In light of this explanation, three questions remain unanswered: What kind of "prey" did Jacob foresee Saul would "devour" in "the morning"? Why does the first clause speak of "prey" (עַד) and the second of "spoils" (שָׁלָל)? And why would a verse which ostensibly foresees the collective future

י וַיִּכְתֹּב בְּשֵׁם הַמֶּלֶךְ אֲחַשְׁוֵרֹשׁ וַיַּחְתֹּם בְּטַבַּעַת
הַמֶּלֶךְ וַיִּשְׁלַח סְפָרִים בְּיַד הָרָצִים בַּסּוּסִים רֹכְבֵי
יא הָרֶכֶשׁ הָאֲחַשְׁתְּרָנִים בְּנֵי הָרַמָּכִים׃ אֲשֶׁר נָתַן
הַמֶּלֶךְ לַיְּהוּדִים ׀ אֲשֶׁר ׀ בְּכָל־עִיר־וָעִיר לְהִקָּהֵל
וְלַעֲמֹד עַל־נַפְשָׁם לְהַשְׁמִיד וְלַהֲרֹג וּלְאַבֵּד אֶת־

---

of the entire Jewish nation allude to the endowment of Haman's estate to two individuals, Mordechai and Esther?

The answer to all three questions is as follows: Both "prey" (עַד) and "spoils" (שָׁלָל) allude to possessions seized by individuals on behalf of the entire Jewish nation. King Saul seized the Amalekites' livestock on behalf of Israel in order to offer the animals as sacrifices to Hashem and thereby express thanksgiving for the victorious campaign against Amalek. Saul thought he was following Moses' example, who built an altar to Hashem immediately after the Israelites' successful battle against Amalek in the desert (see *Exodus* 17:15). As Saul explained to Samuel the Prophet, "The troops took from the spoil. . .to sacrifice to HASHEM your God in Gilgal" (*I Samuel* 15:21).

Samuel the Prophet, however, castigated King Saul for sparing Amalek's livestock and thereby failing to fulfill Hashem's command to exterminate the entire nation. Jacob foresaw Saul's mistake, and for this reason used the word "prey" (עַד) and not "spoils" (שָׁלָל). This alludes to the verse, "The wicked sprout like grass, all evildoers blossom, that they may be destroyed forever (עַד עֲדֵי)" (*Psalms* 92:8) — only on the day when Amalek is completely destroyed will "HASHEM be exalted forever" (ibid. v. 9).

We do see, though, that Saul's intentions were for the sake of Heaven. This is why he merited descendants such as Mordechai and Esther, who repossessed the estate of Haman — an Amalekite — and built the Holy Temple with it. In this manner, they rectified Saul's sin by achieving his original goal — to glorify the Name of Heaven with the spoils seized from Amalek.

11. לְהַשְׁמִיד וְלַהֲרֹג וּלְאַבֵּד אֶת־כָּל־חֵיל עַם וּמְדִינָה הַצָּרִים אֹתָם טַף וְנָשִׁים — To destroy, slay, and exterminate every armed force of any people or province that threaten them, along with their children and women.

Amalek is the only nation we are obligated to annihilate, as the verse says, "Wipe out the memory of Amalek from under the heaven — do not forget!" (*Deuteronomy* 25:19). However, this *mitzvah* is no longer applicable today, for when the Assyrian King Sennacherib conquered the Middle East, he expatriated the nations of the entire region and resettled their homelands with foreigners. Many nations completely disappeared,

[10] *He wrote in the name of King Ahasuerus and sealed it with the King's signet. He sent letters by couriers on horseback, riders of swift mules bred of mares,* [11] *to the effect that the King had permitted the Jews of every single city to organize and defend themselves; to destroy, slay, and exterminate*

---

while others lost their cultural homogeneity. This is why *Rambam* rules that it is no longer possible to identify the nation of Amalek. If so, on what basis did the Jews of Mordechai's generation slay the women and children of their enemies?

My friend R' Akiva Stolper suggested the following answer: Even though we cannot identify the Amalekite nation as a whole, there are certain signs which indicate that particular individuals are of Amalekite descent. In theory, if such signs are perceived on an individual, he should be killed. There are accounts of wise men throughout the ages who were familiar with these signs. For example, it is told that when *R' Chaim of Volozhin* was in Petersburg, he stopped and stared at a youngster called Nikolai. When his disciples asked him what he found so interesting about the gentile boy, R' Chaim answered, "All the signs of Amalek which the *Vilna Gaon* passed down to me are present on this boy!" The boy grew to become the wicked Czar Nikolai.

In Mordechai's day it was even easier to identify individuals of Amalekite descent. Who else but Amalek would dare attack the Jews under such unfavorable circumstances? Haman and his ten sons lay dead, Mordechai was the viceroy of the Persian Empire, Esther — now known to be a Jewess — was the Queen, and King Ahasuerus was passing one decree after the next in favor of the Jews. And nonetheless, despite all the miracles that occurred on behalf of the Jews, small bands of anti-Semites still dared wage war against the Jewish People! Were any more signs necessary to confirm the Amalekite roots of these anti-Semites? They faithfully emulated their wicked ancestors, who dared attack the Jewish People in the desert soon after the miraculous redemption from Egypt and the splitting of the Red Sea, when no other nation dared raise a hand against Hashem's Chosen People. For this reason, the Jews in Mordechai's day permitted themselves to exterminate their enemies, including their wives and children. In this manner, they fulfilled the *mitzvah* to exterminate Amalek.

לְהִקָּהֵל וְלַעֲמֹד עַל־נַפְשָׁם — To organize and defend themselves.

"To organize and defend themselves" appears to be a contradiction in terms: "To organize" implies a state of solidarity and participation in a common struggle. "To defend *themselves*" conveys an individualistic

כָּל־חֵיל עַם וּמְדִינָה הַצָּרִים אֹתָם טַף וְנָשִׁים וּשְׁלָלָם
יב לָבוֹז׃ בְּיוֹם אֶחָד בְּכָל־מְדִינוֹת הַמֶּלֶךְ אֲחַשְׁוֵרוֹשׁ
בִּשְׁלוֹשָׁה עָשָׂר לְחֹדֶשׁ שְׁנֵים־עָשָׂר הוּא־חֹדֶשׁ
יג אֲדָר׃ פַּתְשֶׁגֶן הַכְּתָב לְהִנָּתֵן דָּת בְּכָל־מְדִינָה וּמְדִינָה
גָּלוּי לְכָל־הָעַמִּים וְלִהְיוֹת °היהודיים עתודים לַיּוֹם
יד הַזֶּה לְהִנָּקֵם מֵאֹיְבֵיהֶם׃ הָרָצִים רֹכְבֵי הָרֶכֶשׁ
הָאֲחַשְׁתְּרָנִים יָצְאוּ מְבֹהָלִים וּדְחוּפִים בִּדְבַר הַמֶּלֶךְ
טו וְהַדָּת נִתְּנָה בְּשׁוּשַׁן הַבִּירָה׃ **וּמָרְדֳּכַי**
יָצָא ׀ מִלִּפְנֵי הַמֶּלֶךְ בִּלְבוּשׁ מַלְכוּת תְּכֵלֶת וָחוּר
וַעֲטֶרֶת זָהָב גְּדוֹלָה וְתַכְרִיךְ בּוּץ וְאַרְגָּמָן וְהָעִיר
טז **שׁוּשָׁן צָהֲלָה וְשָׂמֵחָה׃ לַיְּהוּדִים הָיְתָה אוֹרָה**
יז **וְשִׂמְחָה וְשָׂשֹׂן וִיקָר׃** וּבְכָל־מְדִינָה וּמְדִינָה וּבְכָל־

°הַיְּהוּדִים עֲתִידִים ק׳

---

stance, reminiscent of the Talmudic adage, "If two people are walking in the desert and there is only enough water for one of them, the owner of the water should withhold it from his friend, and drink it alone, for his own life takes precedence" (*Bava Metzia* 60a).

The answer is that the words לַעֲמֹד עַל נַפְשָׁם — *to defend themselves* — refers to prayer [as in גּוֹמֵל נַפְשׁוֹ אִישׁ חָסֶד — *A kind man benefits himself,* which refers to prayer (*Rashi, Shabbos* 127b)]. Our Sages teach us two important principles which demonstrate the power of prayer when Jews unite. One is that when a person who has specific needs prays on behalf of a friend with the same needs, the one who is praying will have his needs filled before his friend's are (*Bava Kamma* 97a). The other is that communal prayer is never rejected (*Berachos* 8a). Thus the Jews, by gathering and praying together, were, at the same time, defending *themselves.*

16. לַיְּהוּדִים הָיְתָה אוֹרָה וְשִׂמְחָה וְשָׂשֹׂן וִיקָר — The Jews had light and gladness, and joy and honor.

The Sages said regarding this verse, " 'Light' refers to Torah, as the verse says, 'For the commandment is a *lamp,* and Torah is light' (*Proverbs* 6:23). 'Gladness' refers to the holidays, as the verse says, 'You shall be glad on your holiday' (*Deuteronomy* 16:14). 'Joy' refers to circumcision, as the verse says, 'I rejoice over Your word' (*Psalms* 119:162). 'Glory' refers to *tefillin,* as the verse says, 'All the nations of the world will see that the Name of God is called upon you, and they will be in awe of you' (*Deuteronomy* 28:10)" (*Megillah* 16b).

every armed force of any people or province that
threaten them, along with their children and women,
and to plunder their possessions, 12 *on a single day*
in all the provinces of King Ahasuerus, namely, up-
on the thirteenth day of the twelfth month, that
is, the month of Adar. 13 *The contents of the*
document were to be promulgated in every province,
and be published to all peoples so that the Jews
should be ready on that day to avenge themselves
on their enemies. 14 *The couriers, riders of swift*
mules, went forth in urgent haste by order of the
King, and the edict was distributed in Shushan the
Capital.
15 ***Mordechai left the King's presence clad in***
royal apparel of turquoise and white with a large
gold crown and a robe of fine linen and purple;
then the city of Shushan was cheerful and glad.
16 ***The Jews had light and gladness, and joy and***
honor. 17 *Likewise, in every province, and in every*

It would seem that the Sages omitted another important *mitzvah* which the Jews in Mordechai and Esther's day fulfilled — *teshuvah,* or repentance. As the Talmud states, "[The] removal of [Ahasuerus'] signet ring, [with which Haman sealed his evil decree,] had a greater [effect] than forty-eight prophets. For [while all those prophets] could not return [the Jews] to [the path of] righteousness, the removal of the signet ring *did* return [the Jews] to [the path of] righteousness" (*Megillah* 14a). *Rashi* explains that in response to the removal of Ahasuerus' ring, the Jews decreed public fast days and encouraged each other to repent. Since the Jewish People reached such an unprecedented level of *teshuvah,* it would seem fitting that this historical event be alluded to in the verse, "The Jews had light and gladness, and joy and honor" (v. 16).

The answer is that *teshuvah* is such a fundamental element of this verse that the Sages did not see a need to mention it explicitly. For the sensitive soul of a Jew could not possibly have rejoiced in "light and gladness, and joy and honor" if he would still have been held accountable for having committed a sin against Hashem. Thus, the very fact that the Jewish People were able to feel "light and gladness, and joy and honor" is incontestable proof that they fulfilled the *mitzvah* of *teshuvah* to the highest degree.

ח/יז עִ֣יר וָעִ֗יר מְקוֹם֙ אֲשֶׁ֨ר דְּבַר־הַמֶּ֤לֶךְ וְדָתוֹ֙ מַגִּ֔יעַ שִׂמְחָ֤ה וְשָׂשׂוֹן֙ לַיְּהוּדִ֔ים מִשְׁתֶּ֖ה וְי֣וֹם ט֑וֹב וְרַבִּ֞ים מֵֽעַמֵּ֤י הָאָ֨רֶץ֙ מִֽתְיַהֲדִ֔ים כִּֽי־נָפַ֥ל פַּֽחַד־הַיְּהוּדִ֖ים עֲלֵיהֶֽם׃

Because these four entities — the light of Torah, the gladness of the holidays, the joy of circumcision, the honor of *tefillin* — are the very antithesis of Amalek, one of that evil nation's main objectives is to eradicate them from the world.

This is evident from *Rashi*'s interpretation of the words אֲשֶׁר קָרְךָ בַּדֶּרֶךְ (lit., "that [Amalek] happened upon you on the way"; *Deuteronomy* 25:18) — *Rashi* associates קָרְךָ with קַר, or "cold." This conveys the idea that by attacking Israel, Amalek, as it were, "cooled the heat" of the miracles which occurred by the Red Sea. In this manner Amalek attempted to snuff out the "light," or fire, of the Torah, the force which figuratively melts away all obstructions between Hashem and Man, and allows him to form an eternal bond with the Divine. This is alluded to by the verse, "But you who *cling* to HASHEM" (ibid., 4:4) — heat melts objects together, while cold causes them to contract and remain apart.

Rashi also relates קָרְךָ with מִקְרֶה, which means "natural circumstance." According to this interpretation, Amalek denied the existence of Divine Providence, a theological position which negates the idea of celebrating *Yom Tov,* the holy days on which we commemorate the miracles of the redemption from Egypt. In this manner, Amalek attempted to douse the "gladness" of *Yom Tov* which the Jewish People experienced.

Another association of קָרְךָ which *Rashi* makes is with קֶרִי, a bodily discharge that renders one impure. This interpretation suggests that Amalek tried to eradicate the *mitzvah* of *bris milah* (ritual circumcision). One of the effects of *bris milah* is to curb a person's desires. Amalek could not tolerate this. Thus, that evil nation attempted to eradicate the spiritual "joy" which *bris milah* brought to the Jewish People.

The verse in *Deuteronomy* concludes by defining the root of Amalek's evil — "he did not fear God." Amalek's brand of atheism completely negated the *mitzvah* of *tefillin,* about which the verse says, "All the peoples of the earth will see that *the Name of HASHEM is proclaimed over you,* and they will fear you" (ibid., 28:10). Amalek knew that as long as the Jewish People continued to don *tefillin,* no nation would dare rise up against them, for this *mitzvah* left no doubt in anyone's mind that Israel was God's Chosen People. Amalek decided that the most effective way to overcome this obstacle would be to introduce atheistic concepts to the Jews. If he would do so successfully, he knew, the Jews would stop donning *tefillin,* and then the nations would no longer regard Israel with such awe. For the same reason Haman — the embodiment of Amalek

city, wherever the King's command and his decree reached, the Jews had gladness and joy, a feast and a holiday. Moreover, many from among the people of the land professed themselves Jews, for the fear of the Jews had fallen upon them.

---

in Mordechai's generation — passed a decree prohibiting the *mitzvah* of *tefillin.*

17. וְרַבִּים מֵעַמֵּי הָאָרֶץ מִתְיַהֲדִים כִּי־נָפַל פַּחַד־הַיְּהוּדִים עֲלֵיהֶם — Moreover, many from among the people of the land professed themselves Jews, for the fear of the Jews had fallen upon them.

If "the fear of the Jews" which fell upon the nations in Mordechai's day prompted so many gentiles to convert to Judaism, why did this phenomenon not occur in Moses' generation, when Israel received the Torah? It would seem that "the fear of the Jews" should also have fallen upon the nations at that time, for the Sages teach that the sounds of the reception of the Torah at Mount Sinai were heard in every part of the world, and that the kings of the nations sat quivering and singing songs of praise to Hashem in their palaces (see *Zevachim* 116a).

The answer is that spiritual inspiration can emanate only from the Jewish People. This is evident from the verse "*You* are My witnesses, says HASHEM" (*Isaiah* 43:10) — since the Jewish People are the only nation to merit direct Divine revelation, they alone are Hashem's "witnesses." Other nations can only draw spiritual inspiration from Israel, the repository of spirituality in this world. Even the spiritual yearnings of a prospective convert actually emanate from the Jewish People.

Now, in Moses' day, Hashem had to coerce the Jewish People to accept the Torah. As the Sages said: "[The verse says,] 'Moses brought the people forth from the camp toward God, *and they stood at the bottom of the mountain'* (*Exodus* 19:17). R' Avdimi bar Chama bar Chassa said: This teaches that the Holy One, Blessed is He, held the mountain over [the Jewish People]..and said to them, 'If you accept the Torah, good. But if you do not, that place shall become your graveyard' " (*Shabbos* 88a). Since the Jewish People's spiritual beliefs were based solely on mortal fear of HASHEM, and not on reverence and awe, they did not inspire other nations to serve Him. However, in Mordechai's generation, when the Jewish People voluntarily accepted the Torah [ibid.] and their hearts overflowed with love[1] for HASHEM, their spiritual influence spread far and wide.

---

1. Our father Abraham is called "My beloved" (*Isaiah* 41:8). Because of his great love for Hashem he was able to convert tens of thousands, inspiring them to commit themselves to Torah (*Rambam, Sefer HaMitzvos* #3). (See also *Rambam, Hil. Avodah Zarah* 1:3; *Onkelos, Genesis* 12:5.)

This is a very important principle to keep in mind when trying to strengthen other people's commitment to *mitzvah* observance!

❦ ❦ ❦

The commentators ask: Why did Mordechai's *Beis Din* accept these converts? *Halachah* clearly states that a person who converts to Judaism due to a sense of fear is not considered a legitimate convert (see *Rambam, Hilchos Issurei Biyah,* Ch. 13:15). The reason for this law is that conversion to Judaism must emanate from genuine love of God, and not fear. This is why a gentile who expresses an interest in converting should initially be discouraged to do so. He should be reminded of the Jewish People's miserable condition among the nations and the numerous hardships they constantly encounter. Only if he responds that he nevertheless desires to be a Jew may he be accepted as a prospective convert (see *Yevamos* 47a).

Rama, in *Mechir Yayin,* explains that "The fear of the Jews had fallen upon them" does not mean that the gentiles were *afraid* of the Jews, but rather that they adopted the Jewish fear — Fear of Hashem.

However, one may rightly wonder how the gentiles managed such unprecedented spiritual growth. What prompted them to forsake their heathen customs and suddenly adopt the Torah way of life? It must be that they were greatly influenced by Mordechai. Just as it is said, "The entire world is sustained on the merit of My son Chanina" (*Taanis* 10a), so too, the fear of heaven of the entire world was sustained on the merit of Mordechai.

This explains the wording of the verse, "For Mordechai the Jew was viceroy to King Ahasuerus; he was a great man among the Jews, and found favor with the multitude of his brethren; he sought the good of his *people* (לְעַמּוֹ) and was concerned for the welfare (וְדֹבֵר שָׁלוֹם) of all his *posterity* (זַרְעוֹ)" (10:3). Why are the Jews first called Mordechai's "people," and then, "his posterity"?

The answer is that although Mordechai beseeched HASHEM for "the *good* of his people," he also showed concern for their שָׁלוֹם (translated as "welfare," but the word also means "peaceful relationship") with HASHEM by imbuing them with fear of Heaven. Mordechai knew that nothing in the world can arouse deep-rooted peace between HASHEM and Israel like genuine fear of Heaven. Thus, since the Jewish People's fear of Heaven was nurtured by Mordechai, the verse calls them Mordechai's "posterity," for in the same manner that a son relies completely on his father for sustenance, the Jewish People relied completely on Mordechai to inspire them with genuine fear of Heaven.

Along the same lines, my friend R' Moshe Lieber explained why Zeresh is referred to in the song *Shoshanas Yaakov* as "the wife of my *terrorizer,*" for ostensibly, it would have been more appropriate to call her "the wife of *the wicked man.*" The answer is that the author of *Shoshanas Yaakov* alludes to the paralyzing fear which Haman instilled into the Jews through his evil decree. By brazenly threatening the existence of HASHEM's nation, Haman effectively weakened the faith of the Jews.[1] Consequently, their spiritual zeal waned and they became lax in *mitzvah* observance, which in turn deterred HASHEM from intervening on their behalf. However, in the true spirit of וְנַהֲפוֹךְ הוּא ("complete turnabout"), Mordechai rectified the situation by bolstering the Jewish People's fear of Heaven and faith in HASHEM. This prompted HASHEM to perform great miracles for the sake of the Jews and redeem them from utter destruction.

❧ ❧ ❧

Two questions come to mind: First, as asked above, why did Mordechai's *Beis Din* accept these converts?

The second question is why the *Megillah* exclusively refers to the Jewish People as יְהוּדִים, as in this verse, and never once uses the various other names which appear in Scripture, such as בְּנֵי יִשְׂרָאֵל or בְּנֵי יַעֲקֹב.

To answer both questions, let us first define what prompted Hashem to perform the miracles of Purim. According to *Sfas Emes,* it was the fact that the Jewish People gathered together and formed a single united assembly, in fulfillment of Esther's command, "Go, *assemble* all the Jews. . ." (4:16). In order to awaken such feelings of brotherly love among the Jewish People, the Sages instituted the *mitzvah* of *mishlo'ach manos* (sending portions of food to one another). The love evoked by the miracles of Purim and, later, by the *mishlo'ach manos,* caused Hashem to bring about yet another miracle — the building of the Second Temple. Since the Jews' unity and brotherly love were the foundation stones of the Second Temple, when 420 years later these feelings were replaced by baseless hatred, the Temple was swiftly destroyed.

This also explains why Esther said, "Go, assemble the Jews . . . and fast *for me*" (ibid.). Esther's intention could not have been merely to declare a public fast, since the Jews had been fasting long before she made this decree, as the verse says, "In every province. . .there was great mourning among the Jews, *with fasting. . .*" (4:3). Rather, her intention was to evoke feelings of brotherly love among the Jewish People. Until this point, each Jew had been fasting over the personal hardship that he experienced on an individual basis. Esther introduced the idea that they should also fast for the hardships being experienced by their *fellow Jews,* such as herself.

The focal point of this unprecedented level of solidarity among Jews was the Tribe of Judah. The ability to unite the Jewish People had been

---

1. Haman followed the example of his wicked ancestors, who attacked the Jewish People in the desert (see *Deuteronomy* 25:18). *Rashi* explains that by attacking the Israelites, Amalek dispelled the aura of invincibility which enveloped them following the exodus from Egypt.

bestowed upon this Tribe by Jacob the Patriarch shortly before his death, as the verse says, "Judah, your brothers shall acknowledge you" (*Genesis* 49:8) — this means that Judah would be the source of Jewish leadership and royalty.[1] Some commentators say this is why the *Targum* from this point on in the Pentateuch stops referring to the Jewish People as עִבְרָאֵי ("Hebrews"), and instead calls them יְהוּדָאֵי ("Judahites") — because the Tribe of Judah's unifying qualities fused the other Tribes into a single consolidated nation, it is only fitting that its name symbolize the Jewish nation.[2] Indeed, the word "Jew" is derived from the first three letters of יְהוּדִי ("Yehu"). Judah's unifying role is clearly illustrated in the passage, "Thus said HASHEM: I shall take the staff of Joseph which is in the hand of Ephraim, and of the Tribes of Israel associated with him, *and I will place the staff of Judah upon it and make them into one stick;* they shall be joined in My hand" (*Ezekiel* 37:19). This verse teaches that in the end of days a king of Davidic lineage from the Tribe of Judah will unite Israel under one kingdom. With this, we have answered our second question.

Let us now address our first question — Why did Mordechai's *Beis Din* accept these converts? In reference to the Tribe of Zebulun, the verse says, "The Tribes will assemble at the mount, there they will slaughter offerings of righteousness, for by the riches of the sea they will be nourished, and by the treasures concealed in the sand" (*Deuteronomy* 33:19). According to *Rashi,* one way to interpret the verse is that gentiles will come from afar to trade with Zebulun. The Tribe's merchants will persuade them to go to Jerusalem and see how Jews serve God. The visitors will be so impressed by the sight of the entire Jewish nation worshiping a single God (unlike the polytheistic rituals of heathen nations) and eating the same food (sacrificial offerings) that many will convert and bring offerings to God. From *Rashi*'s interpretation we learn an astounding principle — unity among the Jewish People evokes such intense spiritual power that it can independently induce gentiles to abandon their heathen beliefs and convert to Judaism!

Mordechai and Esther successfully instilled a sense of unity among the Jewish People. Much like *Rashi*'s interpretation of the verse in *Deuteronomy* (33:19), the gentiles of Mordechai's day were also astounded by the palpable sense of unity pervading the community of Jewish exiles. The sight of a united people worshiping the same God and sending *mishlo'ach manos* to each other made the gentiles acutely aware of the inherent disparity of their

1. This is why the brothers instinctively blamed Judah for the incident with Joseph. According to *Rashi* on *Genesis* 38:1, the brothers said to Judah, "You told us to sell him! Had you advised us to send him back to Father, we would have listened!" This illustrates the extent of Judah's influence over the other Tribes.

2. This is why Mordechai is referred to as מָרְדֳּכַי הַיְּהוּדִי ("Mordechai *the Judahite*") even though he was from the Tribe of Benjamin — the *Megillah* refers to his leadership qualities in unifying the Jewish People, not to his lineal ancestry.

own society. This is what the verse means by "the fear of the Jews had fallen upon them" — the contrast between the close-knit Jewish community and their own aloof and impersonal culture became glaringly obvious, and suddenly, they felt frightened at the prospect of continuing to live out their lives as isolated individuals. The comforting harmony and warmth enveloping the Jews beckoned invitingly to these gentiles, prompting them to "profess themselves Jews." Thus, we see that the converts in Mordechai's day were driven by true appreciation of the essence of being Jewish, and not merely by blind fear.

Midrash Shocher Tov in fact alludes to this concept: "You will not find a more difficult and dark period for Israel than the days of Haman, when he said to Ahasuerus, 'There is a certain people *scattered abroad and dispersed* among the peoples in all the provinces of your realm' (3:8). As soon as Esther learned of this, she began saying, 'Go, *assemble* all the Jews' (4:16)." Thus, we see that the stronger sense of unity which Mordechai and Esther instilled among the Jews was the catalyst which brought about the redemption.

Along the same lines, *Shem MiShmuel* explains that since Amalek draws his strength from disunity, the only way to overcome him is through solidarity and cohesion. This is why the *mitzvah* to exterminate Amalek is preceded by the *mitzvah* of appointing a monarch, whose primary responsibility is to unite the Jewish People. We may infer from this that on Purim the Jewish People reached the same degree of unity as in earlier days, when a monarch had ruled over the nation.

The *Shem MiShmuel* then cites *R' Bunim of P'shische*'s interpretation of the verse, "Many are the designs in a man's heart, but it is God's plan that will be fulfilled" (*Proverbs* 19:21) — "God's plan shall be fulfilled" *through the very deeds of a man,* even though God's plans may actually conflict with that man's designs. Haman was a perfect example of such an individual. He and his cronies decided to take the offensive against the Jewish People because they intuitively felt that otherwise the Second Temple would soon be built. However, their efforts backfired — the very decree which they thought would liquidate the Jews actually *united* the Jews, a development which sapped away their Amalekite power and eventually led to their downfall.

The degree of Jewish unity in Mordechai's generation was so great that the Sages allowed themselves to make an unprecedented decision: They set two separate dates for the celebration of Purim (the 14th of *Adar* for unwalled cities, the 15th for walled cities). Traditionally the Sages took great care not to institute such decrees for fear that they would promote factionalism among the Jews. However, when it came to setting the date of Purim, they discerned that the Jewish People's intense brotherly love would compensate for differences of time and space. Thus, they saw no danger in setting two different dates for Purim.

א וּבִשְׁנֵים עָשָׂר חֹדֶשׁ הוּא־חֹדֶשׁ אֲדָר בִּשְׁלוֹשָׁה
עָשָׂר יוֹם בּוֹ אֲשֶׁר הִגִּיעַ דְּבַר־הַמֶּלֶךְ וְדָתוֹ לְהֵעָשׂוֹת
בַּיּוֹם אֲשֶׁר שִׂבְּרוּ אֹיְבֵי הַיְּהוּדִים לִשְׁלוֹט בָּהֶם
וְנַהֲפוֹךְ הוּא אֲשֶׁר יִשְׁלְטוּ הַיְּהוּדִים הֵמָּה בְּשֹׂנְאֵיהֶם׃
ב נִקְהֲלוּ הַיְּהוּדִים בְּעָרֵיהֶם בְּכָל־מְדִינוֹת הַמֶּלֶךְ
אֲחַשְׁוֵרוֹשׁ לִשְׁלֹחַ יָד בִּמְבַקְשֵׁי רָעָתָם וְאִישׁ לֹא־
ג עָמַד לִפְנֵיהֶם כִּי־נָפַל פַּחְדָּם עַל־כָּל־הָעַמִּים׃ וְכָל־
שָׂרֵי הַמְּדִינוֹת וְהָאֲחַשְׁדַּרְפְּנִים וְהַפַּחוֹת וְעֹשֵׂי
הַמְּלָאכָה אֲשֶׁר לַמֶּלֶךְ מְנַשְּׂאִים אֶת־הַיְּהוּדִים כִּי־
ד נָפַל פַּחַד־מָרְדֳּכַי עֲלֵיהֶם׃ כִּי־גָדוֹל מָרְדֳּכַי בְּבֵית
הַמֶּלֶךְ וְשָׁמְעוֹ הוֹלֵךְ בְּכָל־הַמְּדִינוֹת כִּי־הָאִישׁ
ה מָרְדֳּכַי הוֹלֵךְ וְגָדוֹל׃ וַיַּכּוּ הַיְּהוּדִים בְּכָל־אֹיְבֵיהֶם
מַכַּת־חֶרֶב וְהֶרֶג וְאַבְדָן וַיַּעֲשׂוּ בְשֹׂנְאֵיהֶם כִּרְצוֹנָם׃

IX

5. וַיַּכּוּ הַיְּהוּדִים בְּכָל־אֹיְבֵיהֶם מַכַּת־חֶרֶב וְהֶרֶג וְאַבְדָן וַיַּעֲשׂוּ בְשֹׂנְאֵיהֶם כִּרְצוֹנָם — And the Jews struck at all their enemies with the sword, slaughtering and annihilating; they treated their enemies as they pleased

Ne'os Hadeshe asks why this victory is not mentioned in the Purim *Al Hanissim,* the supplementary prayer said in the *Amidah*, much as the Maccabees' military victories over the Greeks *are* mentioned in the Chanukah *Al Hanissim.*

The answer is provided by the *Targum on Megillas Esther* (9:12-17), which teaches that all the gentiles killed by the Jews on Purim were of Amalekite descent. This means that by striking down their enemies, the Jews of Mordechai's generation also fulfilled the Torah-ordained commandment to exterminate Amalek. Hence, the battle is not mentioned in *Al Hanissim* because this supplementary prayer specifically expresses gratitude to Hashem for the *miracles* He performed on our behalf, not for the *mitzvos* He gave us the opportunity to fulfill. The regular daily prayer service already contains several passages in which we express gratitude to Hashem for the opportunity to perform *mitzvos.*

The *Targum's* explanation also clarifies why Esther requested that Ahasuerus grant the Jews an additional day to wage war against their enemies. As the verse says, "Esther replied: 'If it pleases your Majesty, allow the Jews who are in Shushan to act tomorrow as they did today, and let

9/1-5

[1] *And so, on the thirteenth day of the twelfth
month, which is the month of Adar, when the
King's command and edict were about to be en-
forced — on the very day that the enemies of the
Jews expected to gain the upper hand over them —
and it was turned about: The Jews gained the upper
hand over their adversaries;* [2] *the Jews organized
themselves in their cities throughout all the provinces
of King Ahasuerus, to attack those who sought their
hurt; and no one stood in their way, for fear of them
had fallen upon all the peoples.* [3] *Moreover, all the
provincial officials, satraps, and governors and those
that conduct the King's affairs, deferred to the Jews
because the fear of Mordechai had fallen upon them.*
[4] *For Mordechai was now preeminent in the royal
palace and his fame was spreading throughout all
the provinces, for the man Mordechai grew increas-
ingly greater.* [5] *And the Jews struck at all their
enemies with the sword, slaughtering and annihilating; they treated their enemies as they pleased.*

Haman's ten sons be hanged on the gallows' " (9:13). Ostensibly Esther's request seems unnecessary, since by this stage in the war Israel's enemies were subdued and "the fear of the Jews had fallen upon them" (8:17). The answer is that Esther wished to draw a clear distinction between the battle for survival, which had ended victoriously for the Jews, and the fulfillment of the *mitzvah* to exterminate Amalek. She wished to dedicate a separate day exclusively for fulfilling this Torah-ordained commandment. And even though the Jews could have proceeded to kill the Amalekites without the King's explicit consent, Esther knew that it was necessary to obtain royal authorization, for the *mitzvah* may only be fulfilled when the Jewish People are fully empowered to do so (see *Hagahos Maimonios, Hil. Melachim* 5:1). On that additional day which Ahasuerus granted to the Jews, numerous Amalekites were killed. It culminated with Haman and his ten sons being hanged on the very same pole he had prepared for Mordechai. This event was a great sanctification of Hashem's Name in the world.

This explanation provides additional proof for the Sages' contention that the desert generation accepted the Torah out of fear, while Mordechai's generation accepted it out of love (*Shabbos* 88a): From the fact that

ו וּבְשׁוּשַׁ֣ן הַבִּירָ֗ה הָרְג֤וּ הַיְּהוּדִים֙ וְאַבֵּ֔ד חֲמֵ֥שׁ מֵא֖וֹת
ז אִֽישׁ׃ וְאֵ֣ת ׀
פַּרְשַׁנְדָּ֑תָא וְאֵ֣ת ׀
דַּלְפ֖וֹן וְאֵ֥ת ׀
ח אַסְפָּֽתָא׃ וְאֵ֣ת ׀
פּוֹרָ֑תָא וְאֵ֣ת ׀
אֲדַלְיָ֖א וְאֵ֥ת ׀
ט אֲרִידָֽתָא׃ וְאֵ֣ת ׀
פַּרְמַ֙שְׁתָּא֙ וְאֵ֣ת ׀
אֲרִיסַ֔י וְאֵ֣ת ׀
אֲרִדַ֖י וְאֵ֥ת ׀
י וַיְזָֽתָא׃ עֲשֶׂ֗רֶת
בְּנֵ֨י הָמָ֧ן בֶּֽן־הַמְּדָ֛תָא צֹרֵ֥ר הַיְּהוּדִ֖ים הָרָ֑גוּ וּבַּבִּזָּ֕ה לֹ֥א
יא שָֽׁלְח֖וּ אֶת־יָדָֽם׃ בַּיּ֣וֹם הַה֗וּא בָּ֣א מִסְפַּ֧ר הַהֲרוּגִ֛ים
יב בְּשׁוּשַׁ֥ן הַבִּירָ֖ה לִפְנֵ֥י הַמֶּֽלֶךְ׃ וַיֹּ֨אמֶר הַמֶּ֜לֶךְ לְאֶסְתֵּ֣ר
הַמַּלְכָּ֗ה בְּשׁוּשַׁ֨ן הַבִּירָ֜ה הָרְג֨וּ הַיְּהוּדִ֜ים וְאַבֵּ֗ד חֲמֵ֧שׁ
מֵא֣וֹת אִ֗ישׁ וְאֵת֙ עֲשֶׂ֣רֶת בְּנֵי־הָמָ֔ן בִּשְׁאָ֛ר מְדִינ֥וֹת
הַמֶּ֖לֶךְ מֶ֣ה עָשׂ֑וּ וּמַה־שְּׁאֵֽלָתֵךְ֙ וְיִנָּ֣תֵֽן לָ֔ךְ וּמַה־
יג בַּקָּשָׁתֵ֥ךְ ע֖וֹד וְתֵעָֽשׂ׃ וַתֹּ֤אמֶר אֶסְתֵּר֙ אִם־עַל־הַמֶּ֣לֶךְ
ט֔וֹב יִנָּתֵ֣ן גַּם־מָחָ֗ר לַיְּהוּדִים֙ אֲשֶׁ֣ר בְּשׁוּשָׁ֔ן לַעֲשׂ֖וֹת
כְּדָ֣ת הַיּ֑וֹם וְאֵ֛ת עֲשֶׂ֥רֶת בְּנֵי־הָמָ֖ן יִתְל֥וּ עַל־הָעֵֽץ׃
יד וַיֹּ֤אמֶר הַמֶּ֙לֶךְ֙ לְהֵעָשׂ֣וֹת כֵּ֔ן וַתִּנָּתֵ֥ן דָּ֖ת בְּשׁוּשָׁ֑ן

Mordechai's generation requested another day to fulfill the *mitzvah* of exterminating Amalek, we see that they eagerly sought ways to perform as many *mitzvos* as possible. On the other hand, regarding the generation of wandering in the desert the verse says, "They journeyed a three-day distance from the Mountain of HASHEM" (*Numbers* 10:33) — according to *Ramban,* this means that they ran far from Mount Sinai like a child escaping school, lest Hashem decree more *mitzvos.*

9/6-14 6 *In Shushan the Capital, the Jews slew and annihi-*
lated five hundred men. 7 *including*
Parshandatha and
Dalphon and
Aspatha 8 *and*
Poratha and
Adalia and
Aridatha 9 *and*
Parmashta and
Arisai and
Aridai and
Vaizatha 10 *the ten*
sons of Haman, son of Hammedatha, the Jews' enemy; but they did not lay their hand on the spoils.
11 *That same day the number of those killed in*
Shushan the Capital was reported to the King. 12 *The*
King said to Queen Esther, "In Shushan the Capital the Jews have slain and annihilated five hundred men as well as the ten sons of Haman; what must they have done in the rest of the King's provinces! What is your request now? It shall be granted you. What is your petition further? It shall be fulfilled."
13 *Esther replied, "If it pleases His Majesty, allow the Jews who are in Shushan to act tomorrow as they did today, and let Haman's ten sons be*
hanged on the gallows." 14 *The King ordered that*
this be done. A decree was distributed in Shushan,

---

13. וַתֹּאמֶר אֶסְתֵּר אִם־עַל־הַמֶּלֶךְ טוֹב יִנָּתֵן גַּם־מָחָר לַיְּהוּדִים אֲשֶׁר בְּשׁוּשָׁן לַעֲשׂוֹת כְּדָת הַיּוֹם וְאֵת עֲשֶׂרֶת בְּנֵי־הָמָן יִתְלוּ עַל־הָעֵץ — Esther replied, "If it pleases His Majesty, allow the Jews who are in Shushan to act tomorrow as they did today, and let Haman's ten sons be hanged on the gallows."

The *Yeshuah Gedolah* raises the following question: Why did Esther ask the King to grant the Jews an additional day to wage battle against their enemies? Surely she did not think that the Jews would manage to exterminate every last Amalekite in just one more day! If so, why did she make such an impassioned plea for this 24-hour extension?

Once again, the answer lies in a deeper understanding of Esther's life-mission to rectify King Saul's sin (see notes on 4:13). As *Pachad Yitzchak* points out, the Jewish People fought two types of wars against Amalek: In the days of Moses they waged a defensive war in response to Amalek's unprovoked attack, as the verse says, "Amalek came and battled Israel in Rephidim" (*Exodus* 17:8). In King Saul's day the Jewish People took the offensive, as the verse says, "Samuel said to Saul. . .'Now go attack Amalek and seize all that he owns" (*I Samuel* 15:1-3).

Similarly, in Mordechai's day the Jews fought a defensive war on the 13th of *Adar.* On that day, the Jews successfully defended themselves against the gentiles who acted upon Haman's edict and attacked the Jewish People. Esther, however, was not satisfied, for she knew that Saul's sinful reticence against Amalek could only be rectified by the Jewish People waging an *offensive* war against the Amalekites of Haman's generation. This is why Esther begged Ahasuerus to grant the Jews of Shushan one more day to pursue the Amalekites — on the 14th of *Adar* the Jews took the offensive against their enemies, thereby rectifying the sin committed by King Saul years earlier.

❦ ❦ ❦

According to *Rambam,* in the future all the Books of the Prophets and the Writings will be nullified except for *Megillas Esther.* Only the *Megillah* shall endure forever alongside the Pentateuch and the Oral Law. This concept is alluded to in our verse: The word "tomorrow" (מָחָר) can also mean "in the future," as *Rashi* explains regarding the verse, "If your child asks you *tomorrow,* saying, 'What are the testimonies and decrees and the ordinances that HASHEM, our God, commanded you?" (*Deuteronomy* 6:20).

Also, as we have explained earlier, all references to "the King" in the *Megillah* may also be taken as referring to Hashem, the King of Kings. From this perspective, Esther's request takes on new meaning: She requested of "the King" (Hashem) to allow the Jews "tomorrow" (in the Messianic Era) "to act as they did today" (to fulfill the *mitzvah* of exterminating Amalek).

14. וְאֵת עֲשֶׂרֶת בְּנֵי־הָמָן תָּלוּ — And they hanged Haman's ten sons.
The Sages said, "Rabbah bar Ofran introduced [his lecture on] this Scriptural portion [the Book of *Esther*] with the following verse: 'And I will set My throne in Elam and will destroy from there kings and princes' (*Jeremiah* 49:38) — 'king' refers to Vashti, 'and princes,' to Haman and his ten sons" (*Megillah* 10b).

Shem MiShmuel points out that the verse in *Jeremiah* makes unconventional use of the word "throne" (כִּסְאִי), which usually conveys revealed Divine Providence. This kind of manifest Godly supervision can exist only within the Land of Israel, but not in such places as "Elam," a reference to the

Persian and Median exile. Thus, *Shem MiShmuel* concludes, the intention of the verse is unclear.

The explanation may be as follows: As we have mentioned earlier, the Jews of Mordechai's generation fulfilled the *mitzvah* to exterminate Amalek by slaying Haman and his ten sons. In this manner they made Hashem's throne complete, for we know that until the descendants of Amalek are destroyed, Hashem's throne cannot be complete (*Rashi* on *Exodus* 17:16). As a result, an unprecedented event occurred — Divine Providence became manifest in the darkness of exile, outside the boundaries of the Land of Israel. This is why the verse in *Jeremiah* uses the word "throne" in relation to the Persian exile.[1]

Another question arises regarding the Sages' statement quoted above: Why did they associate Vashti with Haman and his ten sons? She was not of Amalekite descent, but rather the daughter of Belshezzar son of Nebuchadnezzar, King of Babylonia.

The answer is that if a person behaves in the manner of an Amalekite, it is as though that person is a direct descendant of that evil nation.[2] According to *Shem MiShmuel*, Shabbos is the very antithesis of Amalek.[3] Vashti

---

1. This principle explains the connection between the miracles of Purim and the Jewish People's decision to reaccept the Torah: As we have explained above, the Jews of Mordechai's generation fulfilled the *mitzvah* to exterminate Amalek by killing Haman and his ten sons, and thereby caused Hashem's Name to become complete. We also know that the Torah is in essence one of Hashem's Divine Names (*Ramban,* introduction to his commentary on the Torah). Thus, when Hashem's Name became complete, the ephemeral light of the Torah correspondingly grew brighter, beckoning the Jewish People to draw closer. The Jews became enraptured by the Torah and immediately reaccepted it from love.

2. See 8:11.

3. *Shem MiShmuel* cites *Pirkei D'Rebbi Eliezer,* which says, "One verse says '*Remember* what Amalek did to you' (*Deuteronomy* 25:17), and another verse says, '*Remember* to sanctify the Shabbos' (*Exodus* 20:8). This verse says 'remember' and this verse says 'remember'! Moses in essence said to [the Israelites], 'There is no similarity between a cup of fine wine and a cup of vinegar — *remember* to sanctify this one, and *remember* to destroy and exterminate the offspring of that one' " (see *Midrash Tanchuma, Parshas Ki Seitzei*). According to the *Shem MiShmuel,* this *Midrash* teaches that Amalek is the antithesis of Shabbos. This concept is also evident in the Sages' statement, "Had the Israelites observed their first Shabbos no enemy would have ruled over them, for it is written, 'It happened on the seventh day that some of the people went out to gather, and they did not find' (*Exodus* 16:27), and a few verses later it is written, 'Amalek came and battled Israel in Rephidim' (ibid., 17:8)" (*Shabbos* 118b).

Haman remained true to his nature when he spoke slanderously of the Jewish People before Ahasuerus. According to the Sages, he said to Ahasuerus, "They waste the entire year, [avoiding the King's work] with excuses such as, 'Today is the Sabbath' [and] 'Today is Passover' " (*Megillah* 13b). It was no coincidence that he spoke contemptuously of Shabbos observance! And why did he specifically mention Passover? He could just as well have spoken of the Jews' unwillingness to work on Sukkos. The answer is that since the Torah refers to Passover as "Shabbos" (see *Leviticus* 23:15), Haman deliberately spoke disparagingly about this holiday.

ט/טו אֲשֶׁר־בְּשׁוּשָׁן גַּם בְּיוֹם אַרְבָּעָה עָשָׂר לְחֹדֶשׁ אֲדָר
וַיַּהַרְגוּ בְשׁוּשָׁן שְׁלֹשׁ מֵאוֹת אִישׁ וּבַבִּזָּה לֹא שָׁלְחוּ
טז אֶת־יָדָם׃ וּשְׁאָר הַיְּהוּדִים אֲשֶׁר בִּמְדִינוֹת הַמֶּלֶךְ נִקְהֲלוּ
ו וְעָמֹד עַל־נַפְשָׁם וְנוֹחַ מֵאֹיְבֵיהֶם וְהָרוֹג בְּשֹׂנְאֵיהֶם
חֲמִשָּׁה וְשִׁבְעִים אָלֶף וּבַבִּזָּה לֹא שָׁלְחוּ אֶת־יָדָם׃

---

proved herself a genuine Amalekite by brazenly desecrating the holiness of Shabbos — the Sages teach that she would undress Jewish girls and force them to do work on Shabbos (*Megillah* 12b). In kind for her sin, she was executed on Shabbos. Thus, by associating Vashti's death to the death of Haman and his ten sons, the Sages taught that she was as much of an Amalekite as they.

15. וַיִּקָּהֲלוּ הַיְּהוּדִים אֲשֶׁר־בְּשׁוּשָׁן גַּם בְּיוֹם אַרְבָּעָה עָשָׂר לְחֹדֶשׁ אֲדָר וַיַּהַרְגוּ בְשׁוּשָׁן שְׁלֹשׁ מֵאוֹת אִישׁ — The Jews that were in Shushan assembled again on the fourteenth day of the month of Adar; and slew three hundred men.

Following the Jews' staggering victories of the previous day, in which they slew 75,000 of their enemies, the very fact that they found anyone against whom to wage war was a miracle in its own right. Very likely, Ahasuerus consented to Esther's request for an additional day of battle because he reasoned that no anti-Semite in his right mind would dare raise a hand against the Jews. He never dreamed that the Jews would manage to find 300 more enemies to slay.

Hashem brought about this miracle in the same manner as in the Israelites' war against King Sihon, about whom the verse says, "Sihon King of Heshbon was not willing to let us pass through it, for HASHEM, your God, *hardened his spirit and made his heart stubborn,* in order to give him into your hand, as on this very day" (*Deuteronomy* 2:30). So too, Hashem instilled into the anti-Semites' hearts a stubborn determination to rise against the Jews despite their overwhelming victories of the previous day. By delivering the anti-Semites into their hands, Hashem demonstrated that the Jews of Mordechai's generation were as beloved to Him as the generation which conquered the Land of Israel in the times of Moses and Joshua.

This also explains why the *Megillah* is read on the 15th of *Adar* only in Shushan and in cities in Israel which were walled in the days of Joshua (as opposed to unwalled cities, which read the *Megillah* on the 14th): Just as Hashem performed a miracle and stirred the enemies of the Jews in Mordechai's time to emerge from their homes and take up arms, He performed the same miracle in the days of Joshua by prompting the Canaanites to choose armed resistance over pursuing peace treaties. As the

that were in Shushan assembled again on the fourteenth day of the month of Adar; and slew three hundred men in Shushan; but they did not lay their hand on the spoils.

16 *The rest of the Jews throughout the King's provinces organized and defended themselves gaining relief from their foes, slaying seventy-five thousand of their enemies — but they did not lay their hand on the spoils.*

---

verse says, "For it was HASHEM's doing to *stiffen their hearts to give battle to Israel,* in order that they might be conquered without compromise and exterminated, as HASHEM had commanded Moses" (*Joshua* 11:20).

With this, we may better understand the words of the *Rambam*: "Even though Shushan the Capital was not walled in the days of Joshua son of Nun, [the *Megillah*] is read on the fifteenth [of *Adar*] because the miracle occurred there, as the verse says, 'and they rested on the fifteenth of the month' (v. 18). And why did [the Sages] make [the date of the *Megillah* reading] conditional on [whether the cities were walled] in the times of Joshua son of Nun? In order to *ascribe honor to the Land of Israel,* which in those days lay in ruins" (*Hilchos Megillah,* Ch. 1, Law 5). How did the Sages "ascribe honor to the Land of Israel" by stipulating that walled cities from the days of Joshua read the *Megillah* on the same day as it is read in Shushan? By reminding us that years earlier, in Joshua's time, Hashem performed the same miracle as in Shushan in order to enable the Israelites to capture the Land of Israel.

This miracle will also take place in the times of Messiah, as the verse says in reference to Gog and Magog, "I will arouse and incite you, and I will take you from the far north and bring you to the mountains of Israel. I will strike your bow from your left hand. . ." (*Ezekiel* 39:2,3) — as *Metzudas David* explains, Hashem will instill the nations with confidence and determination in order to lure them into attacking Israel, and thereby bring about their own destruction.

וּבַבִּזָּה לֹא שָׁלְחוּ אֶת־יָדָם — But they did not lay their hand on the spoils. This phrase is repeated three times in the *Megillah. Sfas Emes* says this teaches that the Jewish People in Mordechai's day rectified the sin committed by Israel in the days of King Saul (see *I Samuel* Chap. 15). At that time, Israel committed three sins: 1. Sparing Agag's life. 2. Taking possession of the Amalekites' livestock. 3. Seizing their gold and silver. Thus, by thrice repeating the phrase, "but they did not lay their hand on the spoils," the *Megillah* conveys that Mordechai's generation rectified these three sins.

ט/יז-יט

יז בְּיוֹם־שְׁלֹשָׁה עָשָׂר לְחֹדֶשׁ אֲדָר וְנוֹחַ בְּאַרְבָּעָה
עָשָׂר בּוֹ וְעָשֹׂה אֹתוֹ יוֹם מִשְׁתֶּה וְשִׂמְחָה׃
יח °והיהודיים אֲשֶׁר־בְּשׁוּשָׁן נִקְהֲלוּ בִּשְׁלֹשָׁה עָשָׂר (°וְהַיְּהוּדִים ק׳)
בּוֹ וּבְאַרְבָּעָה עָשָׂר בּוֹ וְנוֹחַ בַּחֲמִשָּׁה עָשָׂר בּוֹ
יט וְעָשֹׂה אֹתוֹ יוֹם מִשְׁתֶּה וְשִׂמְחָה׃ עַל־כֵּן הַיְּהוּדִים
°הפרוזים הַיֹּשְׁבִים בְּעָרֵי הַפְּרָזוֹת עֹשִׂים אֵת (°הַפְּרָזִים ק׳)
יוֹם אַרְבָּעָה עָשָׂר לְחֹדֶשׁ אֲדָר שִׂמְחָה וּמִשְׁתֶּה

However, this explanation is difficult, for we see that in the end Mordechai took possession of Haman's house. And although some commentators say that it was halachically permissible for Mordechai to do so because it became Ahasuerus' property first, it would still seem that Mordechai did not act in the spirit of the verse, "but they did not lay their hand on the spoils."

The answer is that Mordechai did not personally benefit from Haman's possessions. Rather, he dedicated all of Haman's riches to the construction of the Holy Temple. He did this in order to strengthen the faith of the Jewish People, who had given up all hope of ever being redeemed from exile. Mordechai followed King David's example, who seized treasure from temples of idolatry and dedicated it to the building of the Holy Temple. Once again, in the true Purim spirit of וְנַהֲפוֹךְ הוּא, a complete reversal took place: The possessions of Haman, the wicked man who persuaded the King to interrupt the reconstruction of the Holy Temple, were used to *construct* that very Temple!

17-18. בְּיוֹם־שְׁלֹשָׁה עָשָׂר לְחֹדֶשׁ אֲדָר וְנוֹחַ בְּאַרְבָּעָה עָשָׂר בּוֹ וְעָשֹׂה אֹתוֹ יוֹם מִשְׁתֶּה וְשִׂמְחָה׃ וְהַיְּהוּדִים אֲשֶׁר־בְּשׁוּשָׁן נִקְהֲלוּ בִּשְׁלֹשָׁה עָשָׂר בּוֹ וּבְאַרְבָּעָה עָשָׂר בּוֹ וְנוֹחַ בַּחֲמִשָּׁה עָשָׂר בּוֹ וְעָשֹׂה אֹתוֹ יוֹם מִשְׁתֶּה וְשִׂמְחָה — That was the thirteenth day of the month of Adar; and they gained relief on the fourteenth day, making it a day of feasting and gladness. But the Jews that were in Shushan assembled on both the thirteenth and fourteenth, and they gained relief on the fifteenth, making it a day of feasting and gladness.

An obvious question comes to mind: How could the Jews in the other cities have feasted on the fourteenth of *Adar* knowing that their brethren in Shushan were still in mortal danger?

The answer lies in the verse, "These days should be remembered and celebrated by every single generation, family, province, and city; and these days of Purim should never cease among the Jews, nor shall their remembrance perish from their descendants" (v. 28). *Rashi* explains as follows: "The [Jews] assemble and eat and drink together. In this manner, they accept upon themselves that these days of Purim shall never cease among

17 That was the thirteenth day of the month of Adar; and they gained relief on the fourteenth day, making it a day of feasting and gladness. 18 But the Jews that were in Shushan assembled on both the thirteenth and fourteenth, and they gained relief on the fifteenth, making it a day of feasting and gladness. 19 That is why Jewish villagers who live in unwalled towns celebrate the fourteenth day of the month of Adar as an occasion of gladness and feasting,

---

them." The Sages of that generation permitted the Jews living outside Shushan to partake of this *seudas mitzvah*[1] since they saw it as a means of inducing the Jewish People to reaccept the Torah out of love. Reasoning that the merit of such a *seudas mitzvah* would by far exceed that of a public fast, the Sages decided that the most effective way to help their Jewish brothers still waging battle in Shushan would be by declaring the fourteenth of *Adar* a day of feasting and rejoicing.

17. בְּיוֹם־שְׁלֹשָׁה עָשָׂר לְחֹדֶשׁ אֲדָר וְנוֹחַ בְּאַרְבָּעָה עָשָׂר בּוֹ — That was the thirteenth day of the month of Adar; and they gained relief on the fourteenth day.

The *Targum* interprets the verse as follows: "On the thirteenth day of the month of Adar *they slew the descendants of Amalek,* and they gained. . ."

Shem MiShmuel is of the opinion that the Third Temple will not come before Amalek's lineage is exterminated. For proof, he cites two historical precedents: Joshua led the Israelites in battle against Amalek before the Tabernacle was erected (*Exodus* 17:9), and Mordechai and the Jewish People slew their enemies before the Second Temple was built. The *Tzror HaMor* points out that until the Jews of Mordechai's generation waged war against the Amalekites, they were incapable of even returning to the Land of Israel. This is why the verse, "It will be when you enter the Land. . ." (*Deuteronomy* 26:1), is preceded by the commandment to "wipe out the memory of Amalek" (ibid., 25:19) — just as Amalek prevented the Israelites in the desert from reaching the Promised Land, so too, the Amalekites in Mordechai and Ezra's day prevented the Jews from returning to the Land of Israel.

The roots of Amalek's power are revealed by the *Shelah's* interpretation of the verse, "and he said, 'For the hand is on the throne of God; HASHEM maintains a war against Amalek, from generation to generation" (*Exodus* 17:16). According to *Rashi,* the verse teaches that Hashem's throne will not be complete until Amalek is completely exterminated. This is derived from

---

1. See commentary to verse 26 for another explanation of the importance of the feast.

כ וְיוֹם טוֹב וּמִשְׁלוֹחַ מָנוֹת אִישׁ לְרֵעֵהוּ׃ וַיִּכְתֹּב מָרְדֳּכַי
אֶת־הַדְּבָרִים הָאֵלֶּה וַיִּשְׁלַח סְפָרִים אֶל־כָּל־הַיְּהוּדִים
אֲשֶׁר בְּכָל־מְדִינוֹת הַמֶּלֶךְ אֲחַשְׁוֵרוֹשׁ הַקְּרוֹבִים
כא וְהָרְחוֹקִים׃ לְקַיֵּם עֲלֵיהֶם לִהְיוֹת עֹשִׂים אֵת יוֹם
אַרְבָּעָה עָשָׂר לְחֹדֶשׁ אֲדָר וְאֵת יוֹם־חֲמִשָּׁה עָשָׂר בּוֹ
כב בְּכָל־שָׁנָה וְשָׁנָה׃ כַּיָּמִים אֲשֶׁר־נָחוּ בָהֶם הַיְּהוּדִים

---

the unusual spelling of the words כֵּס יָהּ ("the throne of God") — the letter א has been omitted from the word כֵּס ("throne," usually spelled כִּסֵּא), and the letters וה have been omitted from the Divine Name יָהּ. The three omitted letters, appearing as one word, are alluded to in the verse, "For HASHEM has chosen Zion, He has desired it (אִוָּהּ) for His habitation" (*Psalms* 132:13) — the verse teaches that if these three letters would appear in their appropriate places, then Hashem would choose Zion as His land and the Temple Mount as His habitation.

Chasam Sofer refers to these missing letters in his commentary on the verse, "And so, on the thirteenth day of the twelfth month. . .on the very day that the enemies of the Jews expected to gain the upper hand over them — and it was turned about (וְנַהֲפוֹךְ הוּא)" (v. 1). He explains that the word הוא itself became "turned about," and is actually the compound אוה mentioned above. Only when the Jewish People "retrieved" these three letters from Amalek did they manage to return to the Land of Israel and rebuild the Holy Temple.

Hence, we see that the months of *Adar* and *Nissan* are interrelated. The month of *Adar* marks Israel's purification from the spiritual venom of Amalek, which subsequently clears the way for the construction of the Temple in *Nissan* (for we know that the inauguration of the Tabernacle in the desert occurred on *Nissan*). This link between the two months is also evident in the Sages' statement, "From the onset of *Adar* rejoicing is increased" (*Taanis* 29a) — as *Rashi* explains, the Sages said this because both "Purim *and* Passover (which occurs on *Nissan*) were miraculous times for Israel."

There is a question that we have not yet addressed: What was Amalek's motive? Why did he make such persistent efforts to impede the construction of the Holy Temple?

The answer is that unlike the rest of the world's nations, Amalek is not merely driven by jealousy of the Jewish People's special status as God's Chosen People. His hatred runs much deeper. For we must remember that Amalek is a descendant of Esau (*Genesis* 36:12), who sold the birthright to Jacob, the Patriarch of the Jewish People (ibid., 25:31-34). The birthright included two highly valued privileges: possession of the Land of Israel, and the priesthood. Like his ancestor Esau, Amalek never really came to terms

for holiday-making and for sending portions to one
another.
20 *Mordechai recorded these events and sent letters*
to all the Jews throughout the provinces of King
Ahasuerus, near and far, 21 *charging them that they*
should observe annually the fourteenth and fifteenth
day of Adar, 22 *as the days on which the Jews gained*

---

with losing these two precious gifts to Jacob and his descendants. Therefore, he manifests his indignation by preventing Israel from deriving benefit from either of these two privileges — living in the Land of Israel, and serving in Hashem's Temple.

19. וּמִשְׁלֹחַ מָנוֹת אִישׁ לְרֵעֵהוּ — And for sending portions to one another.

According to *Chasam Sofer,* the *mitzvah* of *mishlo'ach manos* ("sending portions to one another") comes to refute Haman's claim to Ahasuerus that the Jews are "a people scattered abroad and dispersed among the people in all the provinces of your realm" (3:8). By sending gifts to one another, the Jewish People strengthen their solidarity and reaffirm their cultural unity. However, one point still remains unclear: Why does the *Halachah* prefer that the *mishlo'ach manos* be delivered by a third party acting as an envoy? Would it not be a friendlier gesture to deliver the portions of food in person?

The answer is as follows: The Sages said that through his deeds, Mordechai rectified certain long-standing criticisms regarding Jacob the Patriarch's behavior towards his older brother, Esau (*Yalkut Shimoni, Toldos* §115). For example, by calling out in a loud voice in the streets of Shushan, Mordechai counteracted the loud cry let out by Esau when he learned that Jacob took away his blessing (*Genesis* 27:38). By refusing to bow down to Haman, Mordechai rectified Jacob's somewhat effusive prostrations in honor of Esau (ibid., 33:3). Similarly, by sending the *mishlo'ach manos* through an envoy, the Jewish People rectified Jacob's decision to appease Esau with extravagant gifts sent by a series of messengers (ibid., 32:14-17). Therefore, just as Jacob's gifts were delivered by an envoy, our gifts must also be delivered by an envoy.

21. לְקַיֵּם עֲלֵיהֶם לִהְיוֹת עֹשִׂים אֵת יוֹם אַרְבָּעָה עָשָׂר לְחֹדֶשׁ אֲדָר וְאֵת יוֹם־חֲמִשָּׁה עָשָׂר בּוֹ בְּכָל־שָׁנָה וְשָׁנָה — Charging them that they should observe annually the fourteenth and fifteenth days of Adar.

The *sefer Shir Ma'on* cites the following passage from the *Talmud Yerushalmi*: "The terms קיום ('charging' or 'establishing upon') and עשייה ('observe' or 'do') appear in the *Megillah* ten times, for they represent the Ten Commandments."

מֵאֹיְבֵיהֶם וְהַחֹדֶשׁ אֲשֶׁר נֶהְפַּךְ לָהֶם מִיָּגוֹן
לְשִׂמְחָה וּמֵאֵבֶל לְיוֹם טוֹב לַעֲשׂוֹת אוֹתָם יְמֵי
מִשְׁתֶּה וְשִׂמְחָה וּמִשְׁלֹחַ מָנוֹת אִישׁ לְרֵעֵהוּ
כג וּמַתָּנוֹת לָאֶבְיוֹנִים: וְקִבֵּל הַיְּהוּדִים אֵת אֲשֶׁר־
כד הֵחֵלּוּ לַעֲשׂוֹת וְאֵת אֲשֶׁר־כָּתַב מָרְדֳּכַי אֲלֵיהֶם: כִּי
הָמָן בֶּן־הַמְּדָתָא הָאֲגָגִי צֹרֵר כָּל־הַיְּהוּדִים חָשַׁב
עַל־הַיְּהוּדִים לְאַבְּדָם וְהִפִּל פּוּר הוּא הַגּוֹרָל
כה לְהֻמָּם וּלְאַבְּדָם: וּבְבֹאָהּ לִפְנֵי הַמֶּלֶךְ אָמַר עִם־
הַסֵּפֶר יָשׁוּב מַחֲשַׁבְתּוֹ הָרָעָה אֲשֶׁר־חָשַׁב עַל־
הַיְּהוּדִים עַל־רֹאשׁוֹ וְתָלוּ אֹתוֹ וְאֶת־בָּנָיו עַל־הָעֵץ:

The correspondence between the *Megillah* and the Ten Commandments can be better understood in light of the Sages' following statement:

"[The verse says,] 'Moses brought the people forth from the camp toward God, *and they stood at the bottom of the mountain*' (*Exodus* 19:17).

"R' Avdimi bar Chama bar Chassa said: This teaches that the Holy One, Blessed is He, held the mountain over them [the Jewish People] as though it were a barrel and said to them, 'If you accept the Torah, good. But if you do not, that place shall become your graveyard.' "

"R' Acha bar Yaakov said: From this, there is a very strong plea of vindication against the Torah."

"Rava said: Nevertheless, they accepted it again in the days of Ahasuerus, as the verse says, 'The Jews confirmed and undertook upon themselves' (*Esther* 9:27) — they confirmed what they had already undertook in the past [i.e., the Torah]" (*Shabbos* 88a).

From the context of this discussion, it is evident that the Jewish People's decision to celebrate Purim on an annual basis was a manifestation of their desire to voluntarily accept the Torah. This is why their decision, represented by the words קיום and עשייה, is repeated 10 times: This significant number shows that the Jewish People's decision to celebrate Purim was equivalent to a new willingness to accept the Ten Commandments which Hashem had forced upon them at Mount Sinai. When a person celebrates Purim, it is considered as though he were receiving the Ten Commandments again at Mount Sinai!

25. וּבְבֹאָהּ לִפְנֵי הַמֶּלֶךְ אָמַר עִם־הַסֵּפֶר יָשׁוּב מַחֲשַׁבְתּוֹ הָרָעָה אֲשֶׁר־חָשַׁב עַל־הַיְּהוּדִים עַל־רֹאשׁוֹ וְתָלוּ אֹתוֹ וְאֶת בָּנָיו עַל־הָעֵץ — But when she appeared before the King, he commanded by means of letters that the

relief from their enemies, and the month which had
been transformed for them from one of sorrow to
gladness, and from mourning to festivity. They were
to observe them as days of feasting and gladness,
and for sending delicacies to one another, and gifts
to the poor. 23 *The Jews undertook to continue the*
practice they had begun, just as Mordechai had
prescribed to them.
24 *For Haman, the son Hammedatha the Agagite,*
enemy of all the Jews, had plotted to destroy the
Jews and had cast a pur — that is, the lot — to
terrify and destroy them: 25 *but when she appeared*
before the King, he commanded by means of letters
that the wicked scheme, which [Haman] had devised
against the Jews, should recoil on his own head;
and they hanged him and his sons on the gallows.

---

wicked scheme, which [Haman] had devised against the Jews, should recoil on his own head; and they hanged him and his sons on the gallows.

The *Targum Sheini* relates that when Esther appeared before Ahasuerus he said, "I shall surely erase the memory of Amalek from under the heavens" (*Exodus* 17:14)."

Coming from the wicked Ahasuerus, this is indeed a very strange statement. It is totally incongruous with the evil image of Ahasuerus as portrayed by the Sages, for according to them, the King desired to see the destruction of the Jewish People, as much as Haman (see *Megillah* 13a).

The answer must be that Ahasuerus lost his nerve and suddenly began dreading the dire repercussions of having collaborated with Haman in his plot to destroy Hashem's Chosen People. The King's initial reaction to Haman's wicked plan had been, "I am afraid of their God, that He should not do to me as He did to my predecessors" (*Megillah* 13b). However, using sleight of tongue, Haman temporarily dispelled the King's fears. But now that the winds of fortune unpredictably shifted in favor of Israel, Ahasuerus' anxieties returned in full force. Pragmatically, he decided that he had better ingratiate himself with God, and the sooner the better. Thus, he self-righteously announced to Esther that he would forthwith fulfill the *mitzvah* of exterminating Amalek, and hoped that this declaration would mollify God and atone for his trangression.

In light of Ahasuerus' sudden desire to make amends for his sins, it ostensibly seems unfair that the King received no reward. Even the wicked Haman, who remained impenitent until the very end, merited to have de-

כו עַל־כֵּן קָרְאוּ לַיָּמִים הָאֵלֶּה פוּרִים עַל־שֵׁם
הַפּוּר עַל־כֵּן עַל־כָּל־דִּבְרֵי הָאִגֶּרֶת הַזֹּאת וּמָה־
כז רָאוּ עַל־כָּכָה וּמָה הִגִּיעַ אֲלֵיהֶם: קִיְּמוּ וְקִבְּלֻ

---

scendants who "taught Torah in Bnei Brak" (see *Sanhedrin* 96b) in reward for his role in bringing about the miracles of Purim. Since both Haman and Ahasuerus played an equally important role in setting the stage for the miracles of Purim to transpire, why didn't the descendants of both men receive the same reward?

The answer lies in the Talmud's interpretation of the verse, " 'Seek HASHEM, all the humble of the land, who have fulfilled His judgment" (*Zephaniah* 2:3)' — in the place where a man is judged,[1] there his righteous deeds are mentioned" (*Rashi* on *Yevamos* 78b). Since Haman was judged and executed, he merited to have "his righteous deeds mentioned" before the Heavenly Court — that is, he was given credit for setting the stage for the Purim miracles and the sanctification of Hashem's Name. His reward was that his descendants would one day convert to Judaism and teach Torah in Bnei Brak.

Ahasuerus, on the other hand, was not subjected to heavenly judgment, but rather died a natural death. Since he did not merit having "his righteous deeds mentioned," his role in inadvertently bringing about the Purim miracles did not reach the ears of the Heavenly Court. Therefore, he received no reward, and his descendants did not merit converting to Judaism.

Alternatively, Haman merited having his descendants teach Torah in Bnei Brak because of the admission he made in the presence of Mordechai's disciples. The Talmud recounts, "[Haman] asked [Mordechai's disciples]: What topic are you studying?

"They answered: When the Holy Temple was in existence, one who pledged a *minchah* offering brought a fistful of fine flour, through which he would gain atonement.

"[Haman] said to them: Your fistful of flour has supplanted my ten thousand silver talents" (*Megillah* 16a).

From this exchange, it is evident that Haman momentarily glimpsed the dazzling holiness and purity of Torah study. When Haman had set out to look for Mordechai, he had expected to find Mordechai's disciples quivering with fear over their imminent demise, since the date of the planned Jewish genocide was fast approaching. However, to his utter amazement, Mordechai's disciples were diligently plumbing the depths of an obscure law concerning a Temple which no longer existed, seemingly indifferent to the

---

1. Because Hashem's name is sanctified through judgment, the man being judged merits having his righteous deeds mentioned.

 26 *That is why they called these days "Purim" from
the word "pur." Therefore, because of all that was
written in this letter, and because of what they had
experienced, and what has happened to them, 27 *the*

---

events looming over the horizon. At that moment, he grasped the glory of Torah study, which transports one's soul from this murky temporal world to the loftiest heavenly realms. By saying, "Your fistful of flour has pushed aside my ten thousand silver talents," Haman admitted that no corporeal entity — including monetary wealth — can overcome the power of the Torah. Through this admission, Haman inadvertently sanctified Hashem's Name, and as a consequence, his descendants merited to teach Torah in Bnei Brak.

26. עַל־כֵּן קָרְאוּ לַיָּמִים הָאֵלֶּה פוּרִים עַל־שֵׁם הַפּוּר — That is why they called these days "Purim" from the word "pur."

The *Bnei Yisas'char* wonders why Mordechai and his *Beis Din* decided to call the festival "Purim" after the lot (*pur*) cast by Haman, since by doing so they commemorated the Jewish People's darkest hour, when death loomed on the horizon. Why did they not instead choose a name which commemorates the redemption?

The answer is that Purim is a unique festival — it is the only holiday commemorating a redemption which occurred while the Jewish People was in exile. Indeed, it is remarkable that the Sages instituted the festival of Purim at all, for in general Redemption and Exile are mutually exclusive terms. As history has painfully taught us throughout the generations, as long as the Jewish People remain in exile they are never completely safe. Even in Shushan, after all the miracles which transpired and Mordechai's mercurial rise to power, the Jews were by no means safe. True, they had been saved from certain death, but they remained very much under Ahasuerus' iron-handed rule. As they themselves said, "We are still Ahasuerus' slaves!" (*Megillah* 14a).

Thus, we see that Purim is a unique superimposition of Redemption over Exile. It is this rare duality which the Sages wished to preserve for posterity. Significantly, from the verse, "These days of Purim should never cease among the Jews, *nor shall their remembrance perish from their descendants*" (v. 28) the Sages learn that all Jewish festivals will be annulled except Purim.

Every event recorded in the *Megillah* contains an element of this dichotomy: When the Jewish People obtained permission to defend themselves (see 8:11), Haman's original decree calling for the extermination of the Jews was still in effect. Even so, with the battle against their enemies still before them, the verse tells us that, "The Jews had light and gladness, and joy and honor" (ibid., v. 16). Once again, we see that the spark of Redemption appeared in the darkest hour. We must understand, however, how the Jews were able to rejoice at so dark an hour.

The explanation is that Mordechai's generation reached an unprecedented level of faith in Hashem, one which we are almost unable to fathom. In the same manner as they placed their faith in Hashem and rejoiced despite the fierce battle that lay ahead, so too, they never doubted for a moment that Hashem would eventually free them from Ahasuerus' control and return them to the Land of Israel. They had witnessed the miracles of Purim, and although their redemption had by no means been a complete one, they placed their trust in Hashem and waited confidently for Him to consummate their deliverance. This unswerving faith in Hashem is the message the Sages wished to impart to all generations, and it is this lesson that gives Purim its eternal quality.

In this context it is no longer difficult to understand why the Sages chose the name "Purim" after Haman's lot (*pur*), for it is specifically the dichotomy between Redemption and Exile that this festival highlights. In this manner, they wished to teach future generations what true faith is all about — in the face of violent death at the hands of their enemies, the Jewish People had complete faith in their redemption and rejoiced heartily in anticipation, never once doubting Hashem's Divine Providence. This view of Purim is best summed up by *Rambam*: "The Prophets ... instituted these days, and decreed that the *Megillah* be read in its appointed time in order to proclaim the wonders and miracles that Hashem performed for our sake; in order to bless Him and praise Him; in order to teach future generations that the veracity of His assurance, 'For which is a great nation that has a God Who is close to it, as is HASHEM, our God, whenever we call to Him?' (*Deuteronomy* 4:7)."

Alternatively, it is possible the Sages chose the name "Purim" to teach that Haman's casting of the lot *was itself the roots of the Jewish People's redemption.* This idea is derived from the verse, "It is a time of adversity for Jacob, but he shall be delivered *from* it" (*Jeremiah* 30:7) — that is, the deliverance shall actually emerge *from* the "time of adversity." Similarly, the Sages said, "The removal of [Ahasuerus'] signet ring did more than the forty-eight prophets and seven prophetesses who prophesied to Israel, for [they were] all unable to return [the Jews] to the path of righteousness, whereas the removal of the signet ring did return [the Jews] to the path of righteousness" (*Megillah* 14a). As *Rashi* explains, Ahasuerus' gesture prompted the Jewish People to fast and repent for their sins.

In the classical work *Shaarei Teshuvah* (Ch. 2, Sec. 4), *Rabbeinu Yonah* expresses this concept in the following manner: "When a person accepts Hashem's reproof and corrects his deeds and ways, he should rejoice in his hardships, for [in retrospect], they turned out to have been very beneficial to him. He should thank the Almighty for them in the same manner as [he would thank Him] for any other successful venture. As it says, 'I raise the cup of deliverance and call in the Name of HASHEM' (*Psalms* 116:13), and, 'I came upon hardship and distress, and I called in the Name of HASHEM' (ibid., vs. 3-4)."[1]

By choosing the name "Purim," the Sages emphasized that we have as much of an obligation to thank Hashem for the trials our forefathers faced in the days of Haman as for the miracles He performed to redeem us from destruction.[2] As King David said, "I praise You, Hashem, for You have afflicted me and become my deliverance" (ibid., 118:21) — in other words, "You became my deliverance *by afflicting me.*" Isaiah the Prophet expressed the same idea when he said, "I praise You, HASHEM, for although You were furious with me, Your wrath has abated, and You comfort me" (*Isaiah* 12:1).

With this understanding, we may explain *Midrash Talpiot's* comment regarding the Sages' statement, " 'She [Esther] stood in the inner court of the King's palace' (*Esther* 5:1) — R' Levi said: As soon as she reached the chamber of idols [on her way through the palace to Ahasuerus], the Divine Presence departed from her. She exclaimed: My God, my God, why have You forsaken me? Could it be that You regard an inadvertent offense as an intentional one, or an offense committed under coercion as one committed willingly? Or perhaps [You have forsaken me] because I called him [Ahasuerus] a dog, as the verse says, 'Rescue my soul from the sword, my only one from the grip of the dog'? " (*Megillah* 15b). *Midrash Talpiot* writes, "Esther committed a slight transgression by behaving ungratefully towards [Ahasuerus], who generously appointed her as Queen."

At first glance, *Midrash Talpiot's* statement is difficult to understand. Why should Esther show appreciation to the tyrant who "caused the faces of the Jewish People to become as dark as the bottom of a pot" (*Megillah* 11a)?

The answer is that *Midrash Talpiot* was referring to the principle established above — Esther should have been grateful to Ahasuerus for

---

1. This principle is also alluded to in the Sages' statement, "The World to Come is not like This World: In This World, upon hearing bad tidings the blessing 'Blessed are You . . . Truthful Judge' is recited, while in the World to Come, the blessing 'Blessed are You . . . Who is Good and Bestows Goodness' is recited" (*Pesachim* 50a). In the World to Come, the soul perceives that every single event which occurred during its lifetime was ultimately for its own good. Perhaps the reason why all the festivals will be annulled except for Purim is that Purim contains this "World to Come" perspective, and therefore will endure for all eternity.

2. Perhaps this explains why the Sages decreed that on Purim one should drink more wine than usual. According to the *Chayei Adam,* the Sages instituted this *mitzvah* "because the miracle occurred through wine." However, we also know that the *evil decree* which threatened the existence of the Jewish People "occurred through wine" — the Jews were punished for attending Ahasuerus' feast (*Midrash Shochar Tov*). Hence, it would seem inappropriate to drink wine on Purim, for by doing so we also commemorate the Jewish People's sin. However, by keeping in mind the principle that salvation emanates from hardship, it is no longer difficult to understand why the Sages instituted the *mitzvah* of drinking wine on Purim — we call attention to the cause of the hardship *because it proved to be the roots of the redemption.*

mistreating her people, for in this manner he prompted them to shed tears and pray fervently to Hashem. As a result, they reached lofty spiritual heights and came close to Hashem.

27. קִיְּמוּ וְקִבְּל הַיְּהוּדִים עֲלֵיהֶם וְעַל־זַרְעָם וְעַל כָּל־הַנִּלְוִים עֲלֵיהֶם — The Jews confirmed and undertook upon themselves, and their posterity, and upon all who might join them.

Why is the word וְקִבְּל ("undertook upon themselves") spelled without a ו at the end, unlike every other occurrence in Scripture?

The answer lies in *Midrash Tanchuma*: "Israel did not accept the Torah until the Holy One, Blessed is He, suspended the mountain over them like a barrel . . . And if you will say that He suspended the mountain over them [so that they would accept] the *Written* Torah, didn't they all exclaim, 'Everything that HASHEM has said, we will do and we will obey'? (*Exodus* 24:7). This is because [the Written Torah] does not necessitate toil, does not cause distress, and is concise. Rather, He [coerced them into accepting] the *Oral* Torah, which discusses the minute details of light and severe *mitzvos*, and which is harsh as death and severe as the grave."

This *midrash* sheds light on the Sages' statement, "[The Jewish People] accepted [the Torah] again in the days of Ahasuerus, as the verse says, 'The Jews confirmed and undertook upon themselves' (*Esther* 9:27) — they confirmed what they had already undertaken in the past [i.e., the Torah]" (*Shabbos* 88a). According to the *midrash*, in Mordechai's day the Jewish People reaccepted specifically the *Oral* Torah.

We may now understand why the letter ו was omitted from the word וְקִבְּל: The numerical value of ו is 6, representing the 6 Orders of Mishnah, which are the foundations of the Oral Torah. Since in principle it is prohibited to write down a single word of the Oral Torah, the omission of the letter ו alludes to the fact that Mordechai's generation specifically reaccepted the Oral Torah.

Rashi explains that the words, "all who might join them," refers to future converts. However, it is difficult to understand why the *Megillah* emphasizes this point, since it is a well-known fact that converts are bound to observe rabbinical decrees to the same degree as any other Jew. As a matter of fact, if a convert would declare that he accepts every law of the Torah except for one single rabbinical decree, his conversion would not be valid.

The answer lies in *Maharal's* commentary on the verse, "The son of an Israelite woman went out — and he was the son of an Egyptian man — *among the Children of Israel*" (*Leviticus* 24:10). According to *Rashi,* the words "among the Children of Israel" convey that this individual was a convert. *Ramban* finds *Rashi's* interpretation difficult, since the verse explicitly states that he was "the son of an Israelite woman." Why, then, would he have had to convert? Judaism is unquestionably a matrilineal religion. *Maharal* answers *Ramban's* difficulty as follows: All the Israelites who left Egypt were required to undergo a quasi-conversion process, which included circumcision, ritual immersion, and sacrificing an offering (see *Kereisos* 9a). This new covenant only applied to Jews who had been conceived by Jewish fathers. Thus, even though strictly speaking "the son of an Israelite woman" was Jewish, he had not been included in the new covenant with Hashem. Therefore, he could not be considered "among the Children of Israel" until he converted.

Similarly, we may answer that by reaccepting the Torah out of love, the Jews in the days of Mordechai and Esther underwent, as it were, a kind of "conversion." Therefore, our verse saw it necessary to stress that future converts who would join the Jewish nation would also be bound by the laws of Purim even though they themselves did not undergo the process of "conversion" experienced by Mordechai's generation.

In light of the *Maharal's* explanation, however, one might rightly wonder why the laws of Purim do indeed apply to converts. If we were to draw a direct parallel between the son of the Israelite woman in the desert and a gentile who converted after the events of Purim, we would draw the conclusion that a convert *should not* be obligated by law to observe the *mitzvos* of Purim. Just as the son of the Israelite woman was not a full Jew because he was excluded from the "conversion" process which Jews of patrilineal descent underwent, so too, gentiles who converted after Mordechai's time should not be bound to celebrate Purim, when the Jewish People reaccepted the Torah and experienced this "conversion."

The answer to this lies in *Maharal's* contention (see *Gur Aryeh, Vayigash*) that the principle, "A new convert is considered as a new-born infant," did not apply at the time when the Israelites received the Torah at Mount Sinai. *Pachad Yitzchak* explains that although *Halachah* sometimes regards an act or statement evinced through coercion as a true representation of an individual's will, this presumption may only be made on the basis of strong evidence. Thus, when Hashem suspended the mountain over the Jewish People and forced them to accept the Torah, only the direct descendants of the righteous Patriarchs entered Hashem's covenant. Their pious lineage attested to the fact that in the depths of their beings, they truly longed to fulfill Torah and *mitzvos*. However, the converts who were present were excluded from the covenant, since there was insufficient proof that their willingness to observe the Torah was sincere, rather than merely a reaction to the danger threatening them.

ט/כח וְלֹא יַעֲבוֹר לִהְיוֹת עֹשִׂים אֵת־שְׁנֵי הַיָּמִים הָאֵלֶּה
כח כִּכְתָבָם וְכִזְמַנָּם בְּכָל־שָׁנָה וְשָׁנָה: וְהַיָּמִים הָאֵלֶּה
נִזְכָּרִים וְנַעֲשִׂים בְּכָל־דּוֹר וָדוֹר מִשְׁפָּחָה וּמִשְׁפָּחָה
מְדִינָה וּמְדִינָה וְעִיר וָעִיר וִימֵי הַפּוּרִים הָאֵלֶּה
לֹא יַעַבְרוּ מִתּוֹךְ הַיְּהוּדִים וְזִכְרָם לֹא־יָסוּף

This concept only applies to events such as the reception of Torah at Mount Sinai, where coercion was employed to frighten the Jews into accepting Hashem's covenant. However, it *does not* apply to the converts in Mordechai's generation, for then all the Jews — *including the converts* — willingly accepted the yoke of Heaven amidst celebration and unparalleled joy. Thus, although converts were excluded from the covenant at Mount Sinai, they were very much a part of the covenant in the days of Mordechai and Esther. For this reason, all converts — even those who converted after the Purim miracles — are bound to observe the *mitzvos* of Purim forever.

וְלֹא יַעֲבוֹר לִהְיוֹת עֹשִׂים אֵת־שְׁנֵי הַיָּמִים הָאֵלֶּה כִּכְתָבָם וְכִזְמַנָּם בְּכָל־שָׁנָה וְשָׁנָה — To observe these two days, without fail, in the manner prescribed, and at the proper time each year.

The verse teaches that although Purim is celebrated on two different days (residents of unwalled cities celebrate it on the 14th of *Adar,* while residents of walled cities do so on the 15th), it is nevertheless considered as if every Jew, regardless of where he may be, observes *both* days. This concept illustrates the extraordinary degree of national unity reached by the Jewish People in the days of Mordechai — it was so powerful that it spanned differences of time!

The Sages allude to this principle in the following Talmudic passage: "[The verse says] 'The Jews confirmed and undertook upon themselves' (*Esther* 9:27) — they reaccepted the Torah in the days of Ahasuerus" (*Shabbos* 88a). The Sages explain that the Jewish People did not accept the Torah wholeheartedly at Mount Sinai because Hashem coerced them to abide by its laws by suspending the mountain over them. However, in the days of Mordechai, the Jewish People voluntarily reaccepted the Torah as an expression of their love for Hashem. It stands to reason, then, that they attained the same degree of unity which they reached at Mount Sinai, when the "huge multitude of people encamped as though they were *a single person, with a single desire*" (*Rashi* on *Exodus* 19:2).[1]

---

1. This is derived from the verse, "They journeyed from Rephidim and arrived at the Wilderness of Sinai and encamped in the Wilderness; and *Israel* encamped (singular verb) there, opposite the mountain" (*Exodus* 19:2) — the verse suddenly switches from the plural tense to the singular.

to observe these two days, without fail, in the manner prescribed, and at the proper time each year. [28] *Consequently, these days should be remembered and celebrated by every single generation, family, province, and city; and these days of Purim should never cease among the Jews, nor shall their memory perish from their descendants.*

In this respect, the most fitting metaphor for the spiritual struggle which ensued in Mordechai's day is a cosmic balance — on one side of the scale stood the descendants of Jacob, and on the other, the descendants of Esau. As Hashem had told Rebecca when Jacob and Esau were still inside her womb, "Two nations are in your womb. . .*the might shall pass from one regime to the other*" (*Genesis* 25:23). The Sages interpreted this verse to mean that Jacob and Esau would never rise to power simultaneously. Rather, as one would fall, the other would rise (*Megillah* 6a). Similarly, the Sages said, "Tyre became full only from the ruins of Jerusalem" (quoted by *Rashi, Genesis* 25:23). Thus, it is no coincidence that the Scriptural portion which discusses weights and measurements (*Deuteronomy* 25:13-16) appears adjacent to the passage which mentions the *mitzvah* to exterminate Amalek — in this manner, the Torah teaches that the struggle between Israel and Amalek resembles the two sides of a scale.

In his attempt to destroy Israel, Haman utilized the most effective weapon in Amalek's arsenal: sowing discord among the Jewish People. Initially, the scale tipped in Amalek's favor. But then Mordechai and Esther roused the Jewish People to repentance and urged them to pursue harmony and brotherly love with their fellow Jews. The scales suddenly tipped in Israel's favor and ushered in Haman's destruction.

28. בְּכָל־דּוֹר וָדוֹר מִשְׁפָּחָה וּמִשְׁפָּחָה מְדִינָה וּמְדִינָה וְעִיר וָעִיר וִימֵי הַפּוּרִים הָאֵלֶּה לֹא יַעַבְרוּ מִתּוֹךְ הַיְּהוּדִים וְזִכְרָם לֹא־יָסוּף מִזַּרְעָם — By every single generation, family, province, and city; and these days of Purim should never cease among the Jews, nor shall their memory perish from their descendants.

Rashi derives from the words, מִשְׁפָּחָה וּמִשְׁפָּחָה ("every single. . .family"), that the people gathered and feasted together, thereby insuring that the days of Purim never cease from among them. It would seem that *Rashi* bases this remark on the dictum of the Sages that, "Every *mitzvah* which [the Jewish People] accepted upon themselves joyfully, they continue to perform joyfully." (*Shabbos* 130a).[1]

1. One example is [*Bris*] *Milah*, about which the verse says, 'I rejoice over Your word as one who finds a great treasure' (*Psalms* 119:162)" (*Shabbos* 130a). *Rashi* associates the term "joyfully" with eating and drinking.

מִזַּרְעָם׃ כט וַתִּכְתֹּב אֶסְתֵּר הַמַּלְכָּה בַת־
אֲבִיחַיִל וּמָרְדֳּכַי הַיְּהוּדִי אֶת־כָּל־תֹּקֶף לְקַיֵּם אֵת
ל אִגֶּרֶת הַפֻּרִים הַזֹּאת הַשֵּׁנִית׃ וַיִּשְׁלַח סְפָרִים

In keeping with this principle, Mordechai's generation celebrated Purim, the day when they reaccepted the Torah out of love, with feasting and rejoicing. By doing so, they ensured that their love and enthusiasm for Torah would endure forever.

The reasoning behind the Sages' maxim is that if a person rejoices in a *mitzvah* and adheres to it with his entire being, he comes into contact with that *mitzvah*'s eternal spiritual essence. This leaves an indelible impression upon his soul which is then transferred to his descendants down through the generations, ensuring that they, too, will perform this particular *mitzvah* with the same degree of joy.[1]

❧ ❧ ❧

The *Megillas Setarim* interprets the end of the verse to mean that as long as the Jewish People keep observing the *mitzvos* of Purim, "their memory" shall always remain before Hashem.

The *mitzvos* of Purim differ greatly from other *mitzvos*. Most *mitzvos*, such as eating *matzah* on Pesach or picking up the Four Species on Sukkos, are not *a means* to an end, but an end in themselves. In other words, Hashem decreed most *mitzvos* because, in His great wisdom, He deemed it necessary that we perform a particular deed at a specified time, such as eating *matzah* on Pesach and taking the Four Species on Sukkos. In contrast, the *mitzvos* of Purim are not an end in themselves, but a means to an end.

The means is described by the beginning of our verse: "These days should be *remembered* and celebrated by every single generation, family, province, and city." By fulfilling the *mitzvos* of Purim, we keep alive the memory of the miracles that Hashem performed for the sake of our forefathers who lived in Mordechai's time.

The end is described by the end of the verse, "nor shall their memory perish from their descendants." In return for remembering these miracles, the verse continues (according to the *Megillas Setarim*), Hashem keeps alive *our* memory before Him. This is truly a great reward, for whenever the memory of the Jewish People ascends before Hashem, redemption swiftly

---

1. This explains why a festive meal is traditionally prepared in honor of a person's *bar mitzvah* — by joyously celebrating the day when their son becomes obligated to observe the 613 commandments, parents tap into the eternal essence of *mitzvos* and ensure that the *bar-mitzvah* boy will fulfill his obligations with joy throughout his life.

[29] *Then Queen Esther, daughter of Abihail, and Mordechai the Jew, wrote with full authority to ratify this second letter of Purim.* [30] *Dispatches were sent*

---

follows. We learn this concept from the juxtaposition of the verses, "God heard their moaning, and God *remembered* His covenant with Abraham, with Isaac, and with Jacob" (*Exodus* 2:24) and "Moses was shepherding the sheep of Jethro. . .and he arrived at the Mountain of God" (ibid., 3:1) — immediately after God remembered the Israelites, He chose Moses to be their redeemer and bade him to deliver them from the Egyptian house of bondage. [1]

29. וַתִּכְתֹּב אֶסְתֵּר הַמַּלְכָּה בַת־אֲבִיחַיִל וּמָרְדֳּכַי הַיְּהוּדִי אֶת־כָּל־תֹּקֶף לְקַיֵּם אֵת אִגֶּרֶת הַפֻּרִים הַזֹּאת הַשֵּׁנִית — Then Queen Esther, daughter of Abihail, and Mordechai the Jew, wrote with full authority to ratify this second letter of Purim.

In reference to this verse the Sages said the following:

"Eighty-five sages — among them more than thirty prophets — were greatly disturbed by this matter. They said, '[But] it is written, "These are the commandments that HASHEM commanded Moses to the Children of Israel on Mount Sinai" (*Leviticus* 27:34) — Moses in essence said to us, "From now on, no other prophet shall devise new laws for you." And yet, Mordechai and Esther now request to do just that — to devise a new law!' [i.e., to include the *Megillah* in Scripture.]

"The Sages did not leave their places. They considered every aspect of this question until the Holy One, Blessed is He, enlightened their eyes, and they found [the *mitzvah* of Purim] alluded to in the Pentateuch, Prophets, and Writings" (*Talmud Yerushalmi*, *Megillah* Ch. 1, *Halachah* 5).

This account illustrates the extent of the Sages' authority to interpret Scripture as they see fit: Despite the great miracles that occurred as a direct consequence of Mordechai and Esther's deeds, and despite the instrumental role these two righteous individuals played in saving Israel from utter destruction, the Sages adamantly refused to include *Megillas Esther* in Scripture. Only when the Sages themselves found strong allusions to the *Megillah* in all three sections of Scripture did they finally give their consent. This is truly astounding — had Hashem not "enlightened the eyes" of the Sages, the *Megillah* would have been nothing more than an obscure historical record!

---

1. This explains why R' Shimon ben Gamliel ruled that on a leap year the *Megillah* be read on the second *Adar* (see *Megillah* 6b) — the memory of the Jewish People should rise before Hashem on the month adjacent to *Nissan*, when Hashem took us out of Egypt with miracles and wonders, and when He will redeem us in the future. May it come about speedily and in our days!

The last verse in the *Megillah* also underscores the Sages' impartial and steadfast adherence to the principles of Torah: "For Mordechai the Jew was viceroy to King Ahasuerus; he was a great man among the Jews, and popular with *the majority* of his brethren. . ." (10:3). In Tractate *Megillah* (16b), *Rashi* explains why Mordechai was only popular with *the majority* of his brethren, and not with *all* of them: "Some of the members of the *Sanhedrin* (Supreme Torah Tribunal) shunned [Mordechai] because he was forced — due to his duty as viceroy — to neglect his Torah study." Although they owed their very lives to Mordechai, the Sages shunned him because he had — albeit unwillingly — become *lax* in Torah study.

❦ ❦ ❦

The Talmud states, "Esther submitted [the following request] to the Sages: 'Write me down [i.e., the account of the Purim miracles] for all generations' " (*Megillah* 7a). Esther's deeper intention may have been as follows:

As is well known, the written word of the Torah has the power to perpetuate the memory of a thought, person or event. Esther wished not only to eternalize the actual miracles that had occurred on Purim, but also to preserve the *deeds* which had prompted Hashem to perform those miracles. In this manner, she wished to transmit the secret of how to survive the horrors of exile to future generations. In essence, the message Esther imparted to the Jewish People was: "Do not flatter your enemies, but stand indomitably against them and the evil which they represent."

This attitude was best exemplified by Mordechai, about whom the verse says, "But Mordechai would not bow down nor prostrate himself" (3:2). Significantly, the verse does not say, וּמָרְדְּכַי לֹא כָּרַע ("Mordechai *did not* bow down") in the past tense, but rather וּמָרְדְּכַי לֹא יִכְרַע (literally, "Mordechai *will not* bow down"), in the future tense. This conveys that Mordechai's real intention was to demonstrate that not only he, but also future generations of Jews, would never give in to evil. His attitude was the catalyst which brought about the miracles of Purim, and it remains the key to the Jewish People's survival to this very day.

❦ ❦ ❦

Esther mentioned her father's name in order to honor him, as well as to ascribe to him her great courage — the name אֲבִיחַיִל literally means "courageous father." This explains why the *Megillah* was named after Esther despite the fact that Mordechai actually wrote it. As the Sages said, "Whoever ascribes credit to others, others shall ascribe credit to him" (*Berachos* 10b) — because Esther ascribed her courage to her father, others ascribed the *Megillah* to her.

Alternatively, the *Megillah* was named after Esther in order to draw a clear distinction between the first scroll, written independently by Mordechai in the first year (see v. 20), and the second scroll, which was co-authored by Mordechai and Esther in the second year (see v. 29). Since the Sages agreed to "write down for all generations" only this second scroll, they called it "The Scroll *of Esther*," as opposed to the first scroll, which they called "The Scroll of Mordechai."

❦ ❦ ❦

The first letter ת (*tav*) of the word וַתִּכְתֹּב is traditionally written in a larger-sized character. This teaches that just as ת (*tav*) is the last letter of the Hebrew alphabet, so too, the *Megillah* had been completed by Mordechai one year earlier (as *Rashi* explicitly states in his commentary on verse 20). Esther's only contribution was to elevate the *Megillah* from a mere "letter" to a Scriptural work.

This can also explain why the *Megillah* was named after Esther even though Mordechai was the one who actually wrote it — as the Sages said, "A *mitzvah* is named after the one who completes it" (*Sotah* 13b). The *Megillah* was named after Esther because it was she who succeeded in making it an eternal part of the Jewish People for all generations, and instilling it with the sanctity of a Scriptural work.

Immediately after Esther's intervention the verse describes the *Megillah* as, "words of peace and *truth*" (v. 30), which the Sages interpret to mean, "As truthful as Torah" (*Megillah* 16b). Significantly, no such endorsement was made when Mordechai completed writing the *Megillah*, for at that time the *Megillah* had not yet become part of Scripture, and therefore could not be considered "words of *truth*."

Alternatively, the *Megillas Setarim* explains that the *Megillah* was named after Esther because it was she who insisted that the miracles be recorded for posterity and their account be read aloud every year on Purim. Mordechai, on the other hand, was more concerned with establishing Purim as a religiously ordained day of celebration. Thus, it is only fitting that the writing of the scroll be attributed to Esther.

It is also possible that the *Megillah* was named after Esther because of her absolute dedication to save the Jewish People from utter destruction. Just as the Ark of the Tabernacle was ascribed to Bezalel because he devoted himself to the work more than the other wise men, so too, the *Megillah* was ascribed to Esther because she dedicated herself with self-sacrifice to bring about the miracles of Purim. The extent of Esther's self-sacrifice is evident from the verse, "Then I will go in to the King though it's unlawful. And if I perish, I perish" (4:16). As *Rashi* explains, Esther was willing to give up her life to save the Jewish People from destruction.

ט/לא-לב אֶל־כָּל־הַיְּהוּדִים אֶל־שֶׁבַע וְעֶשְׂרִים וּמֵאָה מְדִינָה
לא מַלְכוּת אֲחַשְׁוֵרוֹשׁ דִּבְרֵי שָׁלוֹם וֶאֱמֶת׃ לְקַיֵּם
אֶת־יְמֵי הַפֻּרִים הָאֵלֶּה בִּזְמַנֵּיהֶם כַּאֲשֶׁר קִיַּם
עֲלֵיהֶם מָרְדֳּכַי הַיְּהוּדִי וְאֶסְתֵּר הַמַּלְכָּה וְכַאֲשֶׁר
קִיְּמוּ עַל־נַפְשָׁם וְעַל־זַרְעָם דִּבְרֵי הַצּוֹמוֹת וְזַעֲקָתָם׃
לב וּמַאֲמַר אֶסְתֵּר קִיַּם דִּבְרֵי הַפֻּרִים הָאֵלֶּה וְנִכְתָּב
י/א-ב א בַּסֵּפֶר׃ וַיָּשֶׂם הַמֶּלֶךְ °אחשרש ׀ מַס
°אֲחַשְׁוֵרוֹשׁ ק׳ ב עַל־הָאָרֶץ וְאִיֵּי הַיָּם׃ וְכָל־מַעֲשֵׂה תָקְפּוֹ וּגְבוּרָתוֹ

---

30. דִּבְרֵי שָׁלוֹם וֶאֱמֶת — Words of peace and truth.

In reference to this verse the Sages said, "*Megillas Esther* was [written] with Divine inspiration" (*Megillah* 7a). The Sages concluded this because under normal circumstances, it is humanly impossible to author a work which simultaneously contains words of peace *and* truth: "Truth" means that Mordechai and Esther did not mince words in describing the extent of Ahasuerus and Haman's wickedness; "peace" means that even though Ahasuerus and his ministers read the *Megillah*, they were not offended by the account of their own wickedness.

"Truth" shines forth from the final verse, which concedes that Mordechai was only popular "with *the majority* of his brethren," but was shunned by some of the Sages. We see that even though Mordechai himself wrote the *Megillah*, he did not conveniently omit his own setbacks. Surely only an author with Divine inspiration could have passed up the temptation to omit such damaging information about himself!

31. דִּבְרֵי הַצּוֹמוֹת וְזַעֲקָתָם — The matter of the fasts and their lamentations.

Ibn Ezra explains that "the fasts" refer to the four fasts mentioned in the Book of *Zechariah,* held on the months of *Tamuz*, *Av*, *Tishrei*, and *Teves*. The verse teaches that the Jews of Mordechai's day considered the obligation to rejoice on Purim as binding as that of fasting and lamenting on these four public fast days.

It is evident from the words of *Ibn Ezra* that a correspondence exists between Purim and the four fasts, and that the rejoicing of Purim in a sense counterbalances the sorrow felt on these four days. This concept fits well with the following Talmudic passage: "Yalta said to R' Nachman, 'For everything that the Torah prohibits us, it permits something else in its stead: It prohibits us [to eat] blood, but it permits us [to eat] liver. . .' (*Chullin* 109b). Similarly, the Torah prohibits us to eat on the four fast days, but it *commands*

9/31-32 *to all the Jews, to the hundred and twenty-seven provinces of the kingdom of Ahasuerus — with words of peace and truth —* [31] *to establish these days of Purim on their proper dates just as Mordechai the Jew and Queen Esther had enjoined them, and as they had undertook upon themselves and their posterity the matter of the fasts and their lamentations.* [32] *Esther's ordinance validated these regulations for Purim; and it was recorded in the book.*

10/1-2 [1] *King Ahasuerus levied taxes on both the mainland and the islands.* [2] *All his mighty and powerful acts,*

---

us to feast on one of the four days of Purim (Purim may be celebrated on the 11th, 12th, 14th, or 15th of *Adar* [see *Megillah* 2a]; eating is prohibited on *Taanis Esther*, the 13th of *Adar*).

Along the same lines, the *Pachad Yitzchak* expounds upon the following statement of the Sages:

"R' Yehoshua ben Levi said: Why were they called 'Men of the Great Assembly'? Because they returned the crown to its former place. Moses came and said, 'The great, mighty, and awesome God.' Then came Jeremiah and said, 'Gentiles prance in His sanctuary! Where is His awe?' [From then on, Jeremiah] omitted the word 'awesome.' Then came Daniel and said, 'Gentiles oppress His children! Where is His might?' [From then on, Daniel] omitted the word 'mighty.' Then came [the Men of the Great Assembly] and said, 'On the contrary! This itself demonstrates His might. . .those *are* His awesome deeds! Were it not for the awe of the Holy One, Blessed is He, how could one nation survive among all the nations?' " (*Yoma* 69b).

Pachad Yitzchak points out that through the miracles of Purim the Great Assembly "returned the crown to its former place." The Purim miracles proved beyond doubt that Hashem controls all events, whether they be joyful or sad, and that the only difference between joyous and somber occasions is the degree to which the Divine attribute of Mercy is revealed. With this new realization, the Jewish People accepted upon themselves to observe the four fast days as devotedly as they had observed joyous holidays such as Purim.

X

1. וַיָּשֶׂם הַמֶּלֶךְ אֲחַשְׁוֵרוֹשׁ מַס עַל־הָאָרֶץ וְאִיֵּי הַיָּם — King Ahasuerus levied taxes on both the mainland and the islands.

No verse in the *Megillah* is irrelevant. According to the *Vilna Gaon,* this is why the Sages decreed that unless one hears every single word of the *Megillah* reading on Purim, one has not fulfilled the *mitzvah*: "From the

י/ג וּפָרָשַׁת֙ גְּדֻלַּ֣ת מָרְדֳּכַ֔י אֲשֶׁ֥ר גִּדְּל֖וֹ הַמֶּ֑לֶךְ הֲלוֹא־הֵ֣ם
כְּתוּבִ֗ים עַל־סֵ֙פֶר֙ דִּבְרֵ֣י הַיָּמִ֔ים לְמַלְכֵ֖י מָדַ֥י וּפָרָֽס׃
ג כִּ֣י ׀ מָרְדֳּכַ֣י הַיְּהוּדִ֗י מִשְׁנֶה֙ לַמֶּ֣לֶךְ אֲחַשְׁוֵר֔וֹשׁ וְגָדוֹל֙
לַיְּהוּדִ֔ים וְרָצ֖וּי לְרֹ֣ב אֶחָ֑יו דֹּרֵ֥שׁ טוֹב֙ לְעַמּ֔וֹ וְדֹבֵ֥ר
שָׁל֖וֹם לְכָל־זַרְעֽוֹ׃

---

beginning of the *Megillah* to the end, every single verse, every sentence, has the effect of magnifying the extent of the miracle." Having established this principle, we must now explain why this verse is pertinent to the story of Purim.

It would seem that Ahasuerus levied this new tax in response to a general economic recession in his kingdom which caused a sharp decline in the Crown's annual tax revenues. Yet despite the Crown's desperate need for funds and Ahasuerus' insatiable greed for money, for some strange reason the King decided to confer Haman's estate to Esther. This is truly astounding, especially in light of the Sages' teaching that Haman's estate included the contents of Joseph's vast treasure houses.

Midrash Rabbah (*Terumah* 33:5) explains this amazing turn of events in the following manner:

"When Haman offered silver and gold to Ahasuerus for the right to exterminate the Jewish People, the King said, 'The silver is given to you' (*Esther* 3:11), and he refused it.

"The Holy One, Blessed is He, said, 'How can you sell what is Mine for what is Mine? The verse says, "The Children of Israel are servants to Me, they are *My* servants" (*Leviticus* 25:55), and another verse says, "Silver is Mine and gold is Mine, says HASHEM" (*Haggai* 2:8). By your life, because you said, 'The silver is given to you,' [in the future the verse shall say,] 'That very day, King Ahasuerus gave the estate of Haman. . .to Queen Esther' (*Esther* 8:1)."

In other words, because Ahasuerus refused Haman's silver despite his desperate need for funds, Hashem decreed that the King would eventually[1]

---

1. *Midrash Tanchuma* teaches that "even the mouth is not under Man's control. From where do we learn this? From Balaam and Isaac. From Balaam, for the verse says, 'But HASHEM, your God, refused to listen to Balaam, and HASHEM, your God, *reversed the curse to a blessing* for you. . .' (*Deuteronomy* 23:6). From Isaac, for the Sages said, '[After Jacob took the blessing of the firstborn] and Esau entered, Isaac said, "Who — where — is the one who hunted game, brought it to me, and I partook of all when you had not yet come, and I blessed him?" At this point, Isaac was about to add, "Indeed, he shall be accursed!" but the Holy One, Blessed is He, said [to Isaac], "What are you doing? Do you think your mouth is yours to use as you see fit?" Isaac then said, "Indeed, he shall be *blessed*!" ' "

So too, Ahasuerus was forced to say, "Behold, I have given Haman's estate to Esther," (8:7) against his will.

and a full account of the greatness of Mordechai, whom the King had promoted, are recorded in the book of chronicles of the Kings of Media and Persia.
3 For Mordechai the Jew was viceroy to King Ahasuerus; he was a great man among the Jews, and found favor with the majority of his brethren; he sought the good of his people and was concerned for the welfare of all his posterity.

---

confer Haman's estate to Esther even though he would also then be short of funds. This is why he was forced to levy the tax.

1-3. וַיָּשֶׂם הַמֶּלֶךְ אֲחַשְׁוֵרוֹשׁ מַס עַל־הָאָרֶץ וְאִיֵּי הַיָּם: וְכָל מַעֲשֵׂה תָקְפּוֹ וּגְבוּרָתוֹ וּפָרָשַׁת גְּדֻלַּת מָרְדֳּכַי אֲשֶׁר גִּדְּלוֹ הַמֶּלֶךְ הֲלוֹא־הֵם כְּתוּבִים עַל־סֵפֶר דִּבְרֵי הַיָּמִים לְמַלְכֵי מָדַי וּפָרָס: כִּי מָרְדֳּכַי הַיְּהוּדִי מִשְׁנֶה לַמֶּלֶךְ אֲחַשְׁוֵרוֹשׁ וְגָדוֹל לַיְּהוּדִים וְרָצוּי לְרֹב אֶחָיו דֹּרֵשׁ טוֹב לְעַמּוֹ וְדֹבֵר שָׁלוֹם לְכָל זַרְעוֹ — **King Ahasuerus levied taxes on both the mainland and the islands. All his mighty and powerful acts, and a full account of the greatness of Mordechai, whom the King had promoted, are recorded in the book of chronicles of the Kings of Media and Persia. For Mordechai the Jew was viceroy to King Ahasuerus; he was a great man among the Jews, and found favor with the multitude of his brethren; he sought the good of his people and was concerned for the welfare of all his posterity.**

Another explanation of the relevence of these passages may be that an attempt was made to align the written format of the Purim redemption with that of the redemption from Egypt:

According to the *Baal HaTurim*, Moses' statement to Pharaoh, "You have spoken correctly — I shall never see your face again" (*Exodus* 10:29), conveyed that the plague of the first-born would be the final blow, and that no more plagues would be forthcoming. Following Moses' announcement is a short passage of three verses, concluding with Moses' popularity, *the man Moses was very great in the land of Egypt, in the eyes of the servants of Pharaoh, and in the eyes of the people* (ibid., 11:3).

Similarly, the *Megillah* concludes with a short passage of three verses, concluding with Mordechai's popularity, "For Mordechai the Jew *was viceroy to King Ahasuerus; he was a great man among the Jews, and popular with the majority of his brethren*; he sought the good of his people and was concerned for the welfare of all his posterity" (10:3). Just as the short passage regarding the redemption from Egypt concludes with a verse in praise of Moses, so too, the short passage at the end of the *Megillah* concludes with a verse in praise of Mordechai.

❧ ❧ ❧

Why does the verse use the causative word, "*For* Mordechai the Jew was. . ."?

According to *Ibn Ezra*, the verse explains how Ahasuerus managed to intimidate the inhabitants of even the most remote islands of the kingdom to pay the new tax: Since Mordechai was his viceroy, he succeeded in all his endeavors.

It would seem that the continuation of the verse provides further explanation: It was only because Mordechai remained righteous and God fearing that he brought success[1] to King Ahasuerus.

❧ ❧ ❧

According to the *Vilna Gaon*, "he was a great man" means that Mordechai was an accomplished Torah scholar. Apparently, the *Vilna Gaon* meant that despite Mordechai's difficult and time-consuming governmental responsibilities, he did not forget his Torah knowledge. This was quite a feat, for *Midrash Rabbah* (*Genesis* 79:8) teaches that even the great Joseph failed to retain his Torah knowledge during his term as Pharaoh's viceroy.

It would seem that the source of the *Vilna Gaon*'s interpretation of the term "great man" is the following Talmudic passage:

"What is the intent of the verse, 'And he burned the House of HASHEM, and the King's house, and the houses of Jerusalem, and every *great house* did he burn with fire' (*II Kings* 25:9)?

"One [Sage] said ['every *great house*' refers] to a place in which they *increase* Torah [knowledge; i.e., a study hall] . . . for it is written, 'HASHEM desires because of His righteousness to *increase* Torah and strengthen it' (*Isaiah* 42:21)" (*Megillah* 7a). Thus, we see that the word "great" is associated with Torah study.

Alternatively, "he was a great man" conveys the idea that despite Mordechai's high position, he continued to inspire the Jewish People to follow the ways of the Torah.

This may well be the reason why an infant who has undergone circumcision is traditionally given the blessing, "This little one, may he become *great*." The verse says, "And God made the two great luminaries, the *greater* luminary to dominate the day and the lesser luminary to dominate the night; and the stars" (*Genesis* 1:16). As is well known, "the *greater* luminary" refers to the sun, "the lesser luminary" to the moon. An infant is akin to the moon: Just as the moon can reflect light but not emit,

1. Similarly, Laban admitted to Jacob, "HASHEM has blessed me on account of you" (*Genesis* 30:27).

so too, an infant can receive from his parents, but not give anything of his own. Thus, he is given a blessing to "become *great*" — i.e., to one day have the merit of providing spiritual guidance to others just as the sun provides the entire world with light.[1]

❦ ❦ ❦

The *Yeshuah Gedolah* cites a *midrash* which says, "Every trait you find in Moses, you also find in Mordechai: Just as Moses was humble, also Mordechai was humble, as the verse says, 'he was concerned for the welfare of all his posterity.' " The *Midrash* adds, "Mordechai was as important in his generation as Moses was in his generation . . . Mordechai was as worthy a leader of the Jewish People as Moses, as the verse says, 'There was a Jewish man in Shushan the Capital whose name was Mordechai. . .' "

However, the *Midrash* (*Bereishis Rabbah* 30:8) seems to disagree. It states: *It was said in reference to Moses — this teaches that Moses was destined to become a redeemer. It was said in reference to Mordechai — this teaches that Mordechai was destined for redemption.*

Unlike the *midrash* cited by the *Yeshuah Gedolah*, *Midrash Rabbah* seems to imply that Moses and Mordechai did not share a common spiritual role — Moses was destined to become a *redeemer*, whereas Mordechai was destined for *redemption*.

The difficulty may be resolved as follows: In the same way that Israel has only three Patriarchs, so too, only one person can be considered Israel's Redeemer. Moses was the archetype of this role, and all subsequent individuals who redeemed the Jewish People throughout history drew their strength from him.

This concept is clearly evident in the verse, "HASHEM spoke to Moses, 'Take to yourself Joshua son of Nun, a man in whom there is spirit, and lean your hand upon him. . .*You shall place some of your majesty upon him, so that the entire assembly of Israel will pay heed*' " (*Numbers* 27:18,20). Hashem assured Moses that the Jewish People would obey him, as the verse says, "They will heed your voice" (*Exodus* 3:18). It was the merit of this promise to Moses that empowered subsequent leaders such as Joshua to redeem Israel from destruction.

We may now understand why *Midrash Rabbah* says that Moses was destined to become a *redeemer*, whereas Mordechai was destined for *redemption*. The *Midrash* does not imply that Moses and Mordechai had diverse spiritual roles, but rather that Moses was destined to become the prototype of the Jewish redeemer while Mordechai was destined to draw from Moses' essence and thereby bring about the redemption of Israel.

---

1. See R' Yosef Dov Soloveitchik's homiletical insight on *Genesis* 1:16 as cited in the ArtScroll Stone Edition *Chumash.*

However, had it not been for the spiritual kinship between these two individuals, Mordechai would not have been capable of drawing upon Moses' merit.[1]

❦ ❦ ❦

I heard from my friend R' Zalman Bass that the numerical value of וַיְהִי, the first word in the *Megillah*, together with that of וְזַרְעוֹ, the last word in the *Megillah*, is 314, the numerical value of the Divine Name ש־ד־י.

This numerical equivalence is not accidental. The fundamental lesson taught by the *Megillah* is that even in the deepest darkness of exile, when HASHEM's Presence remains concealed, it is still He Who controls the world. This attribute of concealed Divine supervision is represented by the Divine name ש־ד־י, as *Ramban* explains in reference to *Genesis* 17:1: "It is through this Divine name that hidden miracles occur on behalf of righteous individuals. It saves them from death, sustains them during famine, and delivers them from the sword in times of war. These miracles occur without perceptible variations in the laws of Nature."

Various commentators point out that the *Megillah* consists of 166 verses, equals to the number of words in the two Torah passages that mention the *mitzvah* of exterminating Amalek (*Exodus* 17:8-16, *Deuteronomy* 25:17-19). The sub-value of 166 is also significant: 1 + 6 + 6 = 13.

Thirteen is the numerical value of the word אֶחָד, "one." This teaches that when Amalek is finally exterminated, it will become apparent to the entire world that HASHEM is One and His Name is One, as the verses say, "Redeemers shall ascend Mount Zion and *judge the Mountain of Esau*, and the Kingdom shall be HASHEM's" (*Obadiah* 1:21), and "HASHEM will be King over all the world; on that day HASHEM will be *One* and His Name will be *One*" (*Zechariah* 14:9).

Thirteen is also the numerical value of אַהֲבָה, "love." This alludes to the Messianic Era, when HASHEM's love for Israel will become apparent to all the inhabitants of the earth.

Significantly, the *Megillah* begins with the word וַיְהִי, whose numerical value through *mispar kattan*[2] is 13, and ends with the word וְזַרְעוֹ, [283 = 2 + 8 + 3] whose sub-value is 13. This reoccurrence of the number 13 conveys the idea that from beginning to end, the underlying theme of the *Megillah* is HASHEM's fervent love for His people. Discovering this Divine love in every word, in every nuance, is the primary objective of reading the *Megillah*. If one looks closely enough, it can even be found in the verses which describe the ominous dangers that threatened Israel's existence.

---

1. According to *Rashi* on *Sukkah* 39a, the leading Torah scholar of each generation also draws his strength from Moses.

2. *Mispar Kattan* is a *gematraic* device by which the value of each letter is not affected by the addition of zeros (e.g.: כ, which normally has a value of 20, has a *mispar kattan* value of 2).

The name *Megillas Esther* (מְגִילַּת אֶסְתֵּר) notifies the reader that HASHEM's love for Israel is נִסְתָּר, concealed, and therefore may only be discovered by plumbing the depths of the *Megillah*. It should therefore not come as a surprise that the sub-value of the names מָרְדְּכַי [274 = 2 + 7 + 4] and אֶסְתֵּר [661 = 6 + 6 + 1] is also 13. This teaches that it is possible to discern HASHEM's Oneness (אֶחָד = 13, אֶסְתֵּר = 13) within the darkest הֶסְתֵּר, concealment.

If a *minyan* is present for the *Megillah* reading, the following blessing is recited after the reading.

בָּרוּךְ אַתָּה יהוה אֱלֹהֵינוּ מֶלֶךְ הָעוֹלָם, (הָאֵל) הָרָב אֶת רִיבֵנוּ, וְהַדָּן אֶת דִּינֵנוּ, וְהַנּוֹקֵם אֶת נִקְמָתֵנוּ, וְהַמְּשַׁלֵּם גְּמוּל לְכָל אֹיְבֵי נַפְשֵׁנוּ, וְהַנִּפְרָע לָנוּ מִצָּרֵינוּ. בָּרוּךְ אַתָּה יהוה, הַנִּפְרָע לְעַמּוֹ יִשְׂרָאֵל מִכָּל צָרֵיהֶם, הָאֵל הַמּוֹשִׁיעַ.

After the nighttime *Megillah* reading, the following two paragraphs are recited. the daytime reading, only the second paragraph is recited.

אֲשֶׁר הֵנִיא עֲצַת גּוֹיִם, וַיָּפֶר מַחְשְׁבוֹת עֲרוּמִים.
בְּקוּם עָלֵינוּ אָדָם רָשָׁע, נֵצֶר זָדוֹן, מִזֶּרַע עֲמָלֵק.
גָּאָה בְעָשְׁרוֹ, וְכָרָה לוֹ בּוֹר, וּגְדֻלָּתוֹ יָקְשָׁה לּוֹ לָכֶד.
דִּמָּה בְנַפְשׁוֹ לִלְכֹּד, וְנִלְכַּד, בִּקֵּשׁ לְהַשְׁמִיד, וְנִשְׁמַד מְהֵרָה.
הָמָן הוֹדִיעַ אֵיבַת אֲבוֹתָיו, וְעוֹרֵר שִׂנְאַת אַחִים לַבָּנִים.
וְלֹא זָכַר רַחֲמֵי שָׁאוּל, כִּי בְחֶמְלָתוֹ עַל אֲגָג נוֹלַד אוֹיֵב.
זָמַם רָשָׁע לְהַכְרִית צַדִּיק, וְנִלְכַּד טָמֵא, בִּידֵי טָהוֹר.
חֶסֶד גָּבַר עַל שִׁגְגַת אָב, וְרָשָׁע הוֹסִיף חֵטְא עַל חֲטָאָיו.
טָמַן בְּלִבּוֹ מַחְשְׁבוֹת עֲרוּמָיו, וַיִּתְמַכֵּר לַעֲשׂוֹת רָעָה.
יָדוֹ שָׁלַח בִּקְדוֹשֵׁי אֵל, כַּסְפּוֹ נָתַן לְהַכְרִית זִכְרָם.
כִּרְאוֹת מָרְדְּכַי, כִּי יָצָא קֶצֶף, וְדָתֵי הָמָן נִתְּנוּ בְשׁוּשָׁן.
לָבַשׁ שַׂק וְקָשַׁר מִסְפֵּד, וְגָזַר צוֹם, וַיֵּשֶׁב עַל הָאֵפֶר.
מִי זֶה יַעֲמֹד לְכַפֵּר שְׁגָגָה, וְלִמְחֹל חַטַּאת עֲוֹן אֲבוֹתֵינוּ.
נֵץ פָּרַח מִלּוּלָב, הֵן הֲדַסָּה עָמְדָה לְעוֹרֵר יְשֵׁנִים.
סָרִיסֶיהָ הִבְהִילוּ לְהָמָן, לְהַשְׁקוֹתוֹ יֵין חֲמַת תַּנִּינִים.
עָמַד בְּעָשְׁרוֹ, וְנָפַל בְּרִשְׁעוֹ, עָשָׂה לוֹ עֵץ, וְנִתְלָה עָלָיו.
פִּיהֶם פָּתְחוּ, כָּל יוֹשְׁבֵי תֵבֵל, כִּי פוּר הָמָן נֶהְפַּךְ לְפוּרֵנוּ.
צַדִּיק נֶחֱלַץ מִיַּד רָשָׁע, אוֹיֵב נִתַּן תַּחַת נַפְשׁוֹ.
קִיְּמוּ עֲלֵיהֶם, לַעֲשׂוֹת פּוּרִים, וְלִשְׂמֹחַ בְּכָל שָׁנָה וְשָׁנָה.
רָאִיתָ אֶת תְּפִלַּת מָרְדְּכַי וְאֶסְתֵּר, הָמָן וּבָנָיו עַל הָעֵץ תָּלִיתָ.

If a *minyan* is present for the *Megillah* reading, the following blessing is recited after the reading.

Blessed are You, HASHEM, our God, King of the Universe, (the God) Who takes up our grievance, judges our claim, avenges our wrong; Who brings just retribution upon all enemies of our soul and exacts vengeance for us from our foes. Blessed are You, HASHEM, Who exacts vengeance for His people Israel from all their foes, the God Who brings salvation.

After the nighttime *Megillah* reading, the following two paragraphs are recited. After the daytime reading, only the scond paragraph is recited.

א *Who balked the counsel of the nations and annulled the designs of the cunning,*
ב *When a wicked man stood up against us, a wantonly evil branch of Amalek's offspring.*
ג *Haughty with his wealth he dug himself a grave,*
and his very greatness snared him in a trap.
ד *Fancying to trap, he became entrapped;*
attempting to destroy, he was swiftly destroyed.
ה *Haman showed his forebears' enmity,*
and aroused the brotherly hate of Esau on the children.
ו *He would not remember Saul's compassion,*
that through his pity of Agag the foe was born.
ז *The wicked one conspired to cut away the righteous,*
but the impure was trapped in the pure one's hands.
ח *Kindness overcame the father's error, and the wicked one piled sin on sins.*
ט *In his heart he hid his cunning thoughts, and devoted himself to evildoing.*
י *He stretched his hand against God's holy ones,*
he spent his silver to destroy their memory.
כ *When Mordechai saw the wrath commence, and Haman's decrees be issued in Shushan,*
ל *He put on sackcloth and bound himself in mourning, decreed a fast and sat on ashes:*
מ *'Who would arise to atone for error, to gain forgiveness for our ancestors' sins?'*
נ *A blossom bloomed from a lulav branch — behold!*
Hadassah stood up to arouse the sleeping.
ס *His servants hastened Haman, to serve him wine of serpent's poison.*
ע *He stood tall through his wealth and toppled through his evil —*
he built the gallows on which he was hanged.
פ *The earth's inhabitants opened their mouths, for Haman's lot became our Purim,*
צ *The righteous man was saved from the wicked's hand; the foe was substituted for him.*
ק *They undertook to establish Purim, to rejoice in every single year.*
ר *You noted the prayer of Mordechai and Esther;*
Haman and his sons You hung on the gallows.

The following is recited after both *Megillah* readings.

שׁוֹשַׁנַּת יַעֲקֹב צָהֲלָה וְשָׂמֵחָה, בִּרְאוֹתָם יַחַד תְּכֵלֶת מָרְדְּכָי.

תְּשׁוּעָתָם הָיִיתָ לָנֶצַח, וְתִקְוָתָם בְּכָל דּוֹר וָדוֹר. לְהוֹדִיעַ, שֶׁכָּל קֹוֶיךָ לֹא יֵבֹשׁוּ, וְלֹא יִכָּלְמוּ לָנֶצַח כָּל הַחוֹסִים בָּךְ. אָרוּר הָמָן, אֲשֶׁר בִּקֵּשׁ לְאַבְּדִי, בָּרוּךְ מָרְדְּכַי הַיְּהוּדִי. אֲרוּרָה זֶרֶשׁ, אֵשֶׁת מַפְחִידִי, בְּרוּכָה אֶסְתֵּר בַּעֲדִי, וְגַם חַרְבוֹנָה זָכוּר לַטּוֹב.

The following is recited after both *Megillah* readings:

ש The rose of Jacob was cheerful and glad,
when they jointly saw Mordechai robed in royal blue.
ת You have been their eternal salvation, and their hope throughout generations.

To make known that all who hope in You will not be shamed; nor ever be humiliated, those taking refuge in You. Accursed be Haman who sought to destroy me, blessed be Mordechai the Yehudi. Accursed be Zeresh the wife of my terrorizer, blessed be Esther [who sacrificed] for me — and Charvonah, too, be remembered for good.

◈ Appendix

מצות מחית עמלק —
The Mitzvah to Eradicate Amalek

מפטיר לפרשת זכור

(דברים כה: יז־יט)

יז זָכוֹר אֵת אֲשֶׁר־עָשָׂה לְךָ עֲמָלֵק בַּדֶּרֶךְ בְּצֵאתְכֶם
יח מִמִּצְרָיִם: אֲשֶׁר קָרְךָ בַּדֶּרֶךְ וַיְזַנֵּב בְּךָ כָּל־הַנֶּחֱשָׁלִים
יט אַחֲרֶיךָ וְאַתָּה עָיֵף וְיָגֵעַ וְלֹא יָרֵא אֱלֹהִים: וְהָיָה בְּהָנִיחַ
יהוה אֱלֹהֶיךָ ׀ לְךָ מִכָּל־אֹיְבֶיךָ מִסָּבִיב בָּאָרֶץ אֲשֶׁר

---

17. זָכוֹר אֵת אֲשֶׁר־עָשָׂה לְךָ עֲמָלֵק בַּדֶּרֶךְ בְּצֵאתְכֶם מִמִּצְרָיִם: אֲשֶׁר קָרְךָ בַּדֶּרֶךְ — Remember what Amalek did to you, on the way when you were leaving Egypt, that he happened upon you on the way.

Several questions arise upon reading this passage:

1. What did Amalek do to incur Hashem's wrath to the point that genocide was decreed against the entire nation? Amalek was definitely not the only nation guilty of persecuting Israel. The Egyptians themselves subjugated the Jewish People to unspeakable torture and indiscriminately murdered their male children, yet the Torah did not call for their complete annihilation.

   Furthermore, Amalek did not even gain a decisive victory against Israel in the desert, as the verse says, "Joshua weakened Amalek and its people with the sword's blade" (*Exodus* 17:13). There is also no evidence to indicate that Amalek's attack harmed Israel's interests in any way. It surely did not instill confidence into the inhabitants of Canaan, for as Rahab said to Joshua's spies, "Fear of you has befallen us, and all the inhabitants of the land [of Canaan] are trembling before you" (*Joshua* 2:9). Only in the days of Haman did Amalek become a serious threat to the Jewish People. Why, then, did Amalek incur such severe punishment?

2. Why does the verse repeat the word בַּדֶּרֶךְ ("on the way")? Verse 15:2 in *I Samuel* also places emphasis on this word: "I am exacting punishment for what Amalek did to Israel, for attacking them *on the way,* when they were coming up from Egypt." What is the significance of the word בַּדֶּרֶךְ ("on the way")?

The answer to both questions will emerge in the course of the following discussion:

The verse says, "Now it came to pass on the third day, Esther *clothed herself in royalty* and stood in the inner court of the King's palace facing the King's house" (5:1).

The Sages said in reference to this verse, "[Scripture] should have said [that Esther clothed herself] in *royal garments,* [not *in royalty.* In reply], R' Elazar said in the name of R' Chanina: This teaches that [Esther] clothed herself in the Divine Spirit, for it is written here, "Esther *clothed* herself," and elsewhere it is

MAFTIR FOR PARASHAS ZACHOR

(*Deuteronomy* 25:17-19)

[17] *Remember what Amalek did to you, on the way*
when you were leaving Egypt, [18] *that he happened*
upon you on the way, and he struck those of you who were hindmost, all the weaklings at your rear, when you were faint and exhausted, and he did not fear God.
[19] *It shall be that when* HASHEM, *your God, gives you*
rest from all your enemies all around, in the Land that

---

written, 'And the spirit *clothed* Amasai' (*I Chronicles* 12:19) " (*Megillah* 15a).

Pachad Yitzchak finds this interpretation difficult, since this is the only occurrence in Scripture where the Divine Spirit is referred to as if it were a "royal garment." However, the explanation is as follows:

According to many early authorities, the *mitzvah* to exterminate Amalek is only applicable when the Jewish People have appointed a king. This is why the Israelites crossing into the Promised Land were first commanded to appoint a king, and only thereafter to exterminate Amalek (*Sanhedrin* 20a). If so, *Pachad Yitzchak* asks, how could the Jews in Ahasuerus' day have fulfilled the *mitzvah* of exterminating Amalek by slaying Haman and his sons, since at the time they were not under the sovereignty of a Jewish king?

The answer is that Esther assumed sovereign control over Israel, thereby empowering the Israelites to slay Amalek.

However, merely assuming the throne would not have entitled Esther to lead the Jews in a war against Amalek, for we see that King Saul — the first Jewish monarch to lead an Israelite attack against Amalek — was endowed with both royalty *and* prophecy. This is evident from the verse, "The spirit of HASHEM shall come upon you, you shall prophesy in their midst, and you shall be a different man" (*I Samuel* 10:6). Saul's prophetic revelations caused the people to say to one another, "Is Saul too among the prophets?" (ibid., 10:12).

Esther was a descendant of King Saul (*Megillah* 13b). Since she came to rectify the sin of King Saul, who failed to fulfill his obligation to exterminate Amalek, she too was endowed with prophecy when she rose to the throne. This explains why the Sages interpreted the words, "Esther clothed herself in royalty," to mean that "she clothed herself in the Divine Spirit" — in other words, that she merited to prophecy.

At this point, it is necessary to explain why exterminating Amalek requires both royalty and prophecy. According to *Ramban,* these two preconditions will be required even in messianic times: "Everything Moses and Joshua did to [Amalek] in the past will be done by Elijah and *Mashiach ben Yosef* [to their descendants] in the future" (*Ramban* on *Exodus* 17:9) — Elijah will be the prophet, and *Mashiach ben Yosef* will be the king. The explanation is as follows:

Regarding the battle between the Israelites and the Amalekites in the desert,

כה/יט **יְהוָה־אֱלֹהֶיךָ נֹתֵן לְךָ נַחֲלָה לְרִשְׁתָּהּ תִּמְחֶה אֶת־זֵכֶר עֲמָלֵק מִתַּחַת הַשָּׁמָיִם לֹא תִּשְׁכָּח:**

---

the *Zohar* says: "There had never been such a battle since the creation of the world. Amalek waged war above and below. Therefore, Moses chose Joshua to eternally wage war below, while Moses himself would wage war above. Were it not that Moses overcame them above and Joshua below, Israel would not have defeated them" (*Zohar, Beshalach* 65:2).

The *Zohar* alludes to the Sages' well-known interpretation of the verse, "The might shall pass from one regime to the other" (*Genesis* 25:23), in reference to which *Rashi* says, "They [Jacob and Esau] will not be equal in stature — when this one rises, the other shall fall." Obviously, this inverse relationship between Esau and Jacob exists in both the corporeal and spiritual realms. Thus, when the Jewish People fail to take advantage of one of their most powerful weapons — prayer — this potent force falls into the hands of Amalek, a direct descendant of Esau. Amalek then wages battle against Israel in the heavenly realms by uttering incantations, which, bolstered by the fallen power of Israel's prayer, become formidable weapons. This explains *Rashi*'s commentary on the verse, "Moses said to Joshua, 'Choose *people* for us and go do battle with Amalek' " (*Exodus* 17:9) — "people who know how to neutralize witchcraft."

It is for this reason that the attributes of royalty and prophecy are required to vanquish Amalek: A monarch must lead the Israelites in earthly warfare against Amalek, while a prophet must wage battle in the heavenly spheres against that evil nation.

With this understanding, we may answer our first question: What did Amalek do to incur such severe punishment?

The answer is that Amalek — unlike other nations — is capable of inflicting damage to Israel not only in the physical realm, but also in the spiritual. Just as the Jewish People are able to reach the loftiest heavenly spheres through prayer, so is Amalek able to cause extensive and permanent damage in the heavens. For example, when the Amalekites "cooled down the bath"[1] by audaciously attacking Israel in the desert, they caused a permanent decrease in religious fervor. Until then, the nations of the world were awed by the Israelites and by the Godly presence that surrounded them. Amalek, however, dispelled this aura of reverence by waging an unprovoked attack against the Jewish People. Although the Amalekites were repelled, the very fact that they survived the attack against Hashem's Chosen People became a platform for atheistic notions, which Amalekites have disseminated throughout the world ever since. For this reason, Hashem declared eternal war and annihilation against Amalek.

---

1. See *Rashi* on *Deuteronomy* 25:18.

HASHEM, your God, gives you as an inheritance to possess it, you shall wipe out the memory of Amalek from under the heaven — you shall not forget!

This is the real intent behind the Sages' statement, "There was no one who knew to slander [as skillfully] as Haman" (*Megillah* 13b). Besides the literal meaning of this statement (that Haman was adept at speaking slander against the Jewish People before Ahasuerus), the Sages alluded to the principle established above: Amalek is able to inflict damage upon Israel in the heavenly realms. On this occasion, Amalek focused their power of speech against Israel by accusing them before the Heavenly Tribunal for having become lax in Torah and *mitzvah* observance. In this manner, Amalek undermined the foundations of Hashem's Heavenly Throne — the Jewish People's worship — and in a sense made the Throne "incomplete." In return for this sacrilegious act, Hashem decreed that the Amalekite nation be completely annihilated.

The answer to our second question — why the verse emphasizes the word בַּדֶּרֶךְ ("on the way") — is as follows: The term "on the way from Egypt" does not only describe the Israelites' geographical location, but also the "way of life" towards which they were heading. Upon their redemption from the Egyptian house of bondage, the Israelites discarded the endemic impurity of that land and headed towards Mount Sinai to receive the holy Torah. Amalek, however, intercepted them and attempted to "change their ways" by exposing them to atheistic ideas and a general irreverence for all things holy. Amalek did not merely attempt to cause the Israelites to commit sin, but rather to corrupt their entire outlook on life. They wished to lead to the darkness of hell a holy nation that was on "its way" to enter a covenant of eternal life. Although Amalek's attack was contained, it was not a complete failure — the evil nation nevertheless managed to inflict eternal damage by weakening the nations' faith in God.

Amalek's double-edged sword is represented by the two passages in the Pentateuch which call for that nation's annihilation. The passage in *Parashas Beshalach* (*Exodus* 17:8-15) refers to the Amalekites' metaphysical power, with which they, as it were, make Hashem's Heavenly Throne "incomplete" (this explains why the word כֵּס, or "throne," is written without an א at the end — it conveys the idea that as long as Amalek exists, Hashem's throne remains incomplete). It is for this reason that the passage concludes with the words, "*HASHEM* maintains a war against Amalek from generation to generation" — since the passage refers to the Amalekites' formidable metaphysical powers, HASHEM Himself shall wage battle against them. On the other hand, the passage in *Parashas Ki Seitzei* (*Deuteronomy* 25:17-19) says, "*You* shall wipe out the memory of Amalek from under the heaven," since this passage refers to Amalek's earthly offenses against Israel.

קריאה לפורים

(שמות יז:ח־טז)

ח־ט וַיָּבֹא עֲמָלֵק וַיִּלָּחֶם עִם־יִשְׂרָאֵל בִּרְפִידִם: וַיֹּאמֶר
מֹשֶׁה אֶל־יְהוֹשֻׁעַ בְּחַר־לָנוּ אֲנָשִׁים וְצֵא הִלָּחֵם
בַּעֲמָלֵק מָחָר אָנֹכִי נִצָּב עַל־רֹאשׁ הַגִּבְעָה וּמַטֵּה
י הָאֱלֹהִים בְּיָדִי: וַיַּעַשׂ יְהוֹשֻׁעַ כַּאֲשֶׁר אָמַר־לוֹ מֹשֶׁה
לְהִלָּחֵם בַּעֲמָלֵק וּמֹשֶׁה אַהֲרֹן וְחוּר עָלוּ רֹאשׁ
הַגִּבְעָה:
יא לוי וְהָיָה כַּאֲשֶׁר יָרִים מֹשֶׁה יָדוֹ וְגָבַר יִשְׂרָאֵל וְכַאֲשֶׁר
יב יָנִיחַ יָדוֹ וְגָבַר עֲמָלֵק: וִידֵי מֹשֶׁה כְּבֵדִים וַיִּקְחוּ־אֶבֶן
וַיָּשִׂימוּ תַחְתָּיו וַיֵּשֶׁב עָלֶיהָ וְאַהֲרֹן וְחוּר תָּמְכוּ בְיָדָיו
מִזֶּה אֶחָד וּמִזֶּה אֶחָד וַיְהִי יָדָיו אֱמוּנָה עַד־בֹּא
יג הַשָּׁמֶשׁ: וַיַּחֲלֹשׁ יְהוֹשֻׁעַ אֶת־עֲמָלֵק וְאֶת־עַמּוֹ לְפִי־
חָרֶב:

---

9. וַיֹּאמֶר מֹשֶׁה אֶל־יְהוֹשֻׁעַ בְּחַר־לָנוּ אֲנָשִׁים וְצֵא הִלָּחֵם בַּעֲמָלֵק — Moses said to Joshua, "Choose people for us and go do battle with Amalek.

In *Pirkei Avos* (Ch. 2) the Sages said, "Let your disciple's honor be as dear to you as your own." This principle is deduced from Moses, who said to Joshua, "Choose people for *us,*" and not "choose people for *me.*" In reference to this statement *Pachad Yitzchak* wonders why the Sages derived the obligation to honor one's disciple specifically from this passage, which discusses Amalek's war against Israel?

The answer is that Amalek is the embodiment of spiritual neglectfulness in this world. As we have explained earlier, Amalek was the first nation to dare attack Israel in the desert. Before then the nations had stood in awe of the Israelites, for they knew that Hashem resided in their midst. Amalek, however, brazenly dispelled this aura of reverence by waging war against Israel. As the Sages put it, "Amalek jumped into the boiling tub and cooled it off" (see *Rashi* to *Deuteronomy* 25:18).[1] Amalek is also a spiritual parasite who feeds off the negligent observance of the *mitzvos,* as we find in

---

1. *Pachad Yitzchak* explains that the Amalekite nation inherited its obsession to defile all things holy from Esau, its evil ancestor. As the verse says regarding Esau, "He ate and drank, got up and left; thus, Esau spurned the birthright" (*Genesis* 25:34) — Esau not only sold the birthright for a meal of bread and lentils, but also spurned the holy rights of the first born.

TORAH READING FOR PURIM

(*Exodus* 17:8-16)

8 *Amalek came and battled Israel in Rephidim.*
9 *Moses said to Joshua, "Choose people for us and go*
do battle with Amalek; tomorrow I will stand on top of
the hill with the staff of God in my hand." 10 *Joshua did*
as Moses said to him, to do battle with Amalek; and
Moses, Aaron, and Hur ascended to the top of the hill.
11 *It happened that when Moses raised his hand Israel*
was stronger, and when he lowered his hand Amalek
was stronger. 12 *Moses' hands grew heavy, so they*
took a stone and put it under him and he sat on it, and
Aaron and Hur supported his hands, one on this side
and one on that side, and he remained with his hands
in faithful prayer until sunset. 13 *Joshua weakened*
Amalek and its people with the sword's blade.

Haman's slander of the Jews (*Megillah* 3:8).

Moses was well aware of this aspect of Amalek, which infected all those who came into contact with the evil nation and feeds on negligence to *mitzvos*. In order to counteract it, he consciously paid extra attention to *mitzvos* which people tend to neglect.[1] For example, an offense that is frequently committed is to disregard the honor of individuals of lesser status than oneself. In teacher-student relationships, this tendency is compounded even further by the fact that, in certain circumstances, a teacher is entitled to strike his disciple.[2] As a consequence, teachers tend to take their disciples' honor lightly. However, this is a great mistake on their part, for although a teacher is entitled to *strike* a disciple, it is categorically prohibited for him to *humiliate* one. Knowing Amalek's ability to draw strength from the Jews' weakness in *mitzvah* observance, Moses made a point of honoring Joshua, his faithful disciple.[3] By doing so, he counteracted the enemy and earned merit before the actual war.

---

1. See *Rashi, Deuteronomy* 7:12.

2. *Makkos* 8.

3. The following account underscores this point: Prior to delivering his weekly lecture in the *Etz Chayim Yeshivah,* R' Isser Zalman Meltzer would always make a point of secluding himself in a side room for a few minutes. Once, a curious disciple peeked inside the room to see what the *Rosh Yeshivah* did in that short time. He was dismayed at what he saw: R' Isser Zalman was pacing back and forth while repeating the verse, "You shall love your fellow as yourself" (*Leviticus* 19:18), countless times to himself, over and over again. It would seem that R' Isser Zalman did this in order to prevent himself from inadvertently dismissing a question raised by a disciple during the course of the lecture.

יז/יד־טז יד ישראל וַיֹּאמֶר יְהוָה אֶל־מֹשֶׁה כְּתֹב זֹאת זִכָּרוֹן בַּסֵּפֶר
וְשִׂים בְּאָזְנֵי יְהוֹשֻׁעַ כִּי־מָחֹה אֶמְחֶה אֶת־זֵכֶר עֲמָלֵק
טו מִתַּחַת הַשָּׁמָיִם: וַיִּבֶן מֹשֶׁה מִזְבֵּחַ וַיִּקְרָא שְׁמוֹ יְהוָה ׀
טז נִסִּי: וַיֹּאמֶר כִּי־יָד עַל־כֵּס יָהּ מִלְחָמָה לַיהוָה בַּעֲמָלֵק
מִדֹּר דֹּר:

---

14. כִּי־מָחֹה אֶמְחֶה אֶת־זֵכֶר עֲמָלֵק מִתַּחַת הַשָּׁמָיִם — That I shall surely erase the memory of Amalek from under the heavens.

The Sages said, "Some of Haman's grandchildren taught Torah in Bnei Brak" (*Sanhedrin* 96b). However, the *Mechilta* on *Parashas Beshalach* rules that members of the Amalekite nation may not be accepted as converts to Judaism. If so, how did Haman's grandchildren get to teach Torah in Bnei Brak?

I once heard from *Pachad Yitzchak* that the law only states that Amalekites should not be *accepted* as converts, but not that they *cannot become* converts. In other words, if an Amalekite should express a desire to convert he should be rejected, but if he would conceal his origins and complete the conversion process, he would be considered a true convert.

With this we may resolve the apparent contradiction between the Talmud and the *Mechilta* — Haman's descendants must have kept their origins a secret and converted. Afterwards, they merited to study and teach Torah to the people.

However, it is difficult to understand how Haman's descendants could have managed such a feat, for the Sages of the *Sanhedrin* in those days had *ruach hakodesh* (Divine insight). Surely the Sages would have been able to discern the true identity of Haman's grandchildren! It is known that the *Arizal,* who lived in the 16th century, could discern a person's sins by just looking at his face. It stands to reason that the Sages of the *Sanhedrin* who lived in the era of the Second Temple could do at least as much.[1]

---

1. I heard from R' Shalom Shwadron that R' Isser Zalman Meltzer also possessed this ability. Once, during *Chol Hamo'ed,* R' Isser Zalman asked his attendant to bring him a pen. The attendant was taken aback at this request, since R' Isser Zalman would always scrupulously observe the prohibition against writing unnecessarily during *Chol Hamo'ed.*

Noticing the attendant's astonished look, R' Isser Zalman explained as follows: Due to the countless visitors who would come before R' Isser Zalman during *Chol Hamo'ed,* he made sure to keep before him a piece of paper with the verse, "Let your eyes look forward, your pupils gaze straight ahead" (*Proverbs* 4:25), written upon it. According to the *Nesivos* this verse teaches that when a person discerns faults in others, it is most likely that he himself is guilty of that fault. R' Isser Zalman explained to his attendant that since he could discern people's sins by merely looking at their faces, he could not possibly greet all his visitors congenially without frequently looking down at the verse written before him. Since the piece of paper had been misplaced, it was a matter of immediate importance (צוֹרֶךְ הַמּוֹעֵד) that he write down the verse before his visitors began arriving.

17/14-16

[14] *HASHEM said to Moses, "Write this as a remembrance in the Book and recite it in the ears of Joshua, that I shall surely erase the memory of Amalek from under the heavens."* [15] *Moses built an altar and called its name "HASHEM is My Miracle";* [16] *and he said, "For the hand is on the throne of God: HASHEM maintains a war against Amalek, from generation to generation."*

There is only one answer: It was a heavenly decree that Haman's descendants become Jews. Even though we cannot fully grasp the reason for such a heavenly decree, a plausible explanation may be that Hashem wished to demonstrate that the phenomenon called וְנַהֲפוֹךְ הוּא ("a complete reversal") is not necessarily restricted to the era of Mordechai and Esther. Rather, it is a miraculous process that can potentially occur at any time, the only criteria being the sum of each particular generation's merits. Hashem proved this by transforming descendants of the most evil nation the world has ever known, the very antithesis of everything sacred, into the most holy human beings possible — Torah scholars who taught the people Hashem's ways. From the murkiest recesses of atheism emerged God-fearing individuals who helped strengthen the faith of the Jewish People.

According to the Sages, R' Shmuel bar Shilas, who taught Torah to children, was one of Haman's descendants (*Bava Basra* 9a). This fits well with our explanation, for the Sages said that the Torah-study of children is the key to the continuity of Torah in the world. Thus, we see that the descendants of Haman, the wicked man who would stop at nothing to erase the memory of Torah from the world, dedicated their lives to perpetuate Torah study for all time.

15. וַיִּבֶן מֹשֶׁה מִזְבֵּחַ וַיִּקְרָא שְׁמוֹ יהוה נִסִּי — Moses built an altar and called its name "HASHEM is My Miracle."

Why did Moses build this altar? If it was an expression of gratitude for the miracles that occurred, then why did he not build an altar by the shores of the Red Sea, where a much more spectacular miracle took place?

The *Tzidkas HaTzadik* provides the answer: In every place where the *mitzvah* of exterminating Amalek was fulfilled, the Divine Presence resided there in the form of a synagogue[1] or study hall. Thus, since the Jewish People fulfilled the *mitzvah* of exterminating Amalek in Rephidim, Moses built an altar there. Significantly, this was the first altar every built by the Jewish People.

---

1. This is the reason why the latter section of Tractate *Megillah* discusses the laws pertaining to synagogues and study halls.

This volume is part of
THE ARTSCROLL SERIES®
an ongoing project of
translations, commentaries and expositions
on Scripture, Mishnah, Talmud, Halachah,
liturgy, history and the classic Rabbinic writings;
and biographies, and thought.

For a brochure of current publications
visit your local Hebrew bookseller
or contact the publisher:

Mesorah Publications, ltd

4401 Second Avenue
Brooklyn, New York 11232
(718) 921-9000